D0561360

A CRITIQUE OF
WELFARE ECONOMICS

A CRITIQUE OF
WELFARE ECONOMICS

BY

I. M. D. LITTLE

FELLOW OF NUFFIELD COLLEGE
OXFORD

SECOND EDITION

WITHDRAWN
FROM
UNIVERSITY OF PENNSYLVANIA
LIBRARIES

OXFORD UNIVERSITY PRESS
LONDON   OXFORD   NEW YORK

HB/171/L73/1960/c.4

Oxford University Press

OXFORD LONDON NEW YORK

GLASGOW TORONTO MELBOURNE WELLINGTON

CAPE TOWN IBADAN NAIROBI DAR ES SALAAM LUSAKA ADDIS ABABA

DELHI BOMBAY CALCUTTA MADRAS KARACHI LAHORE DACCA

KUALA LUMPUR SINGAPORE HONG KONG TOKYO

ISBN 0 19 881004 0

First published by the Clarendon Press 1950
Second Edition 1957
First issued as an Oxford University Press paperback 1960
Reprinted 1970, 1973

HB
171
L73
1960
cop.4

Printed in Great Britain
at the University Press, Oxford
by Vivian Ridler
Printer to the University

UNIVERSITY
OF
PENNSYLVANIA
LIBRARIES

CONTENTS

ABBREVIATIONS

THE following abbreviations of the names of periodicals are used:

E.J.	*The Economic Journal*
Q.J.E.	*The Quarterly Journal of Economics*
J.P.E.	*The Journal of Political Economy*
R.E.S.	*The Review of Economic Studies*
O.E.P.	*Oxford Economic Papers*
M.S.	*The Manchester School*
C.J.E.P.S.	*The Canadian Journal of Economics and Political Science*
S.E.J.	*Southern Economic Journal*
A.E.R.	*American Economic Review*

PREFACE TO SECOND EDITION

IN revising for the second edition I have not attempted to enlarge the scope of the book. I have not, for instance, taken note of Professor K. J. Arrow's book *Social Choice and Individual Values*, nor of the discussion, mainly in the *Journal of Political Economy*, arising out of it. I have elsewhere stated that I do not think that this subject has much relevance to classical welfare economics, as expounded and criticized in this book.[1] Nor have I considered either Mr. Fleming's[2] or Mr. Harsanyi's[3] interesting, but not to my mind compelling, attempts to revive the notion that welfare is a sum of utilities.

The following is a brief account of the changes which have been made. In the first chapter the comment on Professor Pigou's views about the interrelation of welfare economics and ethics has been slightly modified and elaborated in response to criticism from Mr. Hugh Dalton. The second chapter has been fairly extensively revised in order to try to meet various criticisms; and the appendix on 'revealed preference', now Appendix II at the end of the book, has a comment added on later developments. I am indebted to Professor Georgescu-Roegen so far as some of these revisions are concerned. A new Appendix I on the logic of strong ordering, written by Mr. C. B. Winsten, has been added. Chapter III has been only slightly revised, somewhat greater stress being placed on the fact that consumption determines tastes, as well as tastes consumption. The former appendix to this chapter, on Utility and Demand Theory, has been suppressed as being an inadequate treatment of the subject (although I have not changed my views). Chapters IV and V are unaltered. Chapter VI, on 'Welfare Criteria', has been extensively rewritten to take account of a justified criticism of the previous analysis by Professor Arrow[4] and other authors.[5] But I have rejected the view put forward by Mr. Kennedy,[6]

[1] I. M. D. Little, 'Social Choice and Individual Values', *J.P.E.*, Oct. 1952.

[2] M. Fleming, 'A Cardinal Concept of Welfare', *Q.J.E.*, Aug. 1952.

[3] J. C. Harsanyi, 'Cardinal Welfare, Individualistic Ethics, and Interpersonal Comparisons of Utility,' *J.P.E.*, Aug. 1955.

[4] K. J. Arrow, 'Little's Critique of Welfare Economics', *A.E.R.*, Dec. 1951.

[5] e.g. R. E. Baldwin, 'A Comparison of Welfare Criteria', *R.E.S.*, 1953-4, No. 55.

[6] See C. Kennedy, 'The Economic Welfare Function and Dr. Little's Criterion', *R.E.S.*, 1952-3, No. 52.

to which some other authors are sympathetic, that this type of analysis is valueless. Chapter VII is marginally altered. In Chapter VIII the treatment of 'external' effects has been slightly elaborated, and in Chapter IX the thesis that it is enough to make prices proportional to marginal costs has been examined at greater length (and more correctly). The related appendix on Direct versus Indirect Taxation has been rewritten in accordance with the analysis in my article of that name in the *Economic Journal*, September 1951, and becomes Appendix IV at the end of the book. Chapter X has been shortened and a number of mistakes removed. Even so I cannot pretend that the treatment of this involved subject of Consumers' Surplus is very satisfactory. Chapter XI has been fairly extensively revised, partly in the light of changes in the rest of the book: but the emphasis and conclusions are hardly affected, except in so far as I have added a stronger plea for profits in the nationalized industries. A few corrections have been made in Chapter XII, and the treatment of 'production potential' has been amended in order to accord better with Professor Samuelson's article 'Evaluation of Real National Income'.[1] In Chapter XIII some corrections have been made as a result of Mr. Baldwin's article cited above, and Professor H. G. Johnson's 'Optimum Tariffs and Retaliation'.[2] Chapters XIV and XV have not been significantly altered. A new appendix (Appendix III) on 'Kinked Behaviour Lines and Boundary Optima' has been added.

I hope I have made some improvements, with the assistance of, among others, the authors here cited. But these improvements may, broadly speaking, be said to be of a technical kind. I have not found that I have wished to alter my views as to the nature or significance of welfare economics, or any part of it. Finally, I am indebted to Mr. C. B. Winsten and Mr. J. Black for reading respectively part of and the whole of the revised text, and to my wife for reading the proofs. But they are in no way responsible for the remaining errors.

Nuffield College
April 1956

[1] *O.E.P.*, Jan. 1950.
[2] *R.E.S.*, 1953–4, No. 55.

PREFACE TO FIRST EDITION

MANY Oxford economists and philosophers have, consciously or unconsciously, contributed to this book. Among philosophers I am particularly indebted to Professor Gilbert Ryle, without whose kindness and encouragement I might not have persevered. Among economists I must thank Professor D. G. Champernowne, Mr. G. D. N. Worswick, Mr. T. Wilson, and Mr. P. W. S. Andrews for reading some or all of an earlier draft, and for making various helpful criticisms. I am also specially indebted to Mr. C. A. R. Crosland, at whose insistence many improvements of style and exposition have been made.

Some of the arguments of this book have been presented in articles in *Economica*, *Oxford Economic Papers*, and the *Review of Economic Studies*. The articles are not reproduced, but I am grateful to the editors of these journals for permission to use again some of the arguments and passages contained therein. Acknowledgements are also due to the Harvard University Press, the Princeton University Press, Macmillan & Co. Ltd., the Blakiston Co., Rinehart and Co. Inc., and Allen & Unwin Ltd., for permission to print passages from books published by them. Finally, it will be clear to most readers that considerable theoretical economy has been made possible by the work of Professor P. A. Samuelson, from whose published writings I have borrowed a great deal.

All Souls College
August 1949

INTRODUCTION

'STATESMEN despise publicists, painters despise art critics, and physiologists, physicists, or mathematicians have usually similar feelings; there is no scorn more profound, or on the whole more justifiable, than that of the men who make for the men who explain. Exposition, criticism, appreciation is work for second-rate minds.'[1]

The men whom some economists thus tend to despise they call 'methodologists'. Perhaps they should be despised. What is the use of the man who studies scientific method? He may explain to students how scientists reached their new theories; but this is unlikely to help the students reach new theories of their own. He may try to generalize, and lay down canons of inquiry. But there is no technique for forming good hypotheses which can be taught. Discussions of scientific method are often trite, and seldom helpful.

This book is not about methodology. Economists have used no methods of scientific research in arriving at their conclusions about economic welfare; and since there are no methods of scientific research involved there can be no methodology. I shall be, on the other hand, concerned with the exposition, the criticism, and the appreciation of the theory of economic welfare.

First there is exposition. Here I do not seek to be completely comprehensive, but only to give an account of the main body of welfare economics. Again, I do not attempt to deduce any new theorems, because the task I set myself is primarily that of the criticism and appreciation of such theory as we already have; and for this purpose there is no need to pursue the theory into every nook and cranny, although I do aim to explore all the important ones. Moreover, I believe that any further extension of welfare theory is unlikely to be at all valuable, except as a mathematical exercise. There is also no attempt to be fashionable, and make the theory dynamic. I do not, for instance, explore the possibilities of making welfare a function of the rate of change of living standards; nor do I bring risk or expectations into the formal theory, except in a very trivial and unrealistic way. My excuse is that any such considerations, though, in principle, they ought to make the theory more realistic, would, in practice, only mean that we could reach

[1] G. H. Hardy, *A Mathematician's Apology*, p. 1.

no specific conclusions, because we would then be dealing formally with factors which are not, in practice, nor even perhaps in
principle, measurable. I only introduce dynamic considerations
in a non-formal manner as affecting the realism of static welfare
theory, which, it seems, must remain static if it is going to be
possible to formulate any definite theorems. It seems better to
reach conclusions, and criticize them in the light of dynamic
considerations, rather than to produce a dynamic theory without
any real content.[1]

But exposition is only ancillary to criticism and appreciation.
In contrast to the undoubted validity of the formal deductions,
what are called the 'foundations' of the theory have always been
shrouded in darkness. What are the foundations of a theory? The
answer is, those postulates from which the theorems are deduced.
But how could they be shrouded in darkness? Surely, it may be
objected, one cannot make valid deductions from vague or ambiguous premises. But this is not true. The validity of the deductions is a matter of formal logic. Whether or not the premises and
conclusions are clear and unambiguous depends on the interpretation of the formal system.

One can, if one chooses, set up a logical system, using only
symbols, and without ever interpreting the symbols—that is,
without giving the system any real meaning. This has not, of
course, been done for welfare economics. The logic has always
been expressed in words. The resultant propositions constitute an
interpretation of the system. Utilitarian economics, or the hedonistic
calculus, was one such interpretation. It was a clear interpretation,
because we all know what words like 'satisfaction' and 'happiness' mean; unfortunately, as we shall show, it was not altogether
plausible. But more recently the word 'welfare' has been employed. It is by no means clear what this word means. It is, to put
it differently, not clear what welfare economics is about.

In spite of this lack of clarity, the theory has certainly influenced
the opinions of many people. It obviously could not have had any
such influence, if its conclusions had been meaningless, or merely

[1] Mr. M. W. Reder in his book *Studies in the Theory of Welfare Economics*
makes an attempt to dynamize the theory. But he only succeeds in reaching
conclusions which are either purely formal, or else negative. Thus he concludes:
'The results of this generalization of welfare economics are mainly negative.
A consideration of dynamic factors merely serves to make us cautious concerning
the application of static welfare criteria to a dynamic world.'

formal and recognized as such. Its conclusions certainly have some real (non-formal) meaning; but no one has bothered very much to try to analyse this meaning, or to show what sort of a meaning it is.

The above paragraph raises two questions. The first is, how can a theory be influential if no one knows what it is about? Physics would hardly influence peoples' actions or beliefs if no one knew what physics was about. What would be the use of reaching conclusions such as 'the earth goes round the sun' if one did not quite know what the words 'earth' and 'sun' meant? One enigma which we will try to solve in this book is precisely this—that welfare conclusions are important and influential, especially among economists, although few economists are clear as to what the word means, or what the theory is about.

The other question is, why has there been so little discussion of the foundations of the theory, and no discussion of the meaning of the word 'welfare', when welfare theory has existed for a long time? One good answer might be that a theory can be true, and very useful, although people are not clear about the meaning of some of its concepts. This is the case with physics. It does not really matter in the least whether one believes that such words as 'electron' or 'molecule' stand for entities of a peculiar kind, or whether one believes that they are merely words which serve a useful theoretical purpose. A discussion of this sort of question is very interesting, but academic. If physicists did not tend to become philosophers, they could afford to be contemptuous.

But drawing analogies between physics and other studies can result in harm. In psychology, for instance, the physical analogy has proved barren. It is not useful to think of the mind as consisting of molecules—feelings and volitions—tugging this way and that, with a resultant force which realizes itself in action. The psychology, which was apparently implied in utilitarian economics, was of this atomistic kind, and not very plausible. To suppose that, because discussions of the foundations of physics are not much use, therefore all such discussions are valueless, may be another example of a fallacy engendered by drawing analogies with that science; and such a supposition may account for the comparative absence of any serious interest in the foundations of welfare economics.

When the foundations of the theory are discussed in print, one gets the impression that the author is impatient—impatient to get on with the job of reaching ambiguous conclusions. A serious economist hardly likes to be caught at the trivial occupation of discussing foundations. Like G. H. Hardy, who excused himself for talking about mathematics, instead of doing mathematics, by saying that he was too old, so any discussion of the foundations of welfare economics is only an excusable occupation for old economists.

I have no doubt that this attitude is sensible as far as mathematics and physics are concerned. I also have no doubt that it is foolish as far as economics is concerned, because, as a result, ideas and opinions have almost certainly been influenced in a way which could not have happened if there had been more clarity about the nature of welfare theory. The analogy with physics breaks down in two important ways, which should lead one to suspect that what holds for one may not hold for the other. First, the concepts of physics, about which people are not clear, do not appear in the conclusions. The conclusions are about macroscopic or microscopic objects, not about electrons. By contrast, in welfare economics, the conclusions are about welfare. Secondly, physicists' conclusions are verified or falsified; ours are not.

My third task is appreciation. Having put the theory on what I believe to be a clear, and widely acceptable, basis, the question whether it is of any use must be asked. In view of the practical impossibility of testing its conclusions, this is a very difficult question to answer; but I do suggest that the reality of the theory has been badly overestimated by some economists. On this question of realism, economists seem to tend to extremes. Some display the greatest contempt for welfare theory. Others put their faith in it to an astonishing degree, and even build their politics upon it. But I know of no serious attempt to test its realism, perhaps because there are no obvious tests, and because it is rather difficult to test a theory if one does not quite know what it is about. Another reason for the lack even of much discussion of its realism may lie in its connexion with ethics. As a result of this connexion, it is a subject which arouses peoples' emotions. The result seems to be a lack of balance, the conclusions of the theory being either passionately attacked or passionately defended. I endeavour, as I go along, to form some judgement about the realism of the theory. Unfortunately, I see no possible way of proving to anyone that my own judgement is balanced, or unbiased. Once again, that would require empirical tests of its conclusions, which are not practicable.

Thus, appreciation of the theory—deciding on its worth—is largely a question of its realism. But in a rather different sense of 'appreciate', one cannot appreciate the importance of the theory without discussing the claims which have been put forward for it; these claims give one a clue as to what kind of an influence, and how much influence, it may have had, and might have in the future. So we are led into a brief political discussion.

I do not suggest that the theory has had, or is likely to have, much direct influence on political events, or economic policy. But in arguing, as I shall do, that it should have little or no influence, I do not believe that I am shadow-boxing, because the theory might well have a considerable indirect influence, by moulding the opinions of undergraduates, and, more important, as a result of some of its conclusions passing into ordinary language and being taken for granted as though they were the most obvious scientific truths. 'Practical men, who believe themselves to be quite exempt from any intellectual influences, are usually the slaves of some defunct economist. Madmen in authority, who hear voices in the air, are distilling their frenzy from some academic scribbler of a few years back . . . soon or late, it is ideas, not vested interests, which are dangerous for good or evil.'[1]

[1] J. M. Keynes, *The General Theory of Employment, Interest and Money*, pp. 383–4.

CHAPTER I

UTILITARIAN ECONOMICS

IF a person says that he undertakes to look after the welfare of a child, then he takes it upon himself to be concerned with everything which may affect the well-being of the child. We are in this book interested in *economic* welfare. There is no part of well-being called 'economic well-being'. The word 'economic' qualifies not well-being, but the causes of well-being or changes in it. If I am interested only in someone's economic welfare, then I interest myself only in the economic things which may affect his well-being.

But what does 'well-being' mean? For the moment it will be assumed that one can substitute the word 'happiness' for the word 'well-being'. The correctness of this substitution will not be fully discussed until Chapter V is reached. Here we will only say that it is in accordance with the usages of utilitarian economics and that, even if there is more to well-being than just happiness, it is at least true that a change in a person's happiness normally plays a large part in determining whether one would say that his well-being had changed. Thus the sentence 'I am interested in the economic welfare of Smith' is to be translated as 'I am interested in the economic causes of (changes in) Smith's happiness'.

It must also be decided which causes are economic, and which are not. The convention adopted about the use of the word 'economic' is not merely a matter of convenience. In this book the economic causes of changes in the happiness of an individual are taken to be those things and services which the individual consumes or enjoys, and which could be exchanged for money, together with the amount and kind of work which the individual does. Similarly, the economic welfare of the community is, by definition, only affected by changes in the amount of things and services consumed, which could be exchanged for money, and the work done by each individual. Everything else, including the methods by which the distribution of such 'goods' is determined, is excluded by the definition of 'economic'. But this limitation of the word 'economic', although convenient, may be misleading if people ordinarily use it in a wider or a narrower sense. The importance of the definition used will be discussed in Chapter V.

We have used the phrases 'the welfare of the community', and 'the well-being of an individual'. Now everyone knows what 'happiness' means with reference to an individual, and most people have a pretty good idea what sort of change may affect the happiness of a person. But when we come to 'the welfare of the community' there are great difficulties. If a person says he is interested in the economic welfare of society, we may make a similar translation as in the case of an individual, and say 'he is interested in the economic causes of the happiness of the community', but that unfortunately does not make it any clearer. Is there really something called 'the happiness of the community' which he is interested in, or is he just trying to create a good impression? Again if a politician stands up and says 'This change which I am proposing will increase social welfare', is he really predicting that something will grow larger, or is he just recommending the change without saying anything about what the results of it would be? In brief, is his statement descriptive or prescriptive, or both?

A very important answer to the kind of question raised above was given by Bentham. The phrase 'the happiness of society' was equivalent to 'the sum total of the happiness of all the individuals in society'. Moreover, Bentham laid it down that the guiding principle of right action was 'the greatest happiness principle'. Utility was a power in objects which would normally create satisfaction, and a man's happiness was the sum total of his satisfactions. Therefore the best principle was also that of the maximization of utility. The question whether one ought to maximize utility was a silly question. It was like asking 'Ought one to do what one ought to do'? To say that an action was the right action in certain circumstances was simply to say that it was the action which, in those circumstances, maximized utility. Again, Bentham held that to say that the 'welfare of the people' was one's guiding principle was just another way of saying that one accepted the greatest happiness principle.

Therefore Bentham would have had no difficulty in understanding the politician who said 'This change which I am proposing will increase social welfare'. He would have understood that the change would increase utility, and happiness, and that therefore it followed logically that it was a good change. He would probably have said that it was one and the same thing to predict an increase in happiness as a result of a change, and to say that the change was good. The politician's statement is, on this view, both scientific and ethical. Utilitarianism is a scientific ethic. It follows from these principles that welfare economics is a branch of ethics. If one maximizes those satisfactions which are the effects of economic causes, then one is maximizing, literally, a part of happiness. So long as this process does not involve making any other part of happiness smaller, then it follows that in striving to maximize economic welfare one is doing one's duty.

The 'maximum happiness principle' invited the application of the differential calculus to the problems of ethical economics, and the development of welfare theory has very largely been the result of applying mathematics to the quantitative ethical concepts which lay ready as a result of Bentham's philosophy.[1] An ethical problem was just another maximum problem, the kind of problem with which applied mathematicians were wont to deal. Edgeworth, in particular, was greatly excited by the possibilities of the science which promised to emerge from this union. To quote:

'Mécanique sociale' may one day take her place along with 'mécanique céleste' throned each upon the double-sided height of one maximum principle, the supreme pinnacle of moral as of physical science. As the movements of each particle, constrained or loose, in a material cosmos are continually subordinated to one maximum sum total of accumulated energy, so the movements of each soul, whether selfishly isolated or linked sympathetically, may continually be realising the maximum energy of pleasure, the divine love of the universe.[2]

Utilitarianism, as a theory of ethics, was, however, generally thought to be inadequate or false by the time that welfare economics, based on utility theory, received its most exhaustive and complete treatment in Professor Pigou's book *The Economics of Welfare*, which was published in 1920, almost 150 years after Bentham first enunciated his famous principle. Professor Pigou himself does not appear to have accepted ethical utilitarianism, but, nevertheless, took over the whole Benthamite doctrine that the welfare of society was the sum total of the welfares of individuals, and that the welfare of an individual was the sum total of the satisfactions he experienced.[3] Economic welfare was said to be a

---

[1] The strictly meaningless formula 'the greatest happiness of the greatest number', which inspired Bentham, was not his invention; it is ascribed to Francis Hutcheson.   [2] *Mathematical Psychics*, p. 12.

[3] Strictly speaking, welfare was held to belong only to states of individuals' minds, but might include 'psychic returns' other than satisfactions. Economic

part of total welfare, to wit that part which 'can be brought directly or indirectly into relation with the measuring rod of money'.[1] Thus Professor Pigou believed that he was discussing the causes of changes in the welfare of society in much the same way as one might discuss the reasons why the level of a river or a pond might change, and in what ways one could influence the level. Economic welfare was like a fluid or a gas which, although perhaps difficult to measure, was in principle measurable, so that changes in the amount of it could be experienced and described, and the causes of such changes discovered. Professor Pigou did not believe, like Bentham, that it followed from the very concept of welfare that it ought to be maximized. This was because, following G. E. Moore, he considered that 'good' and 'welfare' were un-analysable. Nevertheless, he was prepared to affirm that an increase in total welfare was an increase in total goodness. An increase in the satisfaction derived from goods and services (economic welfare) was held to result in an increase in total welfare if no non-economic harm resulted. It is therefore evident that satisfaction was held to be good. This was, apparently, a moral intuition. Thus the science of welfare economics was a science because it dealt with measurable quantities, i.e. satisfactions; it was the science of *welfare* because satisfactions were seen to be good.

The resultant position is not practically different from that of the ethical utilitarians. The latter reached it by a supposed analysis of goodness; Professor Pigou by just knowing what was good. Thus *The Economics of Welfare* purported to be an objective study of the causes of satisfaction; but it was also regarded by its author as an ethical study, although the transition from the one to the other was not, and could not be, analysed. We shall later try to show that *The Economics of Welfare* cannot be regarded as a purely objective study of the causes of welfare, as has sometimes been maintained. We shall also argue that it is indeed an ethical study; but that this follows from the nature of the terminology used, and requires no special moral insight. We will, however, leave this question for the present, and give an outline of the utility theory of welfare economics, as developed by Professor Pigou and his pre-decessors, and of the later developments in utility theory which

welfare, however, consisted only of satisfactions (cf. *Wealth and Welfare*, pp. 3 and 4). Thus, in some places at least, Pigou seemed to believe that 'economic' could qualify 'satisfactions'. [1] *Economics of Welfare*, 4th ed., p. 11.

have been widely accepted as a result of certain criticisms of the Benthamite concepts.

An essential feature of the Pigovian type of welfare economics is the assumption that each individual tries to maximize his own satisfaction. One could never say with much confidence that any change would increase the sum total of satisfaction if individuals were liable to let one down by suddenly trying to make themselves miserable. This assumption fitted in very well with the Marshallian theory of consumers' demand. It was thought that little could be said about the behaviour of prices if demand was not determined by the behaviour of rational individuals, and a rational man, i.e. the 'economic man', was one who tried to maximize his satisfaction. On this assumption the individual spends his money in such a way that the marginal unit of money is expected to yield the same amount of satisfaction on whatever it is spent. From this, it can be deduced that he makes the marginal utilities of every pair of things he consumes proportional to their prices. Then, given the prices of everything, and given the principle of diminishing marginal utility, the way in which each individual spends his money is determined. Thus the theory of value, or price, and the theory of economic welfare were hand in glove, both being based on the utility theory of consumers' behaviour. That each individual behaves in such a way as to maximize his utility was a necessary condition of achieving the maximum total utility which could be obtained from a given set of factors of production.

Certain other necessary conditions could be deduced about the way in which factors of production must be employed, and the way in which the resultant products must be distributed if maximum satisfaction was to be achieved. Exactly what those conditions are, and how they may be proved, will not be stated until we reach Chapter VIII. These conditions will be known as the 'optimum' conditions of production and exchange. They will be referred to, but must for the present be taken on trust. (The word 'optimum' is enclosed in inverted commas, because I do not wish to beg any question as to whether they are, in fact, the best conditions, or even whether they are good in any sense.)

There is a final necessary condition for achieving the maximum possible happiness, which is that the marginal unit of money must yield the same amount of satisfaction to everyone. If this condition is not fulfilled, then happiness can be increased by taking money income away from one man and giving it to another. If we assume a law of diminishing marginal utility of income, this implies that an equalitarian distribution of income will yield the most satisfaction. But there is a trap here. Do we mean to assume that the marginal utility of money decreases as money income increases, or as real income increases?

Marshall seems to have arrived at the law by observing a diminishing marginal utility of money, as money income increases, for a given individual, assuming constant prices. The next step is to assume that everyone has the same tastes, and the same capacity for satisfaction, and is faced with the same set of prices, whence one may pass to the law of diminishing marginal utility of money income with constant prices, to whomsoever that income accrues. In other words, an extra pound will always yield less satisfaction to a man with more money than it will to one with less money. Since at any one moment prices are constant, it follows that at every moment an equal distribution of money income will yield the greatest sum total of satisfaction.

But this is not very plausible. We judge people's tastes by what they buy, and it is not the case that everyone with the same money income buys the same collection of things. To assume an equal capacity for satisfaction would not be enough, even if it were true. Two people with equal money incomes cannot derive equal satisfaction both before and after a change which increases the prices of everything which the one buys and the other does not buy. Thus it appears that we may sometimes want to say that Smith would derive more satisfaction from an extra pound than Jones would, although Smith has more money than Jones.

We will deal with the above problem at greater length later, but here it must be said that Marshall's interpretation of the law of diminishing marginal utility of income is different from that of Bentham who first proposed the law. Bentham, and apparently Professor Pigou, thought that diminishing utility applied in some sense to real income. This raises the question of how one is to compare the real incomes of different people. The real income of a person consists of a heterogeneous bundle of goods and services. There is normally no clear sense in which one such bundle can be said to be larger than another. In order to compare two different collections of goods we have to weight, or value, the different items. If the relative values of different goods are taken to be the same as their relative prices, then the total value of each collection of goods will be equal to, or a given proportion of, the amount of money required to buy it. Therefore, in trying to compare two different men's real income in this way, we would, in fact, only be comparing their money income (given that savings is included as a good). Thus it would appear that the law of the diminishing marginal utility of income cannot refer to real income unless some independent test of relative real income is laid down.

But it has already been seen that it is not very plausible to say that the law refers to money income. How, then, can it be interpreted? The answer is, I think, that it must be supposed to refer to real income; but since no test of relative real income was laid down by the utilitarians, we must interpret the so-called law as a tautology, i.e. a higher marginal utility of money is to be taken as a sufficient criterion of a lower real income. Thus, when Professor Pigou writes: 'Nevertheless it is evident that any transference of income from a relatively rich man to a relatively poor man of similar temperament, since it enables more intense wants to be satisfied at the expense of less intense wants, must increase the aggregate sum of satisfaction',[1] it must be supposed that it is observed that the transference of money income (and therefore real income) from Smith to Jones results in the satisfaction of more intense wants, and *therefore* it is said that Smith is really richer (has a higher real income) than Jones.[2]

Therefore, on the utilitarian view, if the marginal utility of money income is equal for everyone, then satisfaction is maximized, and, by definition, everyone is economically equal; and, by definition, one man is really richer than another when the marginal utility of money is for him lower than for the other. There does not seem to be any other possible interpretation of the doctrine, which is

[1] *The Economics of Welfare*, 4th ed., p. 89.

[2] The phrase 'real income' is ambiguous. The sense of the word 'real' in the phrase differs according to the context in which it is used. If one says 'the real income of the community is the flow of goods and services produced', the force of the word 'real' lies in its reference to things useful for their own sake (as opposed to money). If, on the other hand, knowing that a man's money income has increased, one asks whether his real income has increased, then one is asking, in effect, whether he is better off. The force of the word 'real' here lies in its contrast with 'apparent'. The man is apparently better off, for he has more money—but is he really better off? When one makes real income comparisons (whether interpersonal or not) this latter sense of the word real is, I think, often the operative one. Thus the sentence '*A*'s real income is higher than *B*'s' is, I think, almost equivalent to '*A* is really richer than *B*'.

consistent with the fact that different people do have different tastes and capacities for satisfaction. It may be objected that the obvious utilitarian definition of economic equality is that people are economically equal when they derive the same total satisfaction from economic things. But, if this is the definition, it does not follow that equality produces maximum happiness, which is a central tenet of radical utilitarianism.

Let us now go back to the 'optimum' conditions of production and exchange. If these conditions were not realized, it followed that more satisfaction could be produced so long as putting these 'optimum' conditions into operation did not change the distribution of the goods so much in favour of the rich (as defined above) that any increase in satisfaction which would otherwise have resulted would be wiped out. The main business of welfare theory was to work out these 'optimum conditions', but it can be seen that any conclusion reached always had to be qualified by a reference to distribution. But no means of telling whether income distribution had shifted away from or towards those with higher marginal utilities of money was given. The best that could be done was to take money income as a guide, and use some more or less arbitrary measure of inequality of money incomes.

The general conclusions of utilitarian welfare theory were therefore inevitably tentative. It could never be definitely said that putting the 'optimum' conditions into operation would increase the welfare of the community. Perhaps this was not always sufficiently stressed.

This completes our statement of the basic principles of utilitarian economics. We must now consider the main objections which have been brought against such a theory. First, it is said that satisfactions cannot be added. Therefore it is meaningless to speak of the happiness of the community as the sum total of the happinesses of individuals, and the happiness of individuals as the sum total of their satisfactions. The result of this criticism has been the general acceptance of a theory based on the view that only the ordinal number system, and not the cardinal number system, may be applied to satisfactions. In other words, one can say when one has more or less satisfaction, but one cannot say how much one has. The resulting theory will be discussed in Chapter II, together with the question whether a cardinal or an ordinal utility system best explains the economic behaviour of individuals.

Secondly, it has been held that the satisfactions and happiness of different people cannot be compared in an objective scientific way, and that any such comparison is a value, or an ethical judgement, and not an ordinary empirical judgement about a matter of fact. This criticism, together with a further discussion of the meaning of real income distribution and economic equality, will be dealt with in Chapter IV.

The third criticism, which arises out of the second, is that welfare economics is inevitably a normative study, because no change could be made without harming someone, and since (it has been said) interpersonal comparisons of satisfaction are value judgements, and essential to judgements about the welfare of society, welfare economics is unavoidably ethical. This criticism raises the whole question of the relation of ethics and economics, which will be discussed in Chapter V. Thereafter we will be mostly concerned with the so-called new welfare economics, which has been developed as a result of these criticisms of utilitarian welfare economics.

CHAPTER II

THE ANALYSIS OF
CONSUMERS' BEHAVIOUR[1]

As a result of abandoning the idea that satisfactions can be added, the 'indifference-curve' analysis of the rational consumer's behaviour has largely taken the place of the Marshallian type of analysis. The assumption that the individual tries to maximize his satisfaction is retained. But 'maximizing satisfaction' no longer means 'achieving the largest sum total of satisfaction' but rather 'reaching the highest level of satisfaction'. Satisfaction is like a hill; one can say that one is higher up, or lower down, or at the same height. Like a hill, contour lines can be drawn which mark the same height, but, unlike an ordinary hill, these contour lines are not marked in feet, or units of satisfaction. They are simply given ordinal numbers, first, second, third contours, and so on. Since there is no question of adding up these numbers, for one cannot add ordinals, it does not matter whether they are labelled one, two, three—or one, seven, ten. They could equally well be labelled nine, twenty, thirty. All that matters is the order. A higher contour, representing greater satisfaction, must have a higher number than a lower contour. That is all.

Let us now imagine a world in which there are only two goods, X and Y, and take some one consumer. As far as economic things are concerned his satisfaction as a consumer now only depends on the amounts of X and Y he can consume. The next step is to draw the contour lines on a graph, the two co-ordinates of which represent amounts of X and Y. Any two points on one such contour line thus represent collections of goods which are equally satisfactory to the consumer. In order to draw a contour line, take a given collection of goods, represented by a point A on the graph, and then discover, by asking the consumer, all the other collections of X and Y such that he says he is indifferent between each of these collections B, C, D, &c., and collection A. It is then assumed that

[1] Much of the argument of this chapter is contained in my article 'A Reformulation of the Theory of Consumers' Behaviour', *O.E.P.*, N.S., no. 1, Jan. 1949. I am indebted to Mr. J. Durbin of Cambridge for pointing out some mistakes in the article.

he is indifferent between B and C, C and D, and so on. In other words, it is assumed that indifference is a transitive relation. This means that if a person is indifferent between A and B, and between B and C, then he must be indifferent between A and C. The contour line, which is usually called an indifference curve, is thus determined.[1]

Now give the consumer a little more Y. This brings him to a new point Z, which, let us say, represents $7X$ and $8Y$ whereas A represented $7X$ and $7Y$. Z must be preferred to A. But, one may ask, is it not possible that $7X$ and $7Y$ should give a man more satisfaction than $7X$ and $8Y$? The answer is 'No', because X and Y are *goods*. By definition, a larger collection of goods gives more satisfaction than a smaller collection, and, again by definition, a collection of heterogeneous goods is larger than another collection if there is more of one kind of good, and no less of any kind. This means that if a man likes 7 apples better than 8 apples then for him an apple cannot be called a good. The abstract concept 'good' can only be applied to things in the real world if it is true that more things give more satisfaction than fewer things.

Starting from the new point Z we then go through exactly the same procedure as before, and draw a second indifference curve through this point. This new indifference curve cannot cut the old one. Why?

In Fig. I it has been drawn so as to cut it at a point B. Our consumer is now indifferent between Z and B, and between B and A. But indifference was defined as a transitive relation. Therefore he is indifferent between Z and A, but again by definition Z is preferred to (causes more satisfaction than) A. Our system is evidently contradictory, and therefore indifference curves must not cut. But suppose we find, when they are drawn up for some

[1] This account of how an indifference curve is to be determined follows the usual textbook exposition. A clear statement of the orthodox view is given by R. G. D. Allen, *Mathematical Analysis for Economists*, p. 124, where he states: 'The basic assumption now is that the consumer distributes his expenditure on the two goods according to a definite "scale of preferences". His "tastes" on this assumption are such that he can arrange all possible purchases of the goods in ascending order of preference and, given any two alternative sets of purchases, he can *either* tell which purchases are preferable *or* say they are indifferent to him.' In this context 'preferable' and 'indifferent' cannot be supposed to be meant as uninterpreted symbols, and 'preferable' can thus only mean 'more satisfactory', and 'indifferent' mean 'equally satisfactory'. For this reason I have used the word 'satisfaction' more freely than most authors care to do in this context.

individual, that they do cut. What are we to say about a consumer who insists on being illogical? The answer is simply that we say he is illogical, which means nothing more than that our system of logic does not apply to him. It does not mean that he is irrational, or silly or mad. There are, as we shall see later, plenty of reasons why our system should not apply, which do not imply that we are dealing with a lunatic.

FIG. I

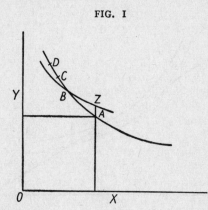

Let us now assume that we have succeeded in drawing up a set of non-intersecting indifference curves, that is a satisfaction map, and remember that we assume that the individual always behaves so as to maximize his satisfaction. The object of the map is to demonstrate what quantities of X and Y our consumer will pur-chase if we give him a certain quantity of Y and then let him trade X for Y at a given price.

In Fig. II the consumer starts off with OA of Y. The price of X in terms of Y is OA/OB. If he gives up any amount of Y, say ΔY, then he can have $\Delta Y \times OB/OA$ of X. Thus the slope of the line AB measures the relative prices of X and Y. Now, since he maximizes his satisfaction, he gives up Y, getting X in exchange (i.e. he travels along the line AB) until he reaches the point E where the line AB touches the highest possible indifference curve.

The question arises whether AB may not touch this highest possible indifference curve at more than one point. If it does there is no telling from the map which of the collections, represented by those points, the consumer will buy. The consumer would be indifferent which collection he bought. But it is inconvenient to have an indeterminate situation, so let us, for the moment, assume that all price lines, such as *AB*, only touch the highest indifference curve at one point. Now if this is to be the case, indifference curves must all be convex or concave towards the origin *O*.[1] If they were everywhere concave the consumer would buy all *X*, or all *Y*, whatever their relative prices, and never some of each. This

FIG. II

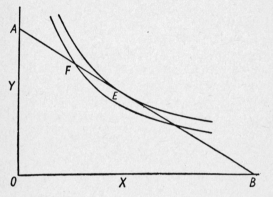

case can be ruled out as unrealistic. It is therefore postulated that the curves are everywhere convex to the origin. This is how they are almost always drawn.

The point *E* is the equilibrium point, that is the point at which *AB* touches the highest indifference curve. What can be said about this point? It is evident that the line *AB* and the indifference curve have the same slope at *E*. The slope of *AB* measures the relative prices of *X* and *Y*. But what does the slope of the indifference curve measure? It measures the rate at which *X* can be substituted for *Y* while remaining at the same level of satisfaction. Therefore the condition for maximizing satisfaction is that the price-ratio of any two goods should be equal to the rate at which the consumer can substitute one for the other without gaining or losing satisfac-

---

[1] It is impossible to deduce that indifference curves are anywhere convex to the origin merely from the definition of equilibrium. A consumer is in equilibrium if he makes a free choice from among the possibilities indicated by the position and slope of the price line. But the fact that he makes one definite choice from among these possibilities does not prove that there is not some other point on the price line which is indifferent to the chosen point.

tion. This condition takes the place of the Marshallian condition that the price-ratio should be equal to the ratio of the marginal utilities of the two goods. Also, the assumption of diminishing marginal utility is replaced by the assumption that we have a diminishing rate of substitution of Y for X if we are to remain on the same level of satisfaction.

We now want to ask ourselves whether this new kind of analysis is an important advance. To answer this we must first discuss the difference between a pure and an applied logical system. In a pure system one uses certain abstract concepts, and defines them by means of axioms. These concepts have no meaning which does not derive from the axioms, and from the way in which they are used within the system itself. They have no reference to anything out-side the system. Every sentence in which such words, or concepts, occur is either an axiom or postulate of the system, or a deduction from the axioms. Such a system is applied by *interpreting* the con-cepts, that is by taking them to refer to, or denote, something out-side the system. For instance, pure geometry is not about space, or about anything at all. It is only about space when its concepts, for instance 'point' and 'line', are taken to refer to real points, such as pin-pricks on paper, and real lines drawn on paper. A logical system can, of course, be perfectly valid (that is, the theories follow from the axioms) even although it has no application to the real world. But it is not only whole logical systems which can be thus abstract. Much the same can be said about words, even if they do not form part of a self-consistent circular logical system. For instance, in formulating the indifference-curve analysis we used the word 'good', and stated that *by definition* more 'goods' give more satisfaction than fewer 'goods'. This was not just arbitrary. The word has, I think, come to be used in this way in economics. But very often it is not easy to tell whether a word used in economics has its ordinary meaning, or whether, by a gradual process of evolution, it has come to have a definition, or a partial definition. It is not always very easy to tell, because definitions can arise by a gradual process and need not to be explicitly laid down. The con-clusions of a logical system are tautologies, for they are deduced from explicit definitions. But there are many tautologies in ordinary speech, although no one has laid down an explicit definition of the words, by virtue of which the tautological statements are tautologies.

Now the important word 'utility' has undergone such a change. For Bentham 'utility' referred to some power in objects to create satisfaction in people. With Marshall and Pigou it was roughly equivalent to 'desiredness'. It was a relation between men and things, although, strictly speaking, maximization of utility could only mean maximization of anticipated satisfaction. But nowadays economists talk of cardinal and ordinal utility systems. In such statements the word 'utility' does not refer to any power in objects or any real relation. It need not refer to anything. A cardinal utility system is an abstract system in which 'utilities' are subject to the operations of addition and multiplication. In ordinal utility systems these processes are excluded.

The difference between Marshall's and the indifference-curve analysis of consumers' behaviour can be described by saying that the former was a cardinal utility system, and the latter is an ordinal utility system. This is a little misleading, because Marshall did not specifically distinguish the pure and applied system. For him utility was not a purely abstract concept. But it would, of course, be easy to pretend that the Marshallian analysis was pure or uninterpreted, in which case 'utility' would cease to refer to some relation between consumers and objects of consumption, and would become an abstract concept. Now, we may ask, what would be the interpretation of 'utility' if we sought to reapply the pure Marshallian analysis? The answer is that 'utility' must be taken to refer to satisfaction, or anticipated satisfaction. We thus see how the word 'utility' has changed its meaning. To put it metaphorically, utility was once thought of as a kind of reflection of satisfaction in the external world, a power in objects to cause satisfaction, but later it came to be thought of as a kind of reflection of satisfactions in logic.

Now in my exposition of the indifference-curve analysis I never mentioned the word 'utility'. I spoke of satisfactions. But if one substitutes the word 'utility' for the word 'satisfactions' one leaves open the question whether the system can be interpreted in terms of satisfaction, or not. Strictly one ought also to regard all the concepts used as abstract or uninterpreted. 'The consumer' should not be taken to refer to any consumer. One must not beg the question whether the system can reasonably be held to have anything to do with real consumers and real satisfactions at all.

After this digression into logic we can now state quite shortly

the advance which the indifference-curve analysis might be supposed to have made. The pure Marshallian type of system subjects
'utilities' to the process of addition. But it is now widely thought
that it makes nonsense to speak of adding satisfactions. If this is
so, the postulate 'the individual maximizes the sum total of utility'
cannot be interpreted as 'the individual maximizes the sum total
of his satisfactions': worse still, how can the law of diminishing
marginal utility be interpreted? The indifference-curve analysis
is, however, in its pure form, an ordinal utility system. Since satisfactions can be arranged at least in order of magnitude, such a
system could, it was thought, be interpreted in terms of satisfaction.

This advance which the indifference-curve analysis would seem
to have made is, however, something of an illusion. It is not true
that it can itself be plausibly interpreted in terms of satisfaction.
It is not denied that it makes sense to say that one satisfaction is
greater than another. Where the chief difficulty lies is in the interpretation of the axiom 'the individual maximizes utility'. We will
seek to show that this cannot reasonably be interpreted in terms of
consumers maximizing their satisfaction. If this were the correct
interpretation it would follow that the system could be applied only
to consumers who did maximize, or at least tried fairly successfully
to maximize, their satisfaction; in other words, economists could
explain only the behaviour of satisfaction-maximizers. For what
economists have done in drawing up a set of indifference curves for
a consumer is to draw a map of the man's preferences and indiffer-
ences. If the man then fails to act in accordance with his preferences how can one explain his behaviour? One must wash one's
hands of him. Even if not mad, he is at least not an example of an
'economic man'. So it would seem that the only people that economists theorize about are satisfaction-maximizers.

In the past economists have often been attacked on the grounds
that their theories applied only to selfish people; such attacks
were brushed aside as absurd. But they were not absurd. It was
the economists who were wrong in suggesting that positive economics had any necessary connexion with satisfactions at all. The
usual way of answering these attacks was to say that an altruistic
man might still be maximizing his satisfaction, because altruism is
itself a pleasure. But this is to deny that one ever suffers, or expects
to suffer, by helping others, which is absurd. For instance, a man

may support a wife who makes his life unbearable, and without getting any pleasure from the fact that he may be doing his duty. It is not at all plausible to say that he is maximizing his satisfaction, and yet, as we shall see, his behaviour may be in perfect conformity with his having a consistent set of 'indifference' curves.

Professor Stigler[1] has tried to get over this difficulty by saying that it does not matter what a man tries to maximize, so long as he tries to maximize something, say his weight or his misery. But this amounts to a determination to say that whenever the economist *can* explain a man's behaviour then that man must be maximizing *something*. It gives no indication whatever as to when the theory can be applied and when not. On the contrary, it uses the successful application of the theory as a test of when a person is maximizing. Instead of saying 'If he maximizes we will get the answers right' it says 'If we get the answers right he is maximizing'. But if we get the answers right, it doesn't matter whether he is maximizing, minimizing, or acting from sheer caprice.

Basically, however, Professor Stigler was on the right lines. He saw that the important principle in utility theory, in so far as the theory has implications about economic behaviour, was that the subject should evaluate all the possibilities open to him according to some common measure, and select the highest valued. That this principle does justice to the wealth and richness of people's motives is repugnant to many people's common sense.[2] But even if people go through no such mental process, they may still behave as if they did. In this case there is no harm (but also, as we saw in the previous paragraph, no advantage), so far as positive economics is concerned, in saying that they maximize 'utility', whatever that may be. But to say this is a considerable disadvantage for welfare economics, for it leads inevitably to interpreting more 'utility' as more satisfaction, or happiness: in so doing the economist merely makes himself seem silly, for nothing is clearer than that there is far from being a perfect link between utility in the above sense, and satisfaction or happiness.

It has become clear that we should first discover what rules of behaviour are implied by the ordinal utility analysis: and then find a better interpretation of 'more utility' than more satisfaction. For this purpose it is necessary to interpret the system in terms of

[1] *The Theory of Price*, p. 64.
[2] See, e.g., Georgescu-Roegen, 'Choice, Expectations and Measurability', *Q.J.E.*, Nov. 1954.

choice.[1] Let us remind ourselves of how, in our exposition above, it was proposed that the set of indifference curves should be drawn up. A certain collection of things was taken, and the individual was asked to name all other collections, such that he was indifferent between each of these and the original collection. Thus an indifference curve, as the name implies, represented all collections between which he was indifferent.

Now the word 'indifference' seems to present an obstacle to our new interpretation. It refers to a state of mind rather than to any single act of choice. In saying this I am not of course maintaining that indifference is a secret sort of feeling. There is no philosophical barrier to using the word, and having an interpretation in terms of choice. We can observe indifference, as someone has remarked.[2] But if we are to produce an exact interpretation we need to say rather more than this. 'Preference' is easy to define in terms of choice: we can translate 'Smith prefers A to B' into 'other things being equal, Smith chooses A rather than B'. But 'indifference' is harder. A statistical definition has been suggested. If we face the individual with the same alternatives many times, and (approximately) half the times he takes one, and half the other, then we say he is indifferent. This is a very unsatisfactory definition. It makes it difficult to distinguish indifference and inconsistency. It also becomes necessary to specify the number of experiments, and fix an arbitrary relative frequency of choices as the boundary of preference and indifference. It also conflicts with the ordinary definitions of preference in terms of a single act of choice: for if we must have a large number of tests to determine indifference, equally we must have a large number to determine preference.

But there is little need to concern ourselves with these puzzles, for it is perfectly simple in principle to arrive at a set of so-called

[1] It should be emphasized that the need to do this has nothing whatever to do with the philosophical or psychological theories of behaviourism. Gibes such as 'Pure behaviourism has not proved a particularly helpful method in psychology proper. Why, at this time of day, we should go out of our way to shackle ourselves with its self-frustrating inhibitions is not at all evident' (L. Robbins, 'Robertson on Utility and Scope', *Economica*, May 1953) are entirely beside the point. There is no doubt that formulating the theory on the basis of certain axioms about the consistency of behaviour has recently stimulated interest in those axioms, and in the question as to what makes people behave consistently or otherwise. It is now much easier to see in what circumstances utility theory is likely to be true or false: and a beginning has even been made with testing it.

[2] V. C. Walsh, 'On Descriptions of Consumers' Behaviour', *Economica*, Aug. 1954.

indifference curves by offering the subject only actual choices between different sets of goods. Let us suppose that we start with a
given collection of things A, and then ask our consumer to say of
every other possible collection whether he would take it rather than
A, or whether he would take A rather than it. It is evident that so
long as we make him name all possible collections we would then
have arrived at the so-called indifference curve as the boundary
between the area representing collections rather than which A
would be taken, and the area representing collections which would
be taken rather than A.[1]

But what of the choices between points which actually lie on the
boundary? If we offer the individual a free choice between two
such points he will select one rather than the other. Therefore if
we wish to say that a person is better off in A than B when he
chooses A rather than B, and this is to mean the same as having
more utility, we cannot call the boundary lines indifference curves.
I have therefore proposed to rechristen them 'behaviour lines'.[2]
If we also assume that his choices between any three points are
transitive, it follows that the boundary points must have a definite
choice order, just as the boundary lines are themselves ordered. We
have then arrived at the simplest of choice theories—to wit, that
all the alternatives can be arranged in order in the manner of links
on a chain, the person selecting the 'highest' link open to him.[3]

Now transitivity of choice is the condition which determines a
set of non-intersecting indifference curves, or behaviour lines, as
we shall now call them. It is left to the reader to prove this for
himself by showing that intransitivity must always occur when two
curves cross. This condition together with invariance of choice

[1] To be strictly rigorous the strong ordering here outlined requires a
different set of axioms to that normally developed for orderings which include indifference. See Appendix I.
[2] 'A Reformulation of the Theory of Consumers' Behaviour', *O.E.P.*, Jan.
1949.
[3] One cannot always have a utility function assigning a different number to
every point in the commodity space—for there are not always enough numbers if
they are to be kept in the right order. If our boundary curves, i.e. behaviour
lines, did not touch each other, then one could define them as iso-utility curves
(or, more paradoxically, as 'indifference' curves), in spite of the fact that the
points on them were ordered by choice. This would suffice for a utility function.
But it has the disadvantage that the relation 'chosen rather than' is not then a
sufficient condition for 'more utility' which is usually identified with 'better off'.
We thus prefer not to assume that a person's choices can necessarily be described
by a utility function: but, on the other hand, see p. 28, note 1.

between every pair of alternatives is what we shall in general mean by consistency of choice.

As we shall see, consistency alone is not sufficient to determine the conventional sets of curves, which have other properties besides not crossing. Let us, however, ignore this for the moment, in order to investigate the meaning which now attaches to our maximization postulate. Suppose, then, that we have a set of non-crossing curves, as in Fig. II. As before, all points on or below the line AB are possibilities for our subject. In order that he should select the point E, it is clear that one must *in abstract terms* have a maximizing postulate. He must seek to reach the highest curve possible. But what interpretation should now be put upon this postulate? The area above any curve represents points which the man said he would take rather than any given point on the curve. If, for instance, the lower of the two curves had been drawn by asking the man to name every set of goods he would choose rather than F, and vice versa, then E would be among the points he said he would choose rather than F. This is also true of any point which is not a point of tangency of AB and one of the curves. If he fails, so to speak, to rise above any given curve when he can, he is failing to do something he said he would do. Thus the interpretation of the postulate that 'utility is maximized' is simply *that the man must behave in the way in which he said he would behave. Roughly speaking, maximizing utility means telling the truth—or, less paradoxically, being able correctly to predict one's own behaviour.*

Let us now return to the already mentioned fact that consistency alone is not sufficient to determine the conventional set of curves, which, apart from not crossing, are also smooth, convex, and never touch each other.

If a behaviour line is not smooth, i.e. has a kink in it as in Fig. III, it is evident that a number of different price-income, or budget, lines[1] can touch[2] it at the same point. If the 'optimum' conditions are to be deduced as necessary conditions for an 'optimum', then this case must be ruled out. On the other hand, if kinked curves are permitted (and it is plausible to argue that such will be a common

[1] If we assume that all prices, except that of x, are constant, then we can put money income instead of y on the vertical axis. The line AB then depicts the position of a consumer with a given income faced with a given price of x. Lines such as AB will be called 'budget lines'.

[2] 'Support' is the correct technical word, 'touch' strictly referring to a condition of tangency.

case),[1] many of the theorems of welfare economics still stand in a slightly modified form. In the text of the book we deal with the conventional statement of these 'optimum' conditions, and for this purpose we assume that each set of goods would be chosen in one and only one price-income situation, which rules out the possibility of kinked curves. The modifications required if this assumption is not made are dealt with in Appendix III.

FIG. III

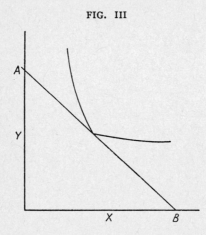

The curves might also be concave in places as in Fig. IV.

In this case there is no telling from the diagram which of the two points E_1 and E_2 would be chosen. The significance of concavity is that no point within the area bounded by the concave part of the curve, and the price-income line (the shaded area in the diagram), would ever be chosen in any price-income situation: for inspection shows that in whatever direction a price line is drawn, it will always touch a higher curve outside such an area than it will in it. For the purposes of welfare economics there is no reason why one should not suppose that the curves are concave in places, so that certain combinations of goods are, as it were, taboo—and would never be chosen in any conceivable price-income situation. If, for other purposes, it were required to rule out this case, then the assumption that every possible set of goods would be chosen in some or other price-income situation does the trick. While, however, some concavity in the preference field is permitted,

[1] See Georgescu-Roegen, *Q.J.E.*, Nov. 1954.

THE ANALYSIS OF CONSUMERS' BEHÁVIOUR 27

the case of lines sloping upwards in a north-easterly direction is
ruled out by the reasonably acceptable assumption that where
there is more of each good that is preferred.[1]

Finally, consistency of choice does not prevent the curves from
merging, as in Fig. V. The diagram is not inconsistent with
transitivity of choice as can be seen by considering the points A,
B, and C; for their positions are consistent with them being chosen

FIG. IV

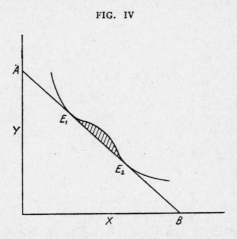

in the order ABC.[2] But on the ordinary indifferent curve analysis,
this case is ruled out, for both A and B would be indifferent to C,
and hence, since transitivity of indifference is assumed, to each
other. But that A and B should be indifferent contradicts the axiom
that a larger set is preferred to a smaller.

[1] It should be noted that, in the case of concave curves, a budget line may
touch both a higher and a lower behaviour line without crossing either in the
neighbourhood of the points of contact. In this case only the point of contact
with the highest curve is assumed to be an equilibrium point—i.e. consumers
are assumed to be long-sighted enough to see and move to any peak higher
than the one they are on.

[2] In the diagram, it can be supposed that either AC or BC is the behaviour
line of C: that is, the subject may have stated that all points above AC, or
alternatively above BC, would be taken rather than C—and vice versa. If BC is
the behaviour line of C, then B and C have a common behaviour line, while AC
is the behaviour line of A, but not of C. If AC is the behaviour line of C, then
A and C have a common behaviour line: while BC is the behaviour line of B,
but not of C.

Merging lines do not prevent one proving the 'optimum' conditions, for these depend only on the requirement that no point on a budget line can be an equilibrium point if it crosses the behaviour line of that point. But they prevent one defining a transitive relation 'equally well off', which is required in welfare economics. Thus Fig. V is inconsistent with our defining a consumer as 'equally well off' if on the same behaviour line—for

FIG. V

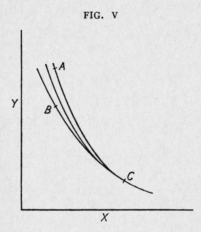

he would then be equally well off at A and B. We must therefore assume that behaviour lines do not merge.[1]

We may now bring together the assumptions we require for the purposes of welfare economics. Apart from the requirements of the above paragraph, they are (1) that larger collections of goods should be chosen rather than smaller ones, (2) that if a person once chooses one collection rather than another, he always does so, (3) that his choices should be transitive, and (4) that any chosen collection of goods should be chosen in only one price-income situation—i.e. any change in relative prices will always cause some change in what is bought.

Given these assumptions, a consistent set of behaviour lines can

[1] The required mathematical assumption is that the differential equation defining the set of curves should have continuous partial derivatives. The meaning of this mathematical condition is that 'indifference' (as defined in note 3 of page 24) should be transitive. This might be said to be the economic interpretation of the required assumption—but it is not one which can be given any meaning in terms of actual choice (since what are, *ex hypothesi*, limiting cases can never be tested).

be drawn up, such that if an individual reaches a point which lies above the curve belonging to the point from which he started, then he has got a collection of goods which is higher'up on the order of his choices than the previous collection. And this will be the criterion (= sufficient condition) used for his being 'better off'. The fulfilment of this criterion may, of course, be taken, by anyone who wishes to do so, to imply that the person is more satisfied. But it is certainly quite possible for someone to be 'on a higher behaviour line', and be less satisfied. In other words, it does not follow logically from the meaning of behaviour lines that anyone who can be said to be 'on a higher behaviour line' must also be said to have more satisfaction—all that follows is that he is in a chosen position. This conclusion may not sound very novel. Indeed, many people have probably thought that the indifference-curve analysis was about choices, and not about satisfactions. But so long as the concept 'indifference' was retained and not defined in terms of choice, a rigorous interpretation in such terms was impossible.

The translation of utility theory into choice theory, which is what has been done above, has, in recent years, become rather confused with what is usually, and rather unfortunately, called 'the Theory of Revealed Preference'. This theory shows how the consumer's behaviour map can in principle be constructed from observations of his purchases in different price-income situations. In such a situation a man is said to choose the collection he buys rather than all the other collections which he could have bought given his income, and the prices. In index-number form he is said to choose collection a rather than any collection x if $\sum p_a q_a \geqslant \sum p_a q_x$.[1] On this procedure the curves are constructed, with the aid of certain assumptions about the rules governing a man's choices, from actual choices. The maximizing postulate disappears altogether, for the highest point a price line touches then represents the same collection of goods which has already been taken before, in exactly the same circumstances, and it is therefore determined simply by the assumption of consistency of choice. But in order to translate

---

[1] $\sum p_a q_a$ stands for the total expenditure (= income) on the collection of goods a. $\sum p_a q_x$ stands for the total sum which results from valuing any other collection of goods x at the prices reigning when the collection a was bought. Thus the condition $\sum p_a q_a \geqslant \sum p_a q_x$ indicates that the expenditure on a would also have sufficed to buy any collection x for which the condition holds. It shows, in other words, that x was a possibility when a was bought: and, hence (by definition) that a was chosen rather than x.

utility theory into choice theory we are not required to limit ourselves to observations of people buying things in perfectly competitive conditions.[1] In principle, choices between pairs of collections of goods, where the only cost of one collection is not having the other, may also be compared. The proof that we can also arrive at behaviour lines, even when limiting our observations to the market, is a piece of pure theoretical virtuosity which adds nothing to an understanding of choice theory. In fact, rather more stringent assumptions are required in order to prove the point than are necessary if observations are not so limited. From the point of view of a critique of welfare economics it would be wrong to make stronger assumptions than are necessary to arrive at the usual conclusions, whose value we are seeking to assess. Consequently further discussion of the 'Theory of Revealed Preference' is relegated to Appendix II.

Some readers may feel that an interpretation of the economic theory of the consumer in terms of choice leaves something out. Surely, they will say, you have not *explained* behaviour if you have not related it to the psychological causes of that behaviour. There is, nearly everyone would agree, no doubt about the value of giving such explanations. It does not follow, however, that anything worth while has been left out: for it is very doubtful whether old-fashioned utility theory was a valuable contribution towards explaining why people behave as they do. We have, in effect, shown that all the conventional theorems of economic behaviour follow from certain axioms of choice, such as transitivity. They also follow from the theory that people can and do value all the possible collections of goods in terms of some common measure such as the satisfaction yielded, and that they choose what gives most satisfaction.[2] The question at issue is really whether this is saying anything which is true and significant, and is not contained in the axioms of choice (which would appear as theorems in old-fashioned utility theory). I myself cannot see that it is. As already stated on p. 21, it seems quite easy to produce examples where it would be a perversion of language to say that a man was maximizing his satis-

[1] The use of a straight budget line implies perfect competition between buyers—i.e. the buyer does not influence prices by varying his purchases.

[2] One cannot sensibly maintain that people weigh up the different components of each set in terms of a common measure, so arriving at a value sum for each collection of goods, because this ignores the relations of complementarity which link the goods in a collection.

faction, and where there is nevertheless no reason to suppose that his behaviour was not explicable in the sense that it obeyed certain rules. Of course, it is always possible to say that the 'economic man' still behaves as if he were maximizing something or other—but that clearly adds nothing whatever to our understanding.

If someone is really convinced that people have preference fields (a 'preference field' being something which the indifference map was supposed to represent) in their minds, or indifference curves on the brain, and that a person's behaviour is determined by reference to these internal maps, let him think so. If he does think this, however, he is arguing from economics to psychology, and not vice versa. We can, for instance, prove to him, since people do not make consistent choices, that these preference fields must jump about a lot. We infer how a person feels from the way he acts.[1] Indeed, if this were not true, we could rule out the possibility of having a welfare economics right from the start. In welfare economics we have to infer from objective facts about consumption to states of mind (assuming that 'welfare' *does* refer to happiness, or anything else which could be called a state of mind).

The exact relevance for welfare economics of the interpretation of the theory of consumers' behaviour which has been outlined above will be discussed in Chapter III. But before we leave the theory of consumers' behaviour, we must take notice of the fact that cardinal utility is not dead. Some people still want to add utilities. It has been argued that an ordinal utility system cannot formalize behaviour when uncertainty or risk enters in.[2] Suppose that instead of offering someone the choice between A and B we

[1] It is, I think, also true to say that a person infers how he himself feels from the way he behaves much more than by introspecting feelings of satisfaction or happiness. For instance, if a person is accused of being cross, he may deny it because he was not seeing red, nor did he have any feeling of constriction in the head, or whatever feeling it is that is associated with being cross. On second thoughts he may realize that he had spoken shortly, or in an irritated tone, and that he had frowned; he may, then, admit that he was cross. Suppose again that a person is asked whether he spent a happy day yesterday. He may reply with certainty, 'Yes', although he cannot recall any feelings of satisfaction or pleasure. Indeed, he may not have had any such thrills, and still may have been happy. It is absurd to suppose that happiness consists of *feelings* of pleasure, or satisfaction. This does not mean that happiness cannot be correctly called a state of mind. 'States of mind' are neither real nor logical constructions out of introspectible feelings.

[2] Cf. W. E. Armstrong, 'Uncertainty and the Utility Function', *E.J.*, Mar. 1948.

offer him the choice between A and a fifty-fifty chance of B or C. Suppose also that he prefers A to B, and C to A. Surely, it is said, which choice he will make depends on *how much* he prefers A to B, and C to A. For instance, if A is much preferred to B, whereas C is only just preferred to A, then he will surely choose A. But unless we say something about how great his preferences are, we cannot begin to say which he is likely to choose. It is quite clear that a person who is faced with such a choice will often, in some sense, compare the relative extent to which he prefers A to B and C to A with the respective chances of getting B or C.

All this is without doubt true. It is also true that an ordinal utility system cannot be applied to the above situation, because differences in the amount of utility do not occur within such a system. In an ordinal utility system there is no significance in asking how much more utility one derives from A than B, or in asking whether the extent to which one prefers A to B is greater or less than the extent to which one prefers C to A. Also it is obvious that in this context 'prefers' means 'likes better'. It is, moreover, true that people do compare differences in satisfaction. To see this we have only to see that, in ordinary language, it makes sense to say 'the satisfaction I get from coffee is *much* greater than the satisfaction I get from tea'. If someone asks 'how much greater?', we can reply, for instance, that the difference is greater than that between China and Indian tea. It does not, however, follow from this that a cardinal utility system can be thought of as measuring satisfactions. For measurement in the fullest sense, we need to be able to compare differences in satisfaction, but also we need a unit and a zero. Both of these are missing. No one would know, at all clearly, what one meant if one said one's satisfaction was at the moment zero, or if one said that it was now equal to seven units of satisfaction. It makes sense to speak of adding and subtracting satisfactions so long as this is only taken to imply that we can roughly compare differences in satisfaction. It must not be taken to imply that there is any possibility of objective measurement.

It may be objected that perhaps it might be possible to define a zero, and a unit, and that the necessary words might pass in ordinary usage. That is not impossible. People do not think of sweetness as measurable, but it is measured; and it is not impossible that people may come to say 'this tastes about ten degrees of sweetness', and 'my sweetness intake from this meal has been twenty units'. Heat also was once a non-numerical concept, but has become numerical, and is spoken of quantitatively in ordinary language. But if such a thing came to pass for satisfactions, it is fairly certain that the satisfaction measurers in economics would realize that they had been barking up the wrong tree. They may want to measure satisfactions because it is thought that they determine behaviour. They would almost certainly have to admit, if satisfactions were measured in a way that was independent of behaviour, that they did not after all determine behaviour. Or they would say that the 'satisfactions', that had been in some sense added, were not the satisfactions they meant. They would have to say one or other of these things, because it is clear from introspection that one's actions are not solely determined by feelings of satisfaction.

The alternative motive for adding satisfactions springs, of course, from ethics. Most people would agree that it is a good thing to make someone happier. If it is thought that happiness consists of satisfactions, then how nice it would be if we could measure them. But suppose we could measure satisfactions. Then either people would give up the naïve idea that happiness consists of feelings of satisfaction, and cease to maintain that one ought to try to maximize satisfactions, or they would say that the satisfaction which was the end of right conduct was not the satisfaction that these scientists measured. Suppose that it was considered immoral to feel feverish, but that there were no thermometers. Then thermometers are invented, and one is said to be feverish if one's temperature is higher than $98 \cdot 4°$ F. Are people going to submit to being told that it is immoral to have a temperature? They are far more likely either to say that the thermometer does not measure one's real feelings, or to cease to say that feverishness is immoral. We can be fairly certain that something similar would happen if it became possible to measure satisfaction. Also, if the measurement of satisfactions is wanted for ethical reasons, we require to add different individuals' satisfactions. This raises questions we deal with later.

But let me, for the moment, beg this question of interpersonal comparisons, and say that I think that people often do employ some rough kind of hedonistic calculus. Nevertheless, I also think that if satisfaction measurers attained their goal, they would realize that it was not where they wanted to be after all. This would be because measurement is a precise objective operation, and if something called 'satisfaction' were really measured, then the very precision of the result would destroy its value for helping to decide ethical issues. A utilitarian would not accept too objectively precise a measurement, because he would want to keep any decision as to what was the best thing to do, in some given circumstances, to himself. So long, however, as the 'measurement', or estimation, of satisfaction is *not* objective, and there is considerable room for disagreement, then it may sometimes be useful and correct to speak of a hedonistic calculus—to speak, that is, of comparing satisfactions, and differences in satisfaction.

A method has been suggested of making 'utility' a number up to a linear transformation. To quote:

Consider three events, C, A, B, for which the order of the individual's preferences is the one stated. Let α be a real number between o and 1 such that A is exactly equally desirable with the combined event consisting of a chance of probability $1-\alpha$ for B and the remaining chance of probability α for C. Then we suggest the use of α as a numerical estimate for the ratio of the preference of A over B to that of C over B.[1]

Here, the phrase 'equally desirable' is used; but, as with the word 'indifferent', it could easily be eliminated. α could be defined as the limiting chance of C, lying between those chances which resulted in A being taken, and those which resulted in the combination 'B or C' being selected. It is quite clear that the system would then have been defined entirely in terms of behaviour, and there would be no need to suppose that it applied to, or measured, satisfactions. Exactly the same remarks apply as do to ordinal utility systems.

Thus it does not follow that a cardinal utility system need be interpreted in terms of satisfaction, any more than an ordinal system need be. The contest between a cardinal and an ordinal system could go on, even if neither side believed that they were really talking about satisfactions. Nevertheless, the reason why some people prefer a cardinal system is that they regard it as useful for welfare economics. And, according to our present interim

[1] Von Neumann and Morgenstern, *Theory of Games and Economic Behaviour*, p. 18. It may be noted that the above scheme seems to be essentially the same as that suggested by F. P. Ramsey, *The Foundations of Mathematics*, pp. 178–9: except that Ramsey went farther, and showed how, in principle, both utility and subjective probability could be simultaneously determined.

definition of 'welfare' (= 'happiness'), it is only of significance for welfare economics if it is thought that we can sometimes argue from objective facts, which require a description in quantitative terms, to states of mind. There is, in this respect, no difference between a cardinal and an ordinal system. 'On a higher behaviour line' does not entail 'more satisfaction', although it does entail 'in a chosen position'. But the fact that a man is 'on a higher behaviour line' may be taken as good evidence for the fact that he may be more satisfied. Similarly, 'a greater amount of utility' does not entail 'more satisfaction', although it entails 'in a chosen position'. Nevertheless, if we can sometimes say that a man has 'a greater amount of utility', we can use this fact as evidence for his being more satisfied.

We must, therefore, ask whether a cardinal system would be better than an ordinal system for formalizing the economic behaviour of a consumer. It is well known that people like or dislike gambling. If someone did not like gambling he would not play roulette knowing that it is 36 to 1 against a number coming up, while he only gets £35 for his £1 if it does come up. Suppose that, in accordance with the system described above, we had given C, A, B, the utility numbers $10\frac{4}{5}$, 10, 9, because the consumer was 'indifferent' between (A certain) and the lottery ticket (C with probability $\frac{5}{9}$ or B with probability $\frac{4}{9}$). It follows that, if we are to have a consistent system of choices which will apply to certainties and uncertainties alike, then, if the consumer is given the choice between B and A, A must be taken. In fact B might well be taken. If the consumer had a distaste for gambling, he might have required, in order that he should select the lottery ticket B or C, that its total risk-discounted utility should be considerably greater than the utility of A. There might be a disutility simply in not knowing whether it would be B or C which he would get. This kind of utility and disutility is specifically ruled out by definition on the above system, and as a result it is unlikely that we should be able to fit it to the facts of actual behaviour when differing risks enter in.[1]

All this is, of course, well known. As we shall see, it is most unlikely that anyone would behave consistently enough for it to be

[1] Since this paragraph was first written an extensive literature has sprung up on the Ramsey-von Neumann-Morgenstern idea. However, it is not in my opinion very much to the point so far as this book is concerned. Some references can be found in, e.g., Sir Dennis Robertson, 'Utility and All That', *E.J.*, Dec. 1954.

theoretically possible to draw up a set of indifference curves. But if we seek to systematize consumers' behaviour in the face of uncertainty, the difficulties are enormously multiplied. In addition to the difficulty raised by the fact that risk and uncertainty itself may be liked or disliked, there is also the fact that, if behaviour is to be predicted, then the uncertainties or risks must be measurable. In economics many of the uncertainties which are important are not measurable.[1]

But risk and uncertainty of the kind discussed above are, in any case, rather irrelevant to the theory of welfare economics (though not, of course, to welfare). In a sense, a consumer's choices are often between lottery tickets. For instance, two goods, one cheap and one expensive, may differ in my eyes only in that it is more likely but not certain that the cheaper will go wrong or last less well (e.g. two watches of identical appearance). But so long as the consumer has a consistent choice ordering of the lottery tickets, that is all that is required. Cardinal utility theory seeks to deduce which option I will select in terms of the strength of my preference as between good and bad watches, and my estimation of the probability that a cheap watch will turn out good, &c. But welfare economics can take over at the point of choice between the two lottery tickets (in the case of consumers' choices the components of the lottery ticket are generally all the same object. Only its attributes are in doubt: when I go to a tailor I know I will get a suit of clothes!). Risk enters more seriously into producers' choices. But 'welfare' theory cannot do more than define optimum production, and state the factors which determine it; the fact that production has to be planned beforehand on very uncertain estimates of costs and prices is one among many factors which make the achievement of any 'optimum' unlikely.

To sum up the reasons why, in the formal parts of this book, we

[1] Formally, the utilities and the subjective probabilities can be simultaneously measured in the manner first suggested by F. P. Ramsey (loc. cit., *supra*). An experiment has been made applying Ramsey's method to very simple risk choices by D. Davidson, S. Siegel, and P. Suppes in 'Some Experiments and Related Theory on the Measurement of Utility and Subjective Probability' (Stanford Value Theory Project, Stanford University). But this does not seem to alter the fact that even if the utilities were all known, together with the subjective probabilities implicit in previous acts of choice, one still could not predict behaviour in the face of a new risk choice unless one could determine an objective probability, and assume precariously that the degree of belief, or subjective probability, would correspond.

use the ordinal utility system, with reference to an individual's behaviour, are (*a*) that it is simpler, (*b*) that all the important conclusions of welfare economics can be made to follow from it, and (*c*) that no different conclusions follow from using a cardinal system. But whenever we find it convenient, we shall not hesitate to make judgements which may imply that differences in satisfaction can be roughly compared. As we shall see, these comparisons are likely to be required only as between different individuals (if we ignore risk, as we do, comparisons of differences in satisfaction for the same person are not necessary). We do not, however, choose to formalize this way of speaking into a cardinal utility system, partly because it is unnecessary, but also because such formalization tends to suggest an element of precision and objectivity which these comparisons certainly lack.

As a result of the above discussion we suggest the following conclusions:

1. Neither cardinal nor ordinal utility systems can be correctly interpreted in terms of satisfactions. A subjective interpretation is ruled out because the system applies if behaviour is consistent, whether or not the consumer, in fact, tries to maximize satisfaction or anything else. *A fortiori* a cardinal utility system cannot be interpreted in terms of satisfaction.

2. There are theoretical grounds for supposing that a cardinal utility system would better explain consumers' behaviour when uncertainty is present. But whether in practice such a system is more applicable is very doubtful: and in any case it would be otiose so far as the derivation of the normal theories of welfare economics are concerned. Therefore, when a theory of consumers' behaviour is required, the ordinal utility analysis, interpreted in terms of choice, will be used. As will be seen later, the factor of uncertainty, when it is present, is, in any case, only one among many reasons why, in fact, we should not expect to be able to apply the theory to any given individual.

3. Welfare economics, so far as the individual is concerned, is, if it is about anything at all, about states of mind. We therefore must argue from behaviour and other objective circumstances to states of mind. The criterion used for an increase in an individual's economic welfare means that he is in a chosen position. This criterion will be discussed at length in the following chapter.

CHAPTER III

THE CHOICE CRITERION

WE saw in the last chapter that 'on a higher behaviour line' entails 'in a chosen position'. In this chapter we will discuss the conditions required to apply the criterion to a real consumer, and, secondly, how far it is a good criterion for 'an increase in economic welfare'.[1]

The first condition is that the consumer is free to choose between the various collections of goods within the limits set by his purchasing power. It is obvious, since the analysis is built up on the basis of choices, and the relation of 'chosen rather than', that one must be able to say that a consumer has chosen one collection rather than another, and that this cannot be said if he is prevented from choosing the alternative collection, other than by its being too expensive. The second condition is that the consumer's choices in relation to every good which enters in the analysis must be consistent for any period of time within which we wish to say 'he is in a chosen position'. We must be able to draw the contours, and, once drawn, they must remain the same.

Thus far the behaviour-line system has been discussed in a timeless manner. So long as one keeps to an abstract logical system, time does not enter in. But, when this logical system of consumers' behaviour is applied, the collections of goods must be interpreted as collections of things chosen over a certain definite period of time. Now if the consumer's income and prices do not change, the condition of consistency of choice implies that exactly the same collection of things must be chosen in every period. If the period is made very short inconsistency will certainly arise, because durable consumption goods are not bought very frequently. Also there is the difficulty that people like a little variety. Even people who, we would say, have very constant tastes do not buy the same collection of goods every week, even when relative prices are unchanged.

---

[1] Strictly speaking that which is defined is always a word or phrase. The *definiendum* should, therefore, always be enclosed in inverted commas to signify that the word or phrase is being *mentioned*, and not *used*. The same is true if we give a criterion for the use of a word or phrase. When this is done, the word or phrase is mentioned, and should therefore be enclosed in inverted commas. Sometimes, however, for the sake of convenience, we loosely speak of, for instance, a criterion for an increase in an individual's welfare (*sic*).

It is clear, then, that a fairly long period is indicated. But here also one is liable to get considerable inconsistency, because, over a longer period, people's tastes change, especially when they are growing up. Even when people are grown up, and their habits formed, it would be extraordinary if they went on doing the same thing year after year.

We must now meet another difficulty. Who is a consumer? Our analysis assumes that the consumer is a chooser. But a very considerable proportion of the population do very little choosing for themselves. Indeed, one may say that only a small minority of the population control their own expenditure for their own benefit. Therefore the analysis could not be applied to many individuals even if individuals were consistent. Should we rather try to apply it to families? But the consumption pattern of a family with children will certainly not remain stable even when prices are unchanged.

We have also to contend with the fact that some things which were available to be bought in one situation may no longer be available in a later situation. This does not raise any serious problem. We can regard the price of this thing as having become infinite. The introduction of new things is more serious. Indeed, they cannot be introduced into the analysis at all. If any new things are bought there must be a new map drawn. If our consumer once bought carriages he must go on buying carriages, even if motorcars are available. This also, of course, raises the problem of classification. When is a thing the same thing? Quality changes must always, at best, blur any precision the analysis might otherwise have had, and, at worst, they may make comparisons very difficult indeed.

We may now briefly list some of the factors which are likely to make for inconsistent behaviour. First, a man's consumption patterns (which are here identified with his tastes) may change for a variety of reasons. The change may be spontaneous, or he may acquire new obligations, as when he marries and has children. Or, a change in the tastes of others may be the cause—he may follow the fashion. Or, a change in his comparative wealth may result in a change of taste, for example, the emulation of *nouveau-riche* friends. Tastes, for the purposes of our analysis, have to be taken as being independent of what is produced. This is because we determine the 'ideal' production by reference to people's tastes, which must therefore be assumed to be independent of that production. Except perhaps in the case of the necessities of life, this is not very true to life. There is no doubt for instance that the production of television sets creates a desire for this kind of entertainment.

There are many other possible causes of inconsistent choices besides change of taste. A person, even when we would not normally say his tastes had changed, may like to experiment. Indeed it is obvious that if a man were really trying to maximize his satisfaction, he would often try out new ways of spending his money. One does not have any innate knowledge of what one likes. Then, too, new goods may become available, or the quality of old goods change, and some durable consumption goods are, in any case, bought too infrequently to enter into a consumption period of reasonable length. As we have seen, a person may also be uncertain what he is going to get for his money, and his estimation of the uncertainties may change, in which case an ordinal utility analysis will not apply very well to his behaviour, and inconsistent choices, as determined by the ordinal analysis, may be made. There are still other factors to consider. Only relative prices enter into our analysis: but sometimes absolute prices are important. Thus some people would buy diamonds only if they were expensive, and would therefore make inconsistent choices if the price fell. This is rather unimportant, but the mention of changing prices brings one on to a factor which *is* important. When prices are expected to change a person's choice is affected, not merely by what he likes and dislikes, but also by what he thinks is going to happen to prices. Rapidly changing prices turn every consumer into a speculator with respect to durable goods. The faster prices change the less durable do consumption goods have to be for future expected prices to influence present choices. So one would not expect the analysis to apply very well to durable goods except when relative price changes are unexpected. No doubt, still other factors could be mentioned which would be likely to make the assumption of consistency of choice unrealistic: but enough has been said to show that there are numerous reasons, besides spontaneous changes of tastes or sheer irrationality, which may make a man behave inconsistently in the economist's sense of the word.

The considerations raised in the above paragraphs amount to the contention that the abstract notion of a consumer being on a higher behaviour line or indifference curve cannot be very well applied to individuals. But to say that someone is in a chosen position may still mean something precise. If, for some individual or family, we can say that $\sum p_2\, q_2 \geqslant \sum p_2\, q_1$, and $\sum p_1\, q_1 < \sum p_1\, q_2$, it follows from the first index-number formula that the goods of the second situation (all the q_2's) were bought when the goods of the first situation could have been bought, and from the second index-number formula it follows that when the goods of the first situation were bought (the q_1's) the goods of the second situation could *not* have been bought. We now define that the second situation is consistently chosen rather than the first. There is also, of course, the case when $\sum p_1\, q_1 \geqslant \sum p_1\, q_2$ and $\sum p_2\, q_2 < \sum p_2\, q_1$, when we say that the first situation is (consistently) chosen rather than the second. But it may be the case that $\sum p_2\, q_2 \geqslant \sum p_2\, q_1$, in which case the second situation is chosen rather than the first (since the goods of the first situation could have been bought), *and* $\sum p_1\, q_1 \geqslant \sum p_1\, q_2$, in which case the first situation, when it was chosen, was chosen rather than the second. This is a case for inconsistent behaviour, and we can say nothing.

Finally, we have the case when

$$\sum p_2\, q_2 < \sum p_2\, q_1 \text{ and } \sum p_1\, q_1 < \sum p_1\, q_2.$$

In this case when the first collection was chosen the second was not a possibility, and vice versa. Thus we cannot show directly that either position was chosen rather than the other, or that there is any indication of inconsistency. In such a case it may, however, be possible to find a third situation, such that we can say that the second is chosen rather than the third, and the third rather than the first, and, therefore, that the second is chosen rather than the first, although it is not possible to say, simply from looking at the first and second situations, that the latter is chosen rather than the former. Let us name the three situations A, B, and C. In symbols the above argument may be written as follows: $\sum p_b\, q_b < \sum p_b\, q_a$, but $\sum p_b\, q_b \geqslant \sum p_b\, q_c$ and $\sum p_c\, q_c \geqslant \sum p_c\, q_a$. Therefore B is chosen rather than A, although $\sum p_b\, q_b < \sum p_b\, q_a$. The meaning of the construction demonstrated in Appendix I is that if consistency is assumed, and if every collection of goods would be chosen in one and only one price-income situation, then it can be shown that, by taking as many mediating positions (such as C) as we like, we can arrive at the ordinary ordinal utility system. (It follows, of course, that if one can say 'X is on a higher behaviour line' then one can also say 'X is in a chosen position'.) But since it is vastly unlikely that any individuals are, in fact, perfectly consistent, it seems that the ordinal utility system is best regarded as an unattainable ideal limit to the successive applications of the index-number criterion to an individual's behaviour. Any inconsistency upsets the behaviour-line analysis (and, of course, the indifference-curve analysis), but it is quite possible that by using index numbers we may reach the conclusion that a person is in a situation which he consistently chooses rather than another situation, although his behaviour may be inconsistent with regard to a wide range of other situations. Thus 'on a higher behaviour line', since it implies perfect consistency, always entails 'in a chosen position'; but 'in a chosen position' does not entail 'on a higher behaviour line', unless we are speaking of a perfectly consistent individual.

We must now discuss the question whether 'being in a chosen position', as defined by the index-number formulae, is a good criterion of increased economic welfare. Henceforth the phrase 'in a chosen position' is to be taken to mean that both index-number formulae are satisfied, unless otherwise indicated. We have said that the statement 'John's economic welfare is greater' means 'economic circumstances have changed in a manner favourable to John's happiness'. The correctness of this translation will not, for the moment, be questioned. We have also limited the use of the word 'economic' so that it refers to those things and services which can be exchanged for money. Thus, 'economic circumstances' is a way of referring to the fact that individual A consumes so much x, y, z, &c., saves so much, and does so much work of such and such a kind in a given time, and, similarly, that individual B consumes so much x, y, z, &c., and so on for all individuals. Or, in short, economic circumstances is taken to refer to (a) the total flow of goods and services consumed by individuals, (b) the amount of work done, and (c) the way in which goods and work are distributed between individuals. For the sake of exposition, we will first assume that the amount and kind of work which our individual does remains constant, and that he saves a constant proportion of his money income.

It is clear that what is most relevant to John's happiness is what he himself consumes, and our choice criterion takes into account only what he himself consumes. But an individual's happiness is also, to some extent, dependent on what others consume. Obviously the standard of living or welfare level of his family is not a matter of indifference to a man. But we do not avoid the difficulty by taking the family as a unit. The standards of living of friends and enemies are still of some account. Again, it is not merely a matter of the standards of living of those people in whom the individual is in some way interested. It has long been recognized that much of the misery of becoming poorer springs from the failure to keep up with the neighbours, or with one's own class; that much of the pleasure of becoming richer lies in moving up the social scale, in rising 'above' one's acquaintances. That this is true of some luxury expenditure is clear. It is needless to elaborate on this theme. The motive of ostentation has been ruthlessly analysed by Veblen.

In formal terms this fact, that what other people have may be of importance, affects our analysis in two ways. It may provide an additional reason for a change of taste on the part of an individual. This may occur when an individual changes his social class. Suppose that a man has become for some time middle class, having previously had what would usually be called a working-class income, and then loses money; and let us compare his last situation with his first. Is he better off? We may tell him that he could still buy what he bought in his original situation (that $\sum p_2 q_2 > \sum p_2 q_1$). He may reply that his tastes have changed. But our index-number criterion may be complete (i.e. $\sum p_2 q_2 > \sum p_2 q_1$ and $\sum p_1 q_1 < \sum p_1 q_2$). He has not, in fact, exhibited any change of taste if we simply compare the two situations by index numbers. Thus, whether the change of taste is caused by his having mixed in 'higher' circles, or spontaneously, the index-number criterion may not take notice of it, although, of course, such change of taste would render the behaviour-line analysis inapplicable.

The question arises whether in the circumstances outlined above we should want to say that the man's economic welfare had increased. Have economic circumstances changed in a manner favourable to his happiness? If we take into account not merely the first and last situations, but the intermediate one as well, that is, so to speak, the route by which the man has travelled, then the answer may be 'No'. And we would then have to admit that the choice criterion had failed us. On the other hand, it is recognized that some people would want to say that the man's economic welfare had increased. They might say that it was, in a sense, the man's own fault if he wasn't happier than he was as a working man. Here we see that ethics is beginning seriously to creep into the discussion. Further consideration of this matter will therefore be deferred till we try to deal with the relationship of ethics and welfare economics in the next chapter.

This brings us on to the wider question of whether one wants to take people's tastes as the arbiter of what should be produced, when those tastes themselves are strongly influenced by other people's consumption, including indeed the consumption of a person's parents and grandparents and their friends. For instance, if tobacco were forbidden, the next generation might not want it at all. An extremist might argue that one's wants and desires for goods are, with the exception of a few necessities, entirely dependent on what others have or have had, and also that it is an illusion to suppose that more of everything for everyone makes anyone better off. We leave this to the reader—with the warning only that the analysis of this book cannot help one in the least to answer such questions, for it is invalid when tastes are interdependent in this manner.

The importance of taking into account the economic circumstances of others may, however, affect our analysis in another way. The individual's tastes may not be changed, and he may be in a chosen position. But if the situation of others has changed in a markedly more favourable manner, we might not want to say that economic circumstances have changed in a manner favourable to his happiness. For instance, a man's standard of living may have risen over a period of years (i.e. he may be in a chosen position) but he may have been left behind in the race. He may have moved down the social scale. Do we want to say that his economic welfare has increased? If my definition, which includes consideration of the circumstances of others, is accepted, then we may not want to answer 'Yes'. This is a case in which the behaviour-line analysis need not be rendered inapplicable, but in which 'on a higher behaviour line' might not be thought to be a good criterion.

Finally, a man may make mistakes. He may buy something and then wish he had not. We clearly do not want to say that someone is better off economically because he is in a chosen position, if he regrets his choice and cannot move back. In the next 'period' he may be able to return to his former situation, or better. But some durable goods are only bought at rare intervals. Mistakes are not always mistakes about the causes of one's own happiness. One may, for instance, buy a motor-car with the mistaken idea that petrol will be available. If it is not, the chosen position may very well be one which is regretted. But, more important than this, we think that some people consistently fail to realize what would make them happy or happier, and to say of such people that they are in a chosen position, or on a higher behaviour line, may not imply that we think that they are in any sense better off. Nevertheless, if this was the only reason why a chosen position might not be a position of greater economic welfare, I think most people would be prepared to admit that for a normal consumer our criterion was, in general, a good one. They would, in fact, accept that those people who are choosers, that is, excluding lunatics and children, know well enough how to order their own affairs to their best advantage. But we must recognize that again most people would think that there are some exceptions.

Relaxing the assumption of a constant amount of work it may happen that our consumer is only able to buy what he bought before, because he works harder. It would seem that one should ask whether he could buy what he had before if he did the same amount of work of the same kind as before; or, alternatively, whether, if he bought exactly what he bought before, he would have more leisure. This answer is, however, rather too simple. It is compli-cated by the fact that leisure, although it is usually conventionally treated as a good in economics, is not universally so regarded, i.e. it is by no means always the case that more would be chosen rather than less. People, for instance, do voluntary unpaid work. Also, it is more often thought that people are bad at estimating how much work they should do to make themselves happy, than it is thought that they are bad at choosing the pattern of consumption which will make them happy. More important still, it is not true that people are free to choose the amount of work they do in the same way as they are, in normal times, free to choose what they will consume. It is obvious that, if a man is unemployed and cannot find work, it would be silly to say that he was better off because, if he did the same amount of work as before, then he would be able to consume more than before. It would be the same if he was forced to work short time, or, again, if he had to work longer hours against his will. The choice criterion cannot very well be extended to apply to work, when it is by no means the general rule that a man can choose how much and what kind of work he does.

For these reasons it seems that it is often better to weigh up any improvement or deterioration in his position as a consumer against any deterioration or improvement in his position as a worker, rather than to attempt to bring both together into a single-choice criterion. Nevertheless, as we shall see later, the formal conclusions of welfare economics depend on the assumption that all economic goods, including leisure, can be fitted into the behaviour-line analysis.

We must now briefly consider savings. Savings do not represent any definite thing, or collection of things, of which we can ask the question 'Could the consumer have the same thing, or collection of things, as before?' Moreover, when prices change, we clearly cannot consider merely the sum of money saved, and ask whether the consumer could have what he had before, and still save the same amount of money. Also we do not know in general what a consumer intends to do with his savings. In these circumstances, we must make some assumption about what savings are intended to buy. The most realistic general assumption we can make is that, when a man saves he is normally saving up to buy a collection similar in composition to that which he is buying when he saves. Therefore, when comparing his welfare for, say, two different years, we must, in effect, scale up his expenditure in the one year until it is equal to his income of that year, and then ask whether, in the other year, he could have bought the scaled-up collection of the one year.

The fact that people save means that the question 'Could he have bought last year's collection of goods?' is ambiguous. If a man has some capital, he may be able to buy last year's collection, but only by spending capital. Thus the question we really need to ask is whether he could this year buy last year's collection without making it, in his opinion, any less probable than it was last year, that he would be able to go on buying at least the same collection as he bought last year in all subsequent years.[1] But this question cannot, of course, have any definite clear-cut answer. We therefore have to admit that our seemingly quite precise choice criterion is not, after all, precise at all. However, the question of savings, and the distinction between income and capital, does not affect our theoretical welfare analysis in a particularly serious manner. We

[1] Cf. J. Hicks, 'The Valuation of the Social Income', *Economica*, May 1940; also *Value and Capital*, ch. xiv.

have to assume that income has somehow been defined. But any failure of the definition to be in accordance with the theoretical question we really want to ask will only be one among many reasons for believing that our welfare criteria are rough and ready.

We must now recognize that the index-number formulae, as criteria of 'chosen rather than', do permit some evaluation of the extent of benefit. Thus, if a man could choose what he had before and have £500 per annum over, we would ordinarily say that he had benefited more than if he could only just buy what he had before. If many of the complicating factors, discussed above, arise to make us doubtful whether to judge that he has benefited or not, then the amount he would have had left over if he had bought what he had bought in the previous situation may be a factor of the greatest importance in determining our decision. The formal (ordinal) criteria 'in a chosen position' and 'on a higher behaviour line' ignore this important element in our judgements. Nevertheless, when we seek to apply the formal theory of 'welfare' to some particular case, we can make some allowance for the extent of benefit which would result if people were consistent (i.e. if the axioms of our behaviour analysis could be precisely applied), and this allowance will normally be of importance in deciding whether people really would be made economically better off.

We have been discussing whether 'in a chosen position' is a precise and acceptable criterion for 'an increase in the economic welfare of an individual'. But let us emphasize that, in order to be able to deduce the 'optimum' conditions of production and exchange, the behaviour-line and not the index-number criterion must be employed. To say that, if a certain change were made, then Smith would be 'on a higher behaviour line' is to say that Smith would be in a chosen position if he were a perfectly consistent economic man. Thus when this latter criterion is used there are two stages of approximation. First, since Smith is not, of course, an economic man it may be false that he would be in a chosen position, if the change in question were made. Secondly, there are, as we have seen, additional reasons for supposing that one might not want to say that his economic welfare had increased, even though he was in a chosen position. These additional reasons may be briefly summed up by saying that people are not independent of each other in respect of welfare, and that they do not always know what would give them most satisfaction.

Before arriving at any final judgement as to the adequacy of our welfare criteria, it is necessary to distinguish short and long periods. Over a comparatively short period, say a few years, most peoples' tastes will not change very much. Also the number of novelties introduced will not be great, and quality changes are not likely to be very important. Thus the behaviour-line analysis will apply better than when the comparison is to be made over a longer period. Again, in the short period, general standards of welfare are not likely to change greatly, and therefore if a person is in a chosen position it is improbable that his social standing will have deteriorated. This removes one of the chief reasons for thinking that the choice criterion is not always a very good criterion of economic welfare.

On the other hand, short periods can sometimes be very abnormal. In a severe inflation, for instance, it becomes very difficult for people to plan their expenditure. The anxiety to exchange money for durable goods as fast as possible turns everyone into a speculator with all the worries, which, for most people, are attendant on great uncertainty. Again, if there are severe shortages of some goods, and rationing is introduced, it may be the case that hardly anyone can be said to be 'in a chosen position', because the choice of the previously purchased collection of goods may be illegal. Nevertheless, we can normally have much more confidence in the applicability and acceptability of the behaviour-line criterion over short periods of time than over long ones. In the limit, if the long period is very long, it becomes quite senseless to discuss any criterion for an increase in individual welfare, because there would be no individual alive both at the beginning and at the end of the period.

We must conclude this chapter by trying to reach some sort of decision as to whether the behaviour-line criterion is good enough for us to have any confidence whatever in the deductions which are made from such a basis. Certainly I find that the arguments, which have been adduced to show that most individuals are liable to be very inconsistent, are formidable. Also I think that the reasons against accepting the criterion 'in a chosen position' are not un-important, especially when the period in question is a fairly long one. Nevertheless, most or all of the arguments brought forward in this chapter are old ones. They have often been presented, though mostly in discussions of demand theory. In spite of this, it

is clear that such arguments are insufficient to upset many economists' faith in welfare economics. I think there is a good reason
for this.

Most people who consider the welfare of society do not, I am
sure, think of it as a logical construction from the welfares of individuals. They think rather in terms of social or economic groups,
or in terms of average, or representative, men. Now it is evident
that representative men are very much more like economic men
than are real individuals. The tastes of an average man do not
change at all rapidly. He does not experiment very much. His life
is not subject to any sudden shocks or crises. The average un-
married male cotton operative will not, for instance, suddenly alter
the pattern of his consumption by getting married. His position
in the social scale will not alter much. The welfare of his friends
and relations is also unlikely to alter greatly. Much more important,
he never dies. (Any prediction that a certain change would increase
the economic welfare of a real man is always liable to be upset by
his death.)

It might be objected that it makes nonsense to apply the behaviour-line analysis to average individuals, or representative men.
This is not true. One of the advantages of getting rid of the idea
of an economic man as a maximizing individual is precisely that we
can now apply the analysis to average individuals. Average men
cannot maximize satisfaction, but they can behave perfectly consistently. We cannot ask average men questions about preference
or indifference, but we can observe the collections of goods which
they take in various price-income situations; and therefore there is
no reason why, in theory, the behaviour-line analysis should not
apply. It might finally be objected that we can hardly speak of an
average man as being in a chosen position. But 'in a chosen position' has been our phrase for describing the fact that the money
income of an individual for period 2 was more than sufficient to
buy the collection of goods bought in period 1. Whatever the
phrase to be used, the fact can certainly be as true of an average
individual as of a real one. Further, there is no reason why one
should not regard such a fact as sufficient reason to say that the
economic welfare of such an average man has increased. There is
also, in any case, no reason why one should not say that an average
man takes (or chooses) one collection of goods rather than another,
because we have defined 'rather than' by saying that A is taken

rather than B, whenever *A* is taken, and *B* could have been taken. Thus, for the rest of this book, the word 'individual' may be loosely interpreted except where the context makes it clear that the reference is to actual individuals.

Whereas it seems to me that one cannot deny that the behaviour-line analysis applies very badly to real individuals, nevertheless it may apply sufficiently well to average men to justify some faith in an analysis which is based on it, so long as the groups, in terms of which we think, are fairly small and reasonably homogeneous. Only a super-individualist would object to this view, on the ground that one may never ignore the differences in the welfare of the actual individuals comprising the average. The present view also has the advantage that it gives at least some sense to comparisons over long periods of time. On the other hand, it must still be admitted that even average men are by no means perfectly consistent, and that people can still reasonably find fault with the choice criterion.

In particular none of the above arguments really answers the fundamental objection that people's tastes are in the long run too much influenced by what is being produced and consumed, and has been produced and consumed in the past, to make the assumptions that they are independent anything but a hollow pretence. Even so I doubt whether this will be for most people a shattering objection to using an analysis which takes people's tastes as given. One would hardly use such an analysis to try to decide whether one ought to stifle aeroplanes or television sets at birth—but once they have been introduced, and tastes have become adapted to them, it may still be worth asking whether people's demands seem to indicate that more or less aeroplanes, &c., should be made.

But we must certainly not pretend that our analysis is anything but rough and ready. As we have already implied, it is particularly inapplicable in respect of choices between jobs, and different hours and kinds of work. Nevertheless, enough has, I think, been said to show that it would be foolish to dismiss the whole of welfare economics solely on the ground that the analysis of 'individual' behaviour, on which it rests, is hopelessly at variance with the facts.

CHAPTER IV

THE DISTRIBUTION OF WELFARE

WE have seen that the utilitarians thought it reasonable to speak of a man's economic welfare as the sum total of his satisfactions which derived from economic causes, and that therefore an increase in his economic welfare was an increase in this total. On the later indifference-curve analysis it no longer made sense to speak of a man's economic welfare as a definite amount of anything. This view is accepted, because we cannot speak of a zero amount of satisfaction, and we have no unit of satisfaction. But it is also accepted for another reason; because one cannot categorize one's satisfactions, and say this one belongs to an economic cause, and that to a political cause, and so on. The picture of a lot of separate satisfactions, each with a label tied round it, is not convincing. One may explain this point more clearly by a metaphor. The utilitarians imagined the mind· to be like a well of known depth into which parcels of satisfaction, duly labelled economic or political or religious, were thrown. The number of parcels could be counted. On the later analysis it is imagined that the mind is like a well of unknown depth, partly filled with water, the level of which could be altered by turning on various taps labelled economic, political, &c. Once the water is in the well there is no way of saying which tap it came from, and also it is impossible to say how much water there is in the well. One cannot therefore significantly ask how much economic welfare someone has; but one can say that the level of the water has risen or fallen as the result of turning the economic tap, if the other taps are not touched, i.e. one can say that economic welfare increased or decreased.

The second picture is undoubtedly an improvement on the first. We have quarrelled with the indifference-curve analysis only in so far as it purported to rest on psychological assumptions. We have interpreted it entirely behaviouristically. We, so to speak, only observe the turning of the taps, and then make inferences about the level of the water. That is the behaviour-line analysis. The indifference-curve analysis traced a logical connexion between the turning of the taps and the level of the water. We have only an

C

empirical connexion based on our general observation of the behaviour of men, and changes in their happiness.

The second important utilitarian thesis was that one could add up the welfares of different individuals to arrive at the welfare of society. That idea has now to be abandoned. To revert to our metaphor, one cannot add up the total amount of water in a number of different wells if one cannot say how much water there is in any well. What, however, is not always noticed is that the utilitarians had no need to add up different people's happinesses in order to prove their thesis that an equalitarian distribution of income would maximize happiness, or for the thesis that one ought to try to maximize happiness. The former theory requires only that one should be able to compare the difference in happiness which an extra pound would make to different people. If one, then, moves money about until a pound more or less makes the same difference to everyone, one has maximized happiness. The addition of happinesses is never required. The addition of differences in happiness may, however, be necessary. If an economic change benefits A, and harms B and C, it would seem that one must be able to add the differences which the change makes to B and C, and compare the result with the difference it makes to A. This is only not necessary if it is possible for A exactly to compensate B and C, in which case one has only to look at A to see whether his happiness is greater or less. Thus if one admits the possibility of full compensation, it becomes true to say that the utilitarian can work quite as happily with an ordinal index as with a cardinal index of satisfaction. To this extent, then, the change-over in economic analysis from a Marshallian to a Pareto concept of utility did not imply a break with utilitarian philosophy. On the other hand, if compensation is impossible, the addition of differences in happiness is required.

We may now ask whether people do compare differences in satisfaction or happiness, and whether they add them. As regards the first, there is no doubt whatever. I can say '£1 would make more difference to Smith than it would to Jones'. Such statements are made, and when such a statement is made it is correct to say that the man who makes the statement is comparing the differences in satisfaction which the addition of £1 to his purchasing-power would make respectively to Smith and to Jones. On the other hand, it is probably incorrect to say that one ever adds such differences.

The statement 'I am about to add together the difference which this change would make to Smith and Jones, and compare the result with the difference it would make to Brown sounds like nonsense. It sounds like nonsense because addition is a precise mathematical operation, which requires the possibility of counting. There is no way in which we can measure units of satisfaction, and so count them. To say that one *adds* Smith's and Jones's satisfaction is wrong, because it is applying far too precise a word to the mental process which we go through when we try, as we may do, to estimate whether making a change (without compensation) would produce more happiness. The conflict, which one may go through, between thinking that utilitarianism is nonsensical and thinking that there must be something in it, results from the endeavour to make it too precise. So long as it remains vague and imprecise, and avoids the use of mathematical operations and concepts such as 'adding', and 'sums total', there is something in it; but it becomes nonsensical if it is pushed too hard in the attempt to make it an exact scientific sort of doctrine. There is little doubt that we do, in fact, make rough comparisons, which, if they were precise, would imply the addition of satisfactions. It makes sense to say, for instance, that the difference between A's and B's increments of happiness is greater than C's increment; in which case we can also say that A's increment is greater than that of B and C put together. We must here add, in order to avoid a possible misunderstanding, that it is by no means maintained that one always ought to try to produce most happiness. The question whether the precepts of utilitarianism can be followed is quite distinct from the question whether they ought to be followed.

It has been said that there is no doubt that we do compare differences in happiness as between different people; there is also no doubt that we compare different people's total happiness (where the word 'total' must not be taken to imply that happiness is a sum of parts). We frequently maintain that A is happier than B, and it is obvious that when we do so we are not talking nonsense. We can, also, roughly compare the amount by which A is happier than B, with the amount by which B is happier than C. In spite of this, part of the reason why the 'indifference-curve' analysis has largely taken the place of the cardinal utility analysis is that it provides no basis for the comparison of different persons' 'levels of preference' (or whatever the phrase may be which is used). Thus this kind of analysis has seemed to give formal recognition to the acceptance among economists of the idea that somehow inter-personal comparisons of satisfaction or happiness are illegitimate, or not objective, or unscientific. Economists, indeed, have said that they 'denied', or that other economists might 'deny', interpersonal comparisons, whatever 'deny' can mean in this context, which is not in the least clear.

No one could 'deny' interpersonal comparisons in the sense that they deny that people make them. Therefore those economists who 'deny' them must think that when a person says 'A is happier than B' he is deluding himself in thinking that he is making a statement of fact. But why should he be deluding himself? Why should it not be a statement of fact? It is probable that what is behind the idea that it is not a statement of fact, that one is not describing something one experiences, when one says 'A is happier than B', is some vague metaphysical doubt about the existence of minds other than one's own. I say about the *existence* of other minds, because nothing short of denying their existence can entitle one to say that other minds cannot be compared. If one admits that another man's behaviour, including his speech, is evidence for his having a mind, then one must admit that one can use such be-haviour as a good basis for saying what sort of mind he has, or what sort of a mental state he is in; that is, for saying that he is stupid or intelligent, happy or miserable, angry or pleased, and so on But if one can say that A is happy and pleased, and B is miserable and angry, then one has compared their mental states. Happy and angry are relative words, but they are not relative merely to some other state of the same man. We can say of a man that he is habitually miserable, or that he has a disposition to be miserable. Obviously we cannot be meaning that he has a disposi-tion to be more miserable than he usually is. We mean that he has a disposition to be more miserable than men usually are. We have some vague standards of happiness and misery. In other words, we use different men's behaviour, in a wide sense of the word, to compare their mental states; and if we say of a man that he is always miserable, basing our judgement on how he looks and behaves, and how we know we would feel if we looked and behaved like that, and on a wide knowledge of his character gathered by observing his behaviour and words in a variety of situations, and on the opinions of all his friends who similarly know him well, then we would think it was just nonsense to say that he might really be deceiving everyone all the time and be the happiest of men. It is a mistake to suppose that another man's mind consists solely of feelings or images which one cannot ever experience (that is, that one's mind is a logical construction of personal feelings and images which are, by definition, not open to inspection by anyone else).

It is clear that if one accepts behaviour as evidence for other minds, then one must admit that one can compare other minds on the basis of such evidence. Therefore those who 'deny' inter-personal comparisons must deny the existence of other minds. The only possible alternative is that they think that, by some extra-ordinary kind of intuition, they can get to know that other minds exist, but that they cannot know anything else about them (for if one could get to know anything else about them, one could compare them). This is not, however, a real alternative, for the suggestion that things can be known to exist, without anything whatever being known about them, is absurd.

We conclude, then, that those who refuse to believe that one can compare other minds must deny their existence. But anyone who says that he does not believe in other minds inevitably contradicts himself, for he cannot help talking about them—that is, he cannot help using mental concepts with reference to other people. Econo-mists are in this matter a little old-fashioned. I doubt whether there is a philosopher today who would be prepared to say that one cannot compare other people's mental states; that one is not saying anything about the real world when one says 'A is happier than B'.

It may be thought that this question of interpersonal compari-sons has been discussed at too great a length, or that no one can really have denied interpersonal comparisons in the sense in which I imply that they have denied them. But their 'denial' in some sense has driven welfare economics into very curious channels. For this reason some discussion of the question is essential.

Two quotations may be put forward, from Professor Robbins, whose thesis it has been that welfare economics is inevitably an ethical study, because it involves interpersonal comparisons, and because interpersonal comparisons are value (or ethical) judge-ments. He writes: 'I still cannot believe that it is helpful to speak as if interpersonal comparisons of utility rest on scientific

foundations—that is upon observation or introspection' and 'But I
still think, when I make interpersonal comparisons, that my judgments are more like judgments of value than judgments of verifiable
fact'.[1] We must insist that it *is* helpful to speak as if interpersonal
comparisons rest on observation or introspection, for the good
reason that they do rest on such foundations. What is the alternative? Evidently, since it is not denied that they make sense, the
alternative is to say that they are value judgements, or (ignoring
the fact that they might be both) at any rate like value judgements.
But surely many such comparisons are not in the least like value
judgements. How is '*A* is happier than *B*' a value judgement? It
clearly does not mean that *A* is better or nobler, or more worthy
than *B*. Does it then mean something like 'If you are going to help
anyone, you ought to help *B* rather than *A*'? Now it is not denied
that something like the latter statement might be implied by the
statement '*A* is happier than *B*' in certain contexts, but certainly
not in all contexts. And even if, which is false, it was so implied in
all contexts, that would not be to say that the statement was simply
and solely a value judgement. The position taken up must surely
be seen to be absurd when it is remembered that it must be
argued that interpersonal comparisons, such as '*A* is angrier than
B', '*A* is more sympathetic than B', '*A* is more intelligent than *B*'
are one and all value judgements. Moreover, since all words like
'happy', 'intelligent', 'angry', &c., are words relative to some norm
of human behaviour, it must be maintained that '*A* is happy', '*A*
is angry', '*A* is intelligent' are value judgements, not judgements of
verifiable fact resting on either observation or introspection. We
will return to this question of value judgements in the next chapter.

It may be remembered that, in Chapter I, we briefly discussed
the question of comparisons of real income, and the question of
when it could be said that two men were economically equal. We
decided that, since people have different tastes, a comparison of
the objective factors, money incomes and prices and available
goods, was insufficient. Even if two people of different tastes had
the same money incomes, and were always faced with the same
available goods at the same prices, it could not very well be said
that they were economic equals both before and after a change
which greatly raised the prices of everything which the one bought
and the other did not buy. It appears that comparisons of real

[1] L. Robbins, *E.J.*, 1938, pp. 640, 641.

income must be comparisons, in part at least, of mental states or changes in mental states.

But what happens if we 'deny' such comparisons? It follows that real income comparisons must also be denied. What then becomes of such a statement as 'You ought to help the poor rather than the rich'? Either the words 'poor' and 'rich' must simply refer to the amounts of money the two people have, or the statement is sheer nonsense, or it is a tautology (the latter if it is thought that an interpersonal comparison such as 'A is really richer than B' means 'B ought to be helped rather than A'). It is obviously not a tautology; nor is it by any means nonsense. Therefore we are committed, if we persist in the absurdity of denying interpersonal comparisons, to saying that we are interested in the amount of money people have, quite regardless of what they can buy with it, and quite regardless of what satisfaction or happiness they get out of spending it. Again this is absurd; we are interested in the distribution of money only because we believe that there is a very good correlation between money incomes and capital, and real income.

Nevertheless, the view has been put forward that comparisons of real income (relative well-being) cannot be made. To quote Professor Lerner:[1]

This does not mean that the prices will not change and that such changes will not make some people better off and others worse off, even though their money incomes remain the same. It does mean, however, *that we must disregard such changes*[2] when they are the result of changes in demand for the various goods or changes in the supply while the optimum allocation of goods is maintained. If we could say that in the old situation the actual relative well-being of consumers was just what we wanted it to be, then, when prices changed, we would want to make some adjustment in the money incomes, to offset the change in prices, and leave the consumers in the same relative position as before. But we have no way of directly comparing the well-being of different consumers. Our only objective general indication is their money income, and this has not changed. We may have good reason for believing that one consumer is better off than he was before and that another is not so well off as he was before, but we have no more reason for supposing that the old situation is better than the new one (that is more like the situation we wish to bring about) than for supposing that the new one is better than the old one.

[1] A. P. Lerner, *The Economics of Control*, p. 24.   [2] My italics.

This passage is highly paradoxical. Either it is assumed that we cannot ever know when the distribution of real income (actual relative well-being) is what we want it to be, or it is assumed that we can know when it is what we want it to be, even although we cannot tell whether it is becoming more or less like what we want it to be, when it is seen to be changing. The latter alternative is absurd, and so it must be supposed that the author is maintaining that one person can never be said to be really better off than another in any sense other than that he has a greater money income. This is a most unconvincing position to take up, although it is, of course, the only possible position if one insists on trying to avoid making interpersonal comparisons of mental states. It amounts to telling people that they ought to ignore everything except money income (and capital?) when they decide what they think the distribution of income ought to be.

It is suggested that our *only* 'objective' criterion of relative well-being is money income. The word 'objective' has many meanings. It may mean 'unbiased' or 'measurable', but, since Professor Lerner holds that one cannot ever say whether one person has more or less satisfaction than another, it appears that he is using the word 'objective' to mean 'empirical'.[1] But how can it possibly be maintained that money income is an indication of relative well-being, when the latter cannot be empirically determined? Relative well-being either appears to become a metaphysical concept, or to become identical with money income. What other alternative is there if money income is our only test? What can money income be a test of, except money income, if no other evidence whatever is admitted?

Professor Lerner has tried to show that we need only be interested in money income, because it can be proved that an equalitarian distribution of money income is more likely than any other to maximize the aggregate amount of satisfaction in the community. It is worth examining how this conclusion is arrived at in the face of a denial of interpersonal comparisons of satisfaction.

It is rather difficult to understand the position which Professor Lerner seeks to maintain. He says that we can know that different people's satisfactions are 'the same kind of thing', and 'it is not meaningless to say that a satisfaction one individual gets is greater

[1] e.g. 'But these things [marginal utilities of income] are not capable of being discovered', op. cit., p. 29.

or less than a satisfaction enjoyed by somebody else'.[1] On the other hand, Professor Lerner insists that it is impossible to discover whether the marginal utility of income is greater or less for A than for B.[2] He also states that when a man says 'Thy need is greater than mine' he may be talking sense, even if it is not possible to discover whether he is right or wrong.

The position thus appears to be one in which it is maintained that it is meaningful to say 'A is happier than B' although this statement cannot in any circumstances be verified or falsified. Thus Professor Lerner is apparently basing his claim, to know that the satisfactions of different people are the same kind of thing, on some special form of intuition. But what is meant by saying that they are 'the same kind of thing'? From the following argument of Professor Lerner's the answer seems to be that he means simply that the satisfactions of different people may be added, although one cannot know whether one is greater or less than another.

Thus the three propositions fundamental to the argument are:

1. The statement 'A is more satisfied than B' is not verifiable.
2. The statement 'One pound would increase A's happiness more than B's' is not verifiable.
3. The statement 'I am adding A's satisfaction to B's' makes sense.

Because one never has, he maintains, any reason whatever for supposing that A has more or less capacity for satisfaction than B, Professor Lerner next assumes that it is equally probable that a shift of money from A to B, when they have equal money incomes, would increase or decrease *total* satisfaction. From this assumption it would follow that, out of a large number of such shifts, 50 per cent. would increase and 50 per cent. would decrease total satisfaction. But the assumption of equiprobability is surely illegitimate. It would be legitimate as a working hypothesis if there was some conceivable way of testing the conclusions. But since the author maintains 'the impossibility of measuring the satisfactions of different people on the same scale',[3] it follows that there is, on his principles, no conceivable way of testing the conclusion. Since from complete ignorance nothing but complete ignorance can follow, it is evident that Professor Lerner must claim an intuitive apprehension of equiprobabilities if this step in his argument is to be valid.

[1] Op. cit., p. 25.   [2] Op. cit., p. 29.   [3] Op. cit., pp. 24, 25.

Finally, in order to arrive at the conclusion that equal money incomes will probably maximize satisfaction, the argument from
total ignorance (or metaphysical intuition) has to be invoked again,
as well as the reasonable assumption of diminishing marginal
utility of income to any given individual.[1]

Thus the contention that we need not worry about anything
except money income, because an equal distribution of money is
most likely to produce most happiness, breaks down. But is the
contention in the least plausible without this support? If we assume an equal distribution of money income, changes in prices
would only alter relative well-being in so far as tastes differed.
There is some plausibility in the view that tastes would not differ
very much if money incomes were equal, and therefore in saying
that money incomes would be an adequate guide to the distribution of real income. But it still would not be very plausible unless
tastes were also assumed to be adaptable and price changes small.
Moreover, it would still only be true that relative money incomes
would be taken as a guide to real incomes. One would always be
ready to abandon the money criterion, if it was observed that some
price change made a great difference to some individual. But, as
soon as we come to consider an inequalitarian society, the view that
it is only money income which is important loses all plausibility.
No one believes that one can simply ignore a large change in the
price-ratio of necessities and luxuries.

Let us now return to the utilitarian argument that an equalitarian distribution of real income will maximize satisfaction. We
have seen that this argument is based on the ability to compare
differences in satisfaction. On certain assumptions, which will be
discussed below, it follows that satisfaction or happiness is maximized when the marginal unit of money makes the same difference
to everyone, that is, when the marginal utility of money is equal for
everyone. It follows again that we have an equalitarian distribution
of purchasing power when the marginal utility of money is equal
for everyone; or, as we have argued before, the statement 'as
one gets really richer the marginal utility of money falls' is a
tautology.

We must now ask whether this statement really is a tautology.
In other words, does it mean the same to say 'A's economic well-
being is greater than B's' as it does to say 'a small extra amount of

[1] See op. cit., pp. 26–32, for a full statement of the argument.

money would make less difference to A's happiness than to B's? (The statement 'A's economic well-being is greater' or 'A is really wealthier', does not, of course, mean the same as 'A is happier'.) Take the case of A, who is a miserable millionaire, and B who has little money, but is happy. A little more money would make no difference at all to A, but it would raise B from happiness to bliss. Such a case, of course, supports the above view, for it would be extremely paradoxical to say that B was really wealthier, although he is, it is admitted, happier. Indeed, it is not very easy to think of a case in which it would not be paradoxical to say that A was really wealthier than B, but a little more money would make more difference to his happiness than it would to B's. The millionaire miser might seem to be an exception. If you give him a little more money his face still lights up, and on this account one might have to say he was really poorer than a man with much less money—so much less that it would seem a paradoxical thing to say. But this may only be a prima-facie exception. One does not think that the little extra money really makes any difference to the miser's happiness, even though it gives him a momentary satisfaction. Happiness is not a sum of satisfactions.

Also the present view is strongly supported by ordinary language and thought. The phrase 'But money means more to me than you' is often used, and shows that people do indeed compare marginal utilities of money. It is also clear that they might equally well have said 'But I am poorer than you'. In a typical context the two phrases would be interchangeable. But, nevertheless, one cannot go so far as to maintain that 'money means more to a poor man' is a tautology. There are exceptions. For instance, one would not want to say that a melancholic with £500 per annum is really as rich (has as high a real income) as a millionaire, just because he is so sunk in misery that no extra amount of money would make any difference to him. It does seem, however, that we have to call in abnormal people to provide exceptions. Thus the utilitarian doctrine that economic equality produces the most happiness is not a correct analysis of how people use the phrase 'economic equality', although it is quite a good analysis.

Of course, if you ask someone to compare the real wealth of two men, the first thing he will look at will be their money incomes. That is perfectly reasonable, because it is a matter of experience that the two are closely correlated. But if there are any rather exceptional circumstances, if their tastes are widely different, if they are faced by different prices, if it is known that one man hates his job and is only just induced to stay in it by a big salary, and so on, then one would want to look farther than money income, or total resources valued in money terms. (The difference between the two is that most people would think that capital has a higher real yield than the actual money income it yields, for example, security and the possibility of using it as a stop-gap while looking for a better job, &c.) One would try to assess in some way the real value of the man's money to him. One might look at the lives both lead, and decide which one would choose oneself. But if one realized that one's own tastes were exceptional, one would try to be more objective; then one might well base one's estimate rather more on the marginal utility of money principle. In conclusion, I think that one can say that, in the last resort, people make such judgements of relative real wealth partly on the basis of their own preferences, but partly by estimating what difference a little more or less money would make to the happiness of the people concerned.

Let us suppose, then, that a man judges that two people have the same real income. Does it follow that it would be impossible to increase happiness by taking money away from one and giving it to the other? We have seen that it doesn't necessarily follow, because we have come to the conclusion that 'an equal marginal utility of money' is not a correct definition of 'economic equality', and therefore that the utilitarian doctrine is not quite right. But, nevertheless, the relative marginal utility of money is a good criterion of relative well-being, and therefore we can say, in general, that an equalitarian distribution of real income would come near to maximizing happiness *if certain assumptions could safely be made.* These are:

(a) that the process of redistribution which may be required does not decrease happiness. (Such a redistribution might require political changes, which some might think would decrease happiness on their own account. Again, the redistribution might be thought to conflict with some ethical principle, such a conflict being, in the long run, unfavourable to happiness.)

(b) if people can be validly treated as independent units whose happiness depends only on what they themselves have and consume;

(c) if the production of goods and services is not adversely affected;

(d) If people's tastes are not changed by virtue of increasing their income so that they get less happiness from a higher income.

To a certain extent, then, and with sweeping assumptions, the thesis that economic equalitarianism produces the maximum amount of happiness is more or less true. But it is very important to realize that, in so far as it is true, it is a linguistic statement. It is almost a tautology. Its truth is discovered by seeing how people tend to judge economic equality. It is a fact about language, that is about a particular usage of the word 'equality', and not a fact about the real world. But, although it is almost a tautology, it is a very important statement which can have much influence, if only because people forget what equalitarianism must mean if it is to be true; people may, for instance, wrongly interpret equalitarianism in such a context as referring to equality of money income, whereas in fact it tells us nothing whatever about what distribution of money would produce most satisfaction. It is this ambiguous nature of the word 'equality', taken in conjunction with the persuasive force of the phrase 'maximum happiness', which can make such a tautology into a powerful and persuasive slogan.[1]

It is obvious that the assumptions referred to above are very important, and that people may disagree greatly as to how realistic they are, and as to the effect on happiness of their not being realized. So long as it was thought that interpersonal comparisons were value judgements, it had to be held that any discussion of the effect on happiness of the failure of these assumptions consisted merely of value statements. Thus a prejudice against an argument which directly involved interpersonal comparisons was set up. If one said that one thought that such and such a distribution of real income would maximize happiness, it was thought that one could only be making propaganda for one's own view of what the social order ought to be.

But to argue that equality would decrease happiness because inequality provides incentives, and an outlet for ambition, or that

[1] It may be noticed that if people judged relative well-being by reference to the marginal welfare of money, and if they regarded 'well-being' as a purely ethical word, then it would be tautological to say that an equal distribution of well-being was the best distribution.

it would decrease happiness because the expenditure of the richer classes adds greatly to other people's happiness in the long run by making possible a higher culture, is not merely propaganda. Nor, on the other hand, is it merely propaganda to maintain that inequality results in envy, hatred, and jealousy, and that the expenditure of the rich therefore has external diseconomies of consumption. (External economies and diseconomies in production have received very wide attention; the process of taking each consumer as an independent unit ignores the economies and diseconomies of consumption, which have been comparatively little noticed, but may be far more important.) We shall see in the next chapter that it is possible to speak of the causes of changes in the happiness of a community in a descriptive manner, but that it is not possible to speak of them in a *purely* descriptive manner. A value element always enters in. But it is not true that the value element enters in because interpersonal comparisons are value judgements.

It has already been implied that, even if people were agreed on the distribution of real income which would produce most happiness, they may still disagree how money incomes should be distributed in order to produce this degree of equality of real incomes. Two people may very well differ in their estimation of whether A or B is really better off. We must notice, however, that the distribution of real income is not a precise concept at all. If all pairs of individuals were taken, and some observer was asked to judge in each case which of the pair was really wealthier, there would be an enormous number of cases in which he would not be prepared to give a definite answer. In most cases where an individual would give a definite answer, then the majority of individuals would probably give the same answer. This means that if it was decided that people should be made economically equal, there would be an infinite number of different distributions of money income which would all correspond with any one individual's idea of equality. At the same time, there would probably be no distribution which would correspond with everyone's idea of equality. The disagreement would come about mainly as a result of each individual being particularly interested in a different small class containing only a few particular pairs of individuals, and he would examine these cases much more closely than others. Nevertheless, such disagreement could easily be exaggerated. If people think on such matters as they normally do, largely in terms of broad social groups, or average individuals, and not about particular cases, there would probably be a wide measure of agreement as to which groups were really wealthier, and which really poorer.

People are not likely to dispute whether a single man with £2,000 per annum is better or worse off than another single man with £500. They might, however, very well dispute whether taxing the former and subsidizing the latter would increase happiness. This would not be a dispute about whether say, the last £100 made more or less difference to the happiness of the rich man. The principle of the diminishing marginal utility of income is not normally a point at issue at all. This principle sets the prima-facie static case for equality of real income; the real arguments follow. Thus it is clear that one such case cannot be treated alone. But if many such cases are considered, then, for instance, the external effects, which are ignored by simply treating each pair of individuals separately as though a transference between them had no effect on anyone else, come in. In fact, the important questions which are left on one side by the assumptions (a), (b), (c), and (d), mentioned above, provide the meat of the real arguments on this subject.

Finally, the question of what distribution of money income would maximize happiness is, *to some extent*,[1] independent of the question how money and property ought to be distributed. Most people would agree that it is a good thing to try to make the country happier, but they would not necessarily agree that this is a consideration which must outweigh all others. In an extreme case, someone might think that it was wrong ever to harm someone in order to benefit someone else. (He might also hold that happiness could never, in the long run, be increased by doing wrong, and therefore that no redistribution of income can increase happiness, even though happiness would be greater in an equalitarian society if it could evolve without one deliberately having to harm some people for the benefit of others). People can also hold moral views about the mechanism of distribution. Thus it has been held that interest is evil, and that a man ought to receive the value of his marginal product. Again, people may hold that it is wrong to 'confiscate' capital,[2] but all right to tax income. Thus the question

---

[1] What is meant by saying it is *to some extent* independent will become clear later.
[2] The word 'confiscate' is enclosed in inverted commas because it is an emotive word.

of how income and property ought to be distributed does not simply depend on the question of what distribution would maximize happiness; all kinds of other ethical issues may be involved, apart from the major ethical premise that, *ceteris paribus*, one ought to increase happiness. In fact, few people would consider that other things ever are equal, or a matter of ethical indifference.

We have, in this chapter, endeavoured to show that:

1. Interpersonal comparisons of satisfaction are empirical judgements about the real world, and are not, in any normal context, value judgements;
2. People are interested in the distribution of *real* wealth, which presupposes interpersonal comparisons of mental states;
3. The distribution of real wealth is a very imprecise concept, and, in particular, economic equality is a very imprecise, rough and ready sort of idea, which will differ from person to person;
4. The utilitarian argument for equality is sound if correctly interpreted, but it tells us nothing about what distribution of money or property will produce equality; furthermore, it presents only a prima-facie case for equality, and is not really a point at issue between those who dispute about such matters;
5. It is possible to discuss the causes and effects of the happiness, both of individuals and countries; such discussions do not consist merely of value judgements; although, as we shall see, a value element is almost always involved;
6. The question what distribution of income would maximize happiness is partly independent of the question how income ought to be distributed.

A discussion of the relation of descriptions and cause and effect statements to value judgements is now overdue; the fact that it has not been considered has, indeed, already begun to cramp our discussion.

CHAPTER V

VALUE JUDGEMENTS AND WELFARE ECONOMICS

In the last chapter we denied that statements such as 'A is happier than B' or '£1 would make more difference to A's happiness than to B's' are merely value judgements. We also held that it is possible to discuss the causes of the happiness, or changes in the happiness, of groups of individuals, and that such discussions certainly do not consist merely of value judgements. Some further discussion of the function of value words, and of the nature of value judgements, and their importance in economics, is now required.

Whether a word is a value word depends on the context. It is clear that 'You ought to go home for your father is dying' is a value judgement, and that in this sentence the 'ought' has a moral force. On the other hand, in the statement 'You ought to go home if you want to avoid being recognized', the 'ought' has no moral implication. Now it is possible that the word 'happiness' may have ethical implications in some contexts. Whereas it has no moral force in 'A is happier than B', it may have in the statement 'That change would increase the happiness of society'. The moral force here would depend on the combination of the word 'happiness' with 'increase' and 'society'.

It is nowadays widely held that ethical judgements do not describe facts. To call someone good is not in the least like calling him tall. It does not describe any fact about him. Nor does it describe any relation which exists between him and the person who says he is good. When I call someone 'good', I am not saying that I am experiencing a certain feeling, which I have whenever I think of him. In other words, ethical statements do not, it is held, describe either external or internal facts.

The above view is too simple. It may be the case that I only call a man good when he has certain characteristics, and lacks others. I may have some rough and ready criterion of goodness, and when I say that a man is good, I am, then, partly describing him. I am saying that there are certain facts about him—facts which I regard as sufficient to warrant the use of the word 'good'. But other people will probably use the word in different ways, and refuse to call him good. There is certainly no settled and agreed descriptive usage for ethical words, as there is, to a much greater extent, for such words as 'tall' or 'brown'. This suggests that there must be a reason why people do not agree on how, and when, to use ethical words. The reason is that ethical statements do more than merely describe.

Now although I have said that the view that ethical statements do not describe anything is too simple, nevertheless in some cases it is correct. The sentence 'You ought not to commit murder' certainly does not describe anything. It tells a person how not to behave. This suggests that all ethical statements may have something in common with such statements as 'You ought not to commit murder', even if they are at the same time descriptive. There may also be an element of telling people how to, or how not to, behave. The word 'telling' is, however, too strong. If I say 'Smith and Jones are good men', I am not telling anyone to emulate their behaviour. Nor if I say 'Hamlet is a good film' am I telling people to see it if they can. But I am certainly suggesting that they go to see it. Such statements may be said to be influential, or persuasive. This is, I think, the reason why people tend to disagree on how ethical words such as 'good' should be used. Different people like to see different kinds of behaviour; they want different sorts of films performed, and pictures painted.

It is not only ethical judgements which have this function of influencing, suggesting, and persuading. Take such a statement as 'That picture is revolting'. Now if the hearer knew what sort of picture the speaker was wont to describe as revolting, the statement might convey to him some information about the picture. But even if no information was conveyed, the statement need not be entirely useless. It might alter the hearer's artistic tastes, and stop him telling others that it was beautiful. Thus aesthetic judgements, even if descriptive, also have the same kind of persuasive or recommendatory force as ethical judgements.

We propose to call all judgements, which have this kind of force, value judgements. We may add, in order to distinguish them from imperatives—commands and requests—that they must be in the indicative mood. For our purposes, in this book, we do not require to have any criterion to distinguish value judgements which are ethical from those which are not. For that we would require a theory of ethics. It is sufficient, for our purposes, to be able to distinguish pure descriptions from descriptions which are also value judgements, and from pure value judgements with no descriptive content. It is, I think, true that the value judgements which enter into welfare economics are of an ethical kind; but that is incidental.

Now the most important kind of value judgement entering into economics is that which is also descriptive. Such judgements describe facts in a way which tends to influence the attitudes which people adopt towards such facts, and hence to influence their characters and behaviour. The way in which this is best done is to take a word which in certain contexts has a strong appeal, say 'democracy', and then to use it to describe something which it was not originally used to describe. The word, by virtue of its having been used to describe states of affairs, which people have come to regard with approval, has itself acquired an emotive force. The new states of affairs, which it is later used to describe, bask under the now favourable light which the word sheds on them. If the word 'democracy' is applied to a certain state, not only does it invest it with a general aura of approbation, but also it serves to emphasize those aspects of the state which may be democratic, and to cover up those aspects in which it is undemocratic. If this sort of thing is done too blatantly the word loses its emotive force, and becomes discredited, as the word 'democracy' is now largely discredited in the eyes of well-educated people. But if the shift in descriptive meaning is not very great, and the emotive word is not too obviously emotive, then these persuasive descriptions may remain persuasive and influential for a long time. The process of defining, whether implicitly or explicitly, an emotive word in such a way that one can or does apply it to something one wants to be persuasively described is known as giving the word a persuasive definition.[1]

Persuasive definitions are very common. For instance, economists would like to have the word 'science' defined or used in such a way that economics can be called a science. Again, sociologists like to be called scientists. Why? Why should it matter to anyone whether their study is called a science or not? The answer is that it matters because the word 'science' is an emotive word. The same

---

[1] Persuasive definitions were brought to light by Professor Stevenson in an article of that title in *Mind*, Mar. 1938.

sort of thing occurs with the words 'gentleman', 'poet', 'productive', and, similarly, most people will try to avoid such labels as 'monopolist', 'rentier', 'capitalist'. People will argue passionately about the correct descriptive usage of such words, for the reason that they are also emotive. Emotive expressions occur in economics to a greater extent than in most other subjects. A good instance of what can be done with persuasive definitions is Mr. Kalecki's conclusion that the share of the capitalist in the national income is equal to the degree of monopoly.[1] Neither of the operative words 'capitalist' or 'monopoly' is used to describe the state of affairs or the class, as a result of describing which they have acquired their emotive force.

Value judgements can, then, be recognized by considering what judgements are likely to influence people, not because they describe in colourless unemotive language facts which people already approve of, but because they describe facts in an emotive way, or because they are merely emotive and describe nothing at all. We may add that it is not sufficient that a value judgement should influence people. One can influence people by pointing out the consequences of the moral or aesthetic attitudes which they have to certain facts. A value judgement is one which tends to influence them by altering these beliefs or attitudes.

We have argued in Chapter IV that interpersonal comparisons are descriptive judgements. Let us first consider an interpersonal comparison such as 'A is happier than B'. Now it is clear that this proposition may be purely descriptive, for in many contexts it would not serve to influence anyone's character or behaviour in any way. It might, however, be influential, and designed to be so, if it was known that someone proposed, for instance, to give the less happy of the two a present. In such a case it still would not be a value judgement, because the present-giver would be influenced only by the actual or supposed truth of a purely descriptive statement, and not by any emotive force which the words themselves have.

Is it a value judgement to say 'A's economic welfare is greater than B's'? This sentence certainly does not appear to recommend that anything should be done. But we have held that, given certain

---

[1] '*The relative share of gross capitalist income and salaries in the aggregate turnover is with great approximation equal to the average degree of monopoly*' (italicized in original), *Essays in the Theory of Economic Fluctuations*, p. 22.

assumptions, it does imply that happiness could be increased by giving money from A to B. On the other hand, these assumptions may be unrealistic, and few people would think that 'A's economic welfare is greater than B's' did imply that happiness could be increased by taking money away from A and giving it to B. If one said 'happiness could be increased by *shifting* money from A to B', that would, I think, be a value judgement, as we shall argue below, but this statement is not entailed by the statement that the marginal utility of money is greater for B, or by the statement that B's economic welfare is lower than A's. Thus we may conclude that interpersonal comparisons of satisfaction, happiness, real income, or welfare are not, in any normal context, value judgements.

Let us now take a statement such as 'this economic change would increase A's happiness'. Is this a value judgement? Of course, to a utilitarian, if we add that no one else would be in any way harmed, it would entail the value judgement that this change ought to be made. Whether utilitarians or not, most people would at least agree that it is a good thing to increase someone's happiness, if no one else is in any way harmed. So it is certainly likely to influence people, but it may influence them only because it describes the effects of a change; effects such that people will approve of the change, because they are already convinced that these effects are good, and worth bringing about. As we have said, this does not necessarily make our judgement a value judgement, because people may be influenced only by the nature of the facts described, and not at all by the way in which they are described.

But we must notice that, since most people approve of happiness, and think that it is a good thing to encourage it, the word 'happiness', or rather the phrase 'increase of happiness', must have acquired considerable emotive force, just as the word 'democracy' acquired emotive force because people approved of democracy. Thus, if we say that some change would increase A's happiness and harm no one else, our audience is liable to be influenced not merely by the described effects, but also to some extent by the way in which they are described. It is, of course, possible to hold that happiness ought not to be increased. But anyone who maintained that a certain change would increase happiness, and would have no other harmful effects whatever, and yet ought not to be carried out, would not merely be maintaining something which few would agree with, but would also be saying something that was slightly paradoxical. It may be concluded that the phrases 'increase of happiness' and 'increase of welfare' are often emotive.

But when these phrases are applied to particular individuals, the emotive or persuasive effect varies very much with the context. It is obvious that the statement 'you would make your mother happy if you visited her occasionally' is not merely a causal statement. It is also persuasive and suggestive. It is not so very different from 'you ought to visit your mother occasionally because it would make her happy'. On the other hand, when a particular individual is named, one cannot very easily misapply the phrase or word 'increase of happiness' or 'happier' and use it to describe in an emotive manner a situation which is not a case of increased happiness, as one can apply the word 'democracy' to a state which is not democratic. The difference is that people know quite well how to judge happiness, and 'an increase of happiness' when applied to a particular individual is a fairly precise description. Such a word as 'democracy' has, in contrast, only a vague descriptive connotation and can be easily misapplied in a persuasive manner.

The case is, however, rather different when we come to discuss a general criterion for an increase in an individual's happiness. Such a criterion could easily be persuasive, because it would be applied to individuals in general, and the results would not be checked by reference to actual individuals. In welfare theory it is simply applied to a variable 'X', which is assumed to stand for any individual. In this context the question of divergence from ordinary descriptive usage is difficult to answer. The criterion will apply well to some individuals, and badly to others. Since the question whether it is, in general, in accordance with ordinary usage is a vague one, there is plenty of room for persuasion. The harder it is to formalize the ordinary usage of an emotive expression, the more scope there is for persuasive criteria, or definitions, of the expression.

Welfare economics is not very much concerned with changes in the welfare of individuals as such. It requires a criterion of an increase in the welfare of individuals only because the welfare of the community is regarded as a logical construction from the welfares of actual or representative individuals. Thus the criterion of an increase in individual welfare is not used with reference to particular individuals, but as a basis from which to deduce conclusions about increases and decreases of welfare or happiness in general. Since people normally think that such increases are *good*, and such decreases *bad*, it follows that any criterion for an increase in individual welfare will be very influential. It should be noted that this is the case, quite apart from the facts of emotive language. People might be deceived, by a criterion for 'an increase in individual welfare', into thinking that a certain change would increase happiness, when it would not, and therefore be deceived into thinking that the change would be good. Thus it is possible that people should be partly deceived and partly influenced into believing that a certain change is a good change. Both the deception and the influence are very much easier to engineer when one's conclusions are about communities, because one cannot check up on whether a community is happier in the same way as one can check up on whether an individual is happier.

We noticed in Chapter III, when discussing the choice criterion for 'an increase in economic welfare', that people might well disagree as to whether one should say, in certain cases, that a man's economic welfare had increased. We instanced the case of a man who had become middle class, having been working class, and then lost money after he had acquired middle-class habits; but he could still buy the goods of his original situation. Should we say that this man's economic welfare had increased in his last situation as compared with his original situation? Someone might well insist on saying that it had, because otherwise it would mean admitting that a person could have more money and less welfare (supposing prices had not changed). But comparing the welfare of the same person before and after any considerable change of taste is very like comparing the welfare of two different people. Thus to refuse to admit that there was an increase of welfare in the above case would be tantamount to denying that an equalitarian distribution of money need be the best distribution. Anyone who held that money ought to be equally distributed would recognize the emotive force of this denial, and might therefore insist on saying that the economic welfare of our specimen had increased. Thus a person who believed in equality of money (no matter why) might seek to press the acceptance of a criterion for an increase in welfare which would serve as a basis for the deduction of the theory that welfare was maximized when money was equally distributed. People with different views would press for different criteria.

So far we have not discussed the *real income* of an individual.

Now in any situation, such as the above one, when the choice criterion is complete (i.e. the individual's present money income is more than sufficient to buy the past collection of goods, and his past money income was insufficient to buy the present collection) some economists may want to say that the individual's real income is, at any rate, greater, even if his economic welfare is not necessarily greater. It is important to see that they would not be making any further descriptive statement by saying this. As we have mentioned before, there is no objective sense in which one bundle of goods is greater than another, except when there is more of every kind of good. But no one wants to say that an individual's real income is higher *only* when this unlikely condition is satisfied. Thus what these economists want to do is simply to substitute the phrase 'has a higher real income' for my phrase 'is in a chosen position'. I prefer not to do this because I think the former phrase tends to beg the question whether it is a good thing for an individual to be in a chosen position. Everyone tends to assume that more real income is a good thing. The phrase is, in other words, suggestive. It is, in fact, suggestive in two ways—(*a*) it suggests that any change, which it is used to describe, is a good change, and (*b*) it suggests that there is something, called real income, which can be said to become larger or smaller in some perfectly objective sense. This latter suggestion is simply false, and the former might be undesirable. The statement '*A* is in a chosen position' is less technical, less misleading, and less colourful than the statement '*A* has a higher real income'. One must first agree that it is a good thing that an individual should be in a chosen position, before one uses the choice criterion as a criterion of increased real income. In this respect there is no difference between changes in welfare and changes in real income.

There is thus a danger that the phrases 'an increase in an individual's welfare' and 'an increase in an individual's real income' may be persuasively defined. But, at the same time, there is a check. It is possible to discuss whether the criterion is, or is not, in reasonable accordance with ordinary usage in a more or less dispassionate manner, because people are fairly well agreed as to what changes would, in the short run at least, increase an individual's happiness.

But when we come to deal with happiness in general the situation is, as we indicated, very much more difficult. We have, for instance, seen that there would be wide agreement that happiness would be increased by transferring money from a man with £2,000 per annum to one with £500 per annum, given certain assumptions. But where the validity of these assumptions is called in question, as it is certain to be, then there would be very considerable disagreement. This disagreement could not, for many reasons, be reconciled by the empirical process of seeing what sort of economic changes did, or did not, increase the happiness of a community.

The two most important reasons are, first, that one cannot make a controlled experiment with a large community; there is sure to be a large number of changes, economic and otherwise, apart from the experimental change. Secondly, and most important, there would be considerable disagreement as to whether the community was happier or not, even if one could make such an experiment. Each individual may mean something descriptive by saying that the community is happier, but no individual can observe the whole community, and each will inevitably take different facts into account. The larger the group of people being considered, the greater the disagreement is likely to be. If the group consisted of only two or three individuals, we might, for instance, get wide agreement as to what changes would increase happiness, especially if the observers were not members of the group. But the group under consideration is normally a whole country. Evidently 'the happiness of the community' can only have the vaguest possible descriptive meaning in such cases, if it has any at all. Also, of course, to say that the happiness of the community would be increased, while it has only a very vague factual meaning, which differs from person to person, has very strong emotive significance. Although people would disagree greatly about whether the community was happier, and even more about the causes of changes in its happiness, there would be wide agreement that anything which would make it happier would normally be a good thing.

It is clear that, in such circumstances, a definition or criterion of 'an increase in the happiness of a community' is certain to be a persuasive criterion, and that any theoretical conclusion to the effect that such and such a change would increase the happiness of the community is certain to be an emotive, influential recommendatory kind of conclusion. It would be a value judgement, tending to alter people's attitudes to the change in question, not because it clearly and unequivocally described some precise sort of result, which they believed to be good, but rather because it stated an effect in terms which would have a different, rather vague, descriptive meaning for everyone, but the same emotive significance for all. In the previous chapter we concluded that judgements about the causes of the happiness of individuals and communities are not merely value judgements. We now see that where the individual is concerned such judgements are mainly descriptive, although a slight value element may be present, but where communities consisting of a very large number of people are concerned, then the descriptive content is nebulous and weak, but the value content strong.

In the above discussion, and in previous chapters, we have used the words 'welfare' and 'happiness' almost as though they were synonymous. It will be remembered that, at the very beginning, we translated 'this change would increase A's economic welfare' into 'this change would alter economic circumstances in a manner favourable to A's happiness'. The descriptive content of the two statements may not be very different. But, in my opinion, the phrase 'increase of welfare' has far greater emotive force than the phrase 'increase of happiness'. The meaning of a statement such as 'X would increase welfare' is much less clear than the meaning of the statement 'X would increase happiness'. It may well be possible to convey an emotive effect by arriving at a welfare conclusion, which would not be possible using the word 'happiness', simply because the descriptive meaning is clearer with the latter terminology, and therefore a conclusion in terms of happiness may make people sit up and say 'I don't believe it', while they might have lain down under the welfare conclusion, simply absorbing the emotive significance without having any very clear idea about the descriptive meaning of the phrase at all.

Some people may say that 'increase of welfare' is a purely ethical expression, and that its only connexion with 'happiness' is that most people would agree that happiness is a good thing, but not the only good thing. If this is correct, then welfare economics is an ethical study right from the start. This seems to me to be almost certainly the correct view, because the sentence 'X would increase welfare' surely does not *entail* any sentence about satisfactions or happiness. Up to this point we have tried to give those economists who hold that welfare economics is, or should be, a positive study of the determinants of happiness the best possible run for their money by supposing that statements about welfare were logically reducible to statements about happiness. But, even if this were true (which it is not), it still could not be claimed that welfare economics is a merely scientific study, because the phrase 'increase of happiness', especially when applied to a society, is emotive. Thus the question whether the word 'welfare' has any descriptive reference is not very important, because any such reference would be to happiness or satisfaction; and the reformulation of welfare economics in terms of satisfactions, or happiness, would not turn it into a purely positive study.

The truth of the contention that welfare conclusions are value judgements is borne out by the ease with which welfare economists slip from talking about economic welfare into using a frankly ethical terminology. It would perhaps be invidious to give specific examples, but we will indicate the kind of language which has come to be frequently used.

First, the word 'economic' usually gets left out. This greatly increases the emotive effect. If I say 'this change will increase economic welfare', it is open to anyone to say 'perhaps, but it will not increase political welfare, or welfare in general'. This reply is not open if I leave out the word 'economic'. Putting it in always suggests that the economist's conclusion is not the last word, and that, therefore, the conclusion is not to be taken as a definite recommendation.

Secondly, the word 'social', or 'community', or 'national' is often inserted where 'economic' is left out. This also increases the persuasive effect, for all these words are highly emotive to different classes of people. Thirdly, instead of 'increase of economic welfare' we very often find the word 'benefit'. 'Benefit' is obviously an ethical word. 'Social benefit' and 'social advantage' have also been used.

It does not seem very likely that these terminological changes could have been so easily made if there was nothing ethical about the word 'welfare' at all, especially as the economists who have made them do not apparently profess to believe in ethical utilitarianism. On the contrary, it has been claimed that welfare economics is a precise objective science, without any ethical presuppositions. That this claim could have been made in the face of the use of expressions such as 'social advantage', 'social benefit', and so on, is extraordinary. It is also difficult to see how one can be very precise or objective about anything so vague as the happiness of the community. (We will say something more about the precision of welfare economics when we deal with the so-called New Welfare Economics in the next chapter.)

The recommendatory force of the new welfare economics has been noticed and contrasted with the apparently more scientific inquiry into the causes of welfare pursued by Professor Pigou. To quote:

> Professor Pigou in his 'Economics of Welfare' does not prescribe; he examines what would increase economic welfare, and leaves it at that. This is important. As the 'economics of welfare' is concerned with the causes of welfare, it follows that it is a positive study, and not a normative study of what ought to be done.
>
> The study of the causes of welfare and prescription are not far apart, the former to most people is only a preparation for the latter. Nevertheless they are two different things.[1]

It is agreed that recent welfare economics has adopted more recommendatory language and is more prescriptive; it also reaches more definite conclusions. The conclusions of Professor Pigou were at least dependent on the proposed changes not causing an unfavourable change in real income distribution, which would undo the good effects which the change might otherwise have brought about. Many recent welfare economists have simply ignored this important qualification. I disagree, on the other hand, with the view that Professor Pigou was merely delving into the causes of welfare in an entirely dispassionate manner. It is maintained that any theory of welfare, if it reaches any conclusions at all, reaches value conclusions even if they are also causal statements. I would, indeed, go rather further, and say that the 'effect', which is an increase in the happiness of a group of many millions of people, is such a nebulous concept that it may be rather misleading to speak of cause and effect in such a case at all.[2] We

---

[1] A. Radomysler, 'Welfare Economics and Economic Policy', *Economica*, Aug. 1946, p. 199.

[2] It is worth noticing that, before Pigou, the word 'welfare' was little used. Economists mostly used the word 'satisfaction'. Pigou appears to have popularized the use of the word 'welfare' by calling his book *The Economics of Welfare*, and, since then, there has been comparatively little use of the 'satisfaction' or 'happiness' terminology. Pigou marked the transition because although his work was called *The Economics of Welfare*, he made considerable use of the word 'satisfaction' in the text, but also spoke of 'benefit', &c. As we have pointed out, the 'welfare' terminology (including such phrases as 'social benefit', 'social advantage') is much more ethical and less descriptive than the 'happiness'

expect 'causes' and 'effects' to be descriptions of things or events the existence or occurrence of which can be fairly objectively determined. (By 'objectively' we mean that there should be more or less precise tests which people would agree on.) The statement 'If you do this, the happiness of the community will increase' cannot be tested in the way in which we expect most of those statements, which we call causal, to be tested. It is, of course, legitimate to say 'such and such would cause an increase in the happiness of the community'. One can also say 'the provision of more school-teachers would cause an improvement in children's morals'. But neither of these statements is like the statement 'pressing the accelerator would cause an increase in the speed of the car'. They are all causal statements, but of quite different kinds. To speak of causes and effects rather suggests scientific tests, and it certainly suggests that there are some more or less generally agreed tests of whether the result of the cause has been the predicted effect. But if 'cause and effect' suggests this, then it is misleading to speak of welfare economics as a study of the causes of the welfare of communities, although it is not misleading to speak of the causes of happiness in the case of particular individuals, or small groups of individuals.

Welfare economics and ethics cannot, then, be separated. They are inseparable because the welfare terminology is a value termino-

terminology. The timing of this change of emphasis is interesting. For the ethical utilitarians of the nineteenth century, value judgements and descriptive judgements were held to be identical. Therefore a 'happiness' economics had a definitely ethical basis. As people ceased to believe in ethical utilitarianism (Pigou himself did not accept this theory of ethics—the teaching of G. E. Moore on the subject of naturalistic fallacies had probably inhibited such views at Cambridge) this logical connexion between ethics and economics vanished. Yet people study economic welfare largely for the purpose of discovering the best thing to do, and for making recommendations. It was therefore not unnatural that welfare economists should, without realizing it, restore the ethical force which descriptive happiness judgements now seemed to lack. This is, at any rate, a possible explanation of the definite growth in the emotive and suggestive force of the terminology of economics in this century.

It may be noted that Dr. Myint in his book *Theories of Welfare Economics* traces the development of what he calls welfare economics from Adam Smith to the present day. We would prefer to say that welfare economics began with Pigou. Before that, we had 'happiness' economics; and, before that, 'wealth' economics. After all, Smith wrote of the wealth, not the welfare, of nations. I do not think this is a trifling distinction. The suggestive force, and the implications of the three phrases, 'This would increase the welfare of society', 'This would increase the happiness of society', and 'This would increase the wealth of the nation' are not the same.

logy. It may be suggested that welfare economics could be purged by the strict use of a technical terminology, which, in ordinary speech, had no value implications. The answer is that it could be, but it would no longer be welfare economics. It would then consist of an uninterpreted system of logical deductions, which would not be about anything at all, let alone welfare. As soon as such a system was held to be about anything, for example, welfare or happiness, it would once again be emotive and ethical. Getting rid of value judgements would be throwing the baby away with the bathwater. The subject is one about which nothing interesting can be said without value judgements, for the reason that we take a moral interest in welfare and happiness.

The fact that the conclusions of welfare economics are inevitably, in part at least, value judgements raises the question of whether it would be best to take the view that welfare economics simply draws out the logical conclusions of a set of consistent value axioms which are laid down for the welfare economist by some priest or parliament or dictator. This view represents a clean break with the utilitarian tradition of English economics. Its supporters[1] deny, in effect, that welfare economics need be, in any way, a study of happiness. They subscribe, in fact, since such a study is still called welfare economics, to the view that the word 'welfare' is a purely ethical word, without, of course, denying that value judgements may be influenced greatly, or even entirely, by considerations of happiness. In this, I think, they are right. But, even if they are right, this is not to say that there is nothing descriptive, nothing empirical, about a study of happiness. Whereas it has been maintained that any statement about increases or decreases in the happiness of a community is a value judgement, it has also been maintained that there is some descriptive element involved (although it is possible that there is nothing descriptive about the phrase 'increase of general welfare').

The difference between the two views may be illustrated by taking the case of an increase in the welfare of an individual. On the 'happiness' approach we might argue about whether an individual was likely to be happier if he was in a chosen position. On the purely ethical approach, the economist merely deduces what fol-

---

[1] The chief representatives of this view seem to be Professor A. Bergson in 'A Reformulation of Certain Aspects of Welfare Economics', *Q.J.E.*, Feb. 1938, and Professor P. A. Samuelson in *Foundations of Economic Analysis*, ch. viii.

lows from the postulate 'It is a good thing that an individual should be in a chosen position'.

There is, to my mind, little doubt which is the best approach. What, after all, is the object of welfare economics? Surely it is to find out what is the best thing to do in various situations. Even those who would claim that welfare economics is a study of the economic causes of happiness must admit that that is not the be-all and end-all of it. As Radomysler, in the quotation given above, said, such a study would only be a preparation for prescription. It may be argued that one could have a purely historical interest in welfare, and seek to be able to compare economic welfare for two different periods. As a result, one could conclude that welfare had increased or decreased over the period in question. It seems unlikely that this problem, although historical, would also be academic in the sense that this result would simply satisfy a craving for knowledge of historical facts. It would be invoked to support historical judgements about the goodness or badness of a certain system or régime. A judgement does not cease to be a value judgement, or to be influential or persuasive, because it is in the past tense.

It is, however, clear that if economists wait for someone to come along and give them a consistent set of value premises they would wait for ever. It is not impossible to anticipate the arrival of such a superman[1] by investigating the theories which can be deduced from a set of value judgements, which, it seems plausible to suppose, might be acceptable to at least some people in a particular country at a particular time. If we are to be able to make intelligent guesses about the kind of value premises that people might think reasonable, it is certain that we must study what kinds of things are relevant to people's happiness. Also if we propose to use a certain criterion for an increase in the economic welfare of an individual—that he is 'on a higher behaviour line'—we must

[1] It is important to notice that putting the necessary value postulates into the mouth of a superman is only an expository device for the purpose of separating off those postulates which are value judgements from those which are not. It must not be taken to imply that the economist has to wait for someone literally to give him his value premises. That would imply a somewhat servile view of the functions of the welfare economist. The economist can, of course, investigate what follows from any set of value premises he likes to choose. If the value premises are made explicit, and are not hidden, the result will be informative and interesting—and cannot be misleading. So long as there are some people who would be prepared to accept the stated premises, the result cannot be entirely useless.

clearly explain what this means in ordinary language or no one would be willing to say whether he considered it a good thing that someone be on a higher behaviour line or not. Further than this, most people would want to know what effects a certain change would have on someone's happiness before they would be prepared to say whether that change would be good or not. Therefore, in any community in which the individual is held to be of importance, it is still essential that the welfare economist should inquire into the causes of the happiness of individuals. Thus, even though there is no alternative to the view that welfare conclusions must be deduced from value premises, that does not mean to say that considerations such as those raised in earlier chapters, where, as far as possible, we tried to concern ourselves with happiness, are unimportant.

It may be remembered that, in Chapter I, we laid it down, by definition of the word 'economic', that the only things which are relevant to the economic welfare of society are the quantities of each good consumed by each individual, together with the amount and kind of work done, and the savings made. This definition is not a value judgement so long as we emphasize the word 'economic'. We must, however, take care that people are not misled. We can only ensure this by emphasizing our definition, and by pointing out some of the considerations which are left out, and which people might think were economic considerations. For instance, someone may think that whether or not a man gets a fair wage is a matter of economic welfare. But we exclude this, since we concern ourselves only with how much he gets and what he does, and not with the question whether one is fair in relation to the other. Some people may think that individuals ought to get the value of their marginal product; or that consumers ought not to be charged for necessities; or even that price ought not to equal marginal cost; or that it is not fair that people should get something free when the taxpayer pays for it. Any such considerations may be important to welfare, but they are excluded from economic welfare. We are concerned with what people get, and not why they get it, and with what work they do, and not with how they are paid for it.

It is, however, important to remember that we can never conclude that something ought to be done, from the proposition that economic welfare has increased. The means of increasing economic welfare may decrease welfare in general. If we treat 'welfare' as a purely ethical expression, it is a tautology that welfare ought to be increased; but if we say that economic welfare would be increased, that only means that welfare would be increased by the change if the other non-economic effects were not unfavourable.

In the next two chapters we will discuss the foundations of the so-called New Welfare Economics, and see whether any conclusions reached could be considered to follow from value premises which might be acceptable to a reasonable number of people.

CHAPTER VI

THE NEW WELFARE ECONOMICS (1):
WELFARE CRITERIA

THE New Welfare Economics is new in that it claims to have established the 'optimum' conditions of production and exchange without adding the 'utilities' of different persons. In this respect it has broken with the utilitarian tradition in economics. The founder of the New Welfare Economics was Pareto, who not only used the concept of ordinal preference, but also defined, for a society, an 'optimum' position which was independent of any necessity for adding satisfactions, or comparing the satisfactions of different individuals. An 'optimum' position was one in which it was impossible to put any individual 'on a higher indifference curve' (or, as we shall now phrase it, 'on a higher behaviour line') without causing someone to drop to a lower one. It must be emphasized at once that there are an infinite number of such 'optima', and that only '*the* optimum' (the best of these 'optima') is necessarily better than any other position. In other words, and roughly speaking, an 'optimum' situation (as so defined) which corresponds to a bad distribution of income, may well be worse than a 'sub-optimum' position corresponding to a good distribution of income. It therefore follows that it cannot be said that an increase in welfare would follow from putting the 'optimum' condition into practice, even assuming that there was a community to which the analysis could be applied.

The results were therefore essentially the same as those of the utilitarian analysis, in which any statement about how welfare could be increased, had to be qualified by a reference to whether the distribution of income would be favourably or unfavourably affected. It may also be noticed that, since the analysis relied on the 'on a higher behaviour line' criterion for an individual being better off, it could apply strictly only to a community of perfectly consistent individuals, in which no one died or was born. It is clear that if an individual were to alter his tastes while a change was being effected which was designed to make him better off, then the change might be wrong. The case is even worse if one refuses to admit interpersonal comparisons (Pareto held that the utilities of different persons were incommensurable) for, if an old individual is replaced by a new individual while the change is being made, then nothing whatever can be said.

It follows from the fact that one is always dealing with a changing community that one cannot both 'deny' interpersonal comparisons and base one's system on individuals; it would be impossible ever to say that any change was an improvement. Pareto did not, indeed, clearly say when one situation could be said to be better than another. He only laid down some of the *necessary* conditions which must be fulfilled if it is to be impossible to make some individual 'better off' without making any other 'worse off'.

Since Pareto, the theory has developed in rather different ways. We may make a threefold classification of the various positions which have been taken up. These categories represent fairly distinct groups of writers. First there is the class of theory which treats 'welfare' as a purely ethical concept; welfare conclusions can be deduced only from ethical premises which must be 'given' by someone. Let us call him 'superman'. Little or no attention is paid by this school to satisfaction or happiness, although, of course, superman may take it into account. There is, however, no necessary reason why superman should decide that the welfare of particular individuals is relevant to the welfare of the community at all. It is therefore possible that a criterion for an increase in individual welfare would not be required. Only if superman decided that the welfare of society was a logical construction from the welfares of individuals would such a criterion be necessary. Even then he might decide on some criterion which would evade the difficulty that people are inconsistent, and that 'on a higher behaviour line' cannot be very well applied to actual individuals. He might decide that satisfaction and happiness were irrelevant to welfare.

The ideal distribution of income is also, of course, treated as an ethical concept, and nothing can be said about welfare unless account is taken of this and all other factors which superman considers to be of ethical importance. Formally there is no reason why such a system should stop at economic welfare. This school is concerned with deductions from consistent ethical premises, and any ethical variable to which superman is prepared to give values can be thrown in.

The above is a sketch of the conceptual framework of one school of thought. Given this framework, the usual 'optimum conditions' can be derived only if the range of variables is severely limited. Widespread assumptions both of fact and of ethical indifference on the part of superman have to be made, and a number of value judgements must be imputed to him. What these assumptions and value judgements are will be shown in Chapter VIII, when we discuss the 'optimum' conditions and how they may be deduced. Here we will only say that this school is undoubtedly right in laying emphasis on the fact that welfare economics is an ethical study.

There is a second school of thought of which the following sketch may be made. The ethical nature of the subject is not recognized. Welfare economics is still held to be essentially a study of the causes of satisfaction. It is, however, recognized that welfare conclusions cannot be reached without considering the distribution of income. An ideal distribution of income is therefore presupposed. Interpersonal comparisons are in some sense denied; yet it is held that it can be proved that some distributions of income give more satisfaction to the community, and even that an equalitarian distribution of money income is, in this sense, probably best. In earlier chapters we have endeavoured to show that welfare economics is essentially an ethical study; that a study of happiness is important, but not logically essential (i.e. statements about welfare do not entail any statements about happiness, whereas they *are* value judgements); that one can and does compare different people's satisfaction; and, finally, that one cannot prove anything about the welfare of a community. We therefore disagree with every one of the logical presuppositions of this school. It differs from utilitarianism only by 'denying' interpersonal comparisons, thereby rendering utilitarianism nonsensical.

The above two schools have this in common, that they deduce the 'optimum' conditions of production and exchange as necessary conditions of '*the* optimum'. An 'ideal' distribution of income is also regarded as a necessary condition of '*the* optimum'. They say little or nothing about how it can be determined whether one 'sub-optimum' position is better or worse (or yields more or less satisfaction) than another 'sub-optimum' position. The impression is thus given that it is a matter of 'all or nothing'. Any 'optimum' position, as defined by Pareto, except '*the* optimum', is just one of these 'sub-optimum' positions. The Pareto 'optima' are thus comparatively unimportant. In application, or in the hands of those members of these schools who seek to apply the system, or assume it can be applied, this conception of welfare economics corresponds to 'utopian' planning.

The third school of thought, with which we shall be concerned for the rest of this chapter, corresponds, on the other hand, to 'piecemeal' planning.[1] Retaining the above terminology, any Pareto 'optimum' is treated as being necessarily better than any position which is not a Pareto 'optimum' position. In other words, it is simply decided that the distribution of income is irrelevant to the question whether one situation is a situation of greater economic welfare than another. In the eyes of utilitarians this amounts to an assumption that £1 yields the same amount of satisfaction to whomsoever it is given, rich or poor. Presumably most people would agree that such an assumption is ridiculous. In the eyes of the first school of thought it amounts to the value judgement 'income distribution ought to be neglected in considering whether one position is better than another'. Actually it is quite clear that the new welfare economists of this third school did not intend to make either the above assumption, or the above value judgement. They did, or do, think that interpersonal comparisons are illegitimate. Therefore they defined the phrase 'an increase in economic welfare' without reference to the distribution of real income. At the same time they did not understand that 'increase of welfare' is an ethical phrase, and so did not recognize the value judgement which is implicit in their definition.

This raises the question of what this group of new welfare economists thought welfare economics was about. As with the second group mentioned above, they have based their system on the individual. An individual is said to be 'better off' if he is 'on a higher indifference curve'. But according to the orthodox interpretation of the theory of consumers' behaviour, 'A is on a higher indifference curve' entails 'A is more satisfied'. It would therefore appear that it was considered that welfare economics was about satisfaction or happiness. But their conclusions, if interpreted in terms of satisfaction, require that £1 yields the same satisfaction to whomsoever it is given. They surely never intended to make this

[1] The use of the words 'utopian' and 'piecemeal' in this context is borrowed from K. Popper, *The Open Society and its Enemies*, ch. 9.

assumption. So it cannot really be held that they thought welfare economics was about the satisfaction or happiness of communities. But it has been claimed that welfare economics is 'objective' and 'scientific', and not ethical. In other words, it is claimed that welfare economics is a science about the causes of something, or about laws governing the increase or decrease of something, called 'welfare'. But if this welfare is not identical with satisfaction, or happiness, what is it?

Let us see how this line of thought was developed. In an article entitled 'Welfare Propositions of Economics and Interpersonal Comparisons of Utility',[1] Mr. Kaldor wrote:

> In all cases, therefore, where a certain policy leads to an increase in physical productivity, and thus of aggregate real income, the economist's case for the policy is quite unaffected by the comparability of individual satisfactions; since in all such cases it is *possible* to make everybody better off than before, or at any rate to make some people better off without making anybody worse off. . . . In order to establish his case, it is quite sufficient for him to show that even if all those who suffer as a result are fully compensated for their loss, the rest of the community will still be better off than before.

and again in a footnote to the same article:

> This principle, as the reader will observe, simply amounts to saying that there is no interpersonal comparison of satisfaction involved in judging any policy designed to increase the sum total of wealth just because any such policy *could* be carried out in a way as to secure unanimous consent.

First, we must note that the article is entitled 'Welfare Propositions of Economics and Interpersonal Comparisons of Utility'. This suggests that Mr. Kaldor thought that welfare propositions could be based on the hypothetical compensation definition put forward. But in the text and footnote he, in fact, defined the following phrases (*a*) 'an increase in general physical productivity', (*b*) 'an increase in aggregate real income', (*c*) 'an increase in the sum total of wealth' all in terms of hypothetical compensation.

A short digression is required to explain the meaning of these phrases, although the 'production' and 'real income' of a community are dealt with at length in Chapter XII. As we shall there contend, there is no criterion of general productivity distinct from

[1] *E.J.*, Sept. 1939, p. 549.

a criterion of real income. But what about the sum total of wealth? As far as I know 'wealth' is not a term with any precise meaning in economic theory, which is distinct both from 'real income' and from 'welfare'. We may therefore confine ourselves to the expression 'aggregate real income'. Now Mr. Kaldor, in the above passages, laid down the following *necessary* proposition (i.e. the partial definition): 'When aggregate real income increases it is possible to make some people better off, without making anyone worse off'. But even if the aggregate Index-Number formulae $\sum P_2 Q_2 \geqslant \sum P_2 Q_1$ and $\sum P_1 Q_2 > \sum P_1 Q_1$ (where the Q's refer to the total quantities of goods summed for all the 'individuals' in the community) are satisfied, that does not prove[1] that the gainers could overcompensate the losers[2] for a movement from situation 1 to situation 2. Thus Mr. Kaldor was proposing a new, and unusual, sufficient criterion of 'an increase in aggregate real income'.

We have already, in the previous chapter, discussed 'real income' with reference to individuals. We did not want to substitute the phrase 'increase of real income' for the phrase 'in a chosen position', because the former phrase suggests that any change it is used to describe is a good change. Nevertheless, if one is willing to accept that it is a good thing that an individual should be in a chosen position, then the substitution is permissible. We also pointed out that there is no objective sense in which real income can be said to be larger or smaller, because 'real income', in economics, is a phrase which refers to a collection of incommensurable items.

An analogous argument may be used against Mr. Kaldor's definition. Instead of saying 'as a result of this change the gainers could overcompensate the losers' Mr. Kaldor wishes to say 'This change would result in an increase of aggregate real income'. But, given that we have an acceptable criterion for an individual being better off, the first sentence describes clearly and precisely the effects of the change. The second sentence, given Mr. Kaldor's definition, describes exactly the same effects. Yet it gives the im-

[1] See Ch. XII. The prices in the formulae could refer either to market-prices or to (marginal or average) costs of production. In neither case is it proved that the gainers could overcompensate the losers.

[2] The phrase 'the gainers could overcompensate the losers' is shorter and means the same as 'it is possible to make some people better off without making anybody worse off'. The phrase was suggested to me by Mr. George Paul.

pression of saying something more—something more important. The truth is that it does not make any further statement.[1] But it gives the impression of so doing because it is a suggestive sentence. It suggests (a) that some objective magnitude is greater, and (b) that this is a good thing. As we have said before, everyone tends to assume that more real income, more wealth, &c., is a good thing. I do not object to its being said that an individual's real income is greater if he is in a chosen position, because on the whole I approve of individuals being enabled to reach chosen positions. But before the substitution of the phrase 'increase of aggregate real income' for the phrase 'possibility of overcompensation for the losers' is permitted, it should first be judged that changes, such that the gainers could overcompensate the losers, are good changes.

What has been said above about the phrase 'increase of aggregate real income' applies, of course, *a fortiori* to the phrase 'increase of general welfare'—*a fortiori* because the latter phrase is considerably more emotive and influential than the former. Whether Mr. Kaldor was prepared to define 'an increase in welfare' also in terms of the possibility of overcompensation is not absolutely clear. But, since he suggests that the economist's case for a change can be established merely by showing that the gainers could overcompensate the losers, it rather appears that he did consider all such changes to be economically desirable. Certainly many subsequent writers have, with some justification, assumed that Mr. Kaldor was also defining 'an increase in welfare'.

It seems improbable that many people would, in England now, be prepared to say that a change, which, for instance, made the rich so much richer that they could (but would not) overcompensate the poor, who were made poorer, would necessarily increase the welfare of the community. Admittedly people might be prepared to say that such a change would increase aggregate real income, so long as the proviso was always added that it would probably decrease welfare. If this proviso were added, the suggestive force of the first half of the sentence would be offset, or more than offset, by the second half. But one cannot rely on the proviso being added. And, in any case, it is much clearer to say that the rich gainers could, but would not, overcompensate the poor losers.

[1] For short I speak of sentences making statements, &c., instead of speaking of the utterer of the sentences making statements.

The hypothetical-overcompensation criterion has been attacked in an article by Professor W. J. Baumol.[1] In his reply[2] to this article, Mr. Kaldor writes:

'Political postulates' are undoubtedly involved in any question concerning income distribution—in the maintenance of the existing as well as its changes. The point of my original article[3] was to show that they are *only* involved in questions concerning income distribution and not in those relating to production; and I suggested a test by which these two elements could be separated from each other. The important point surely is that, when the production of wealth goes up, some income distribution could be found which makes some people better off, and no one worse off than before.

It is presumed that the importance of the postulates being 'political' is that they are value judgements. Mr. Kaldor then says that they are *only* involved in questions concerning income distribution. Presumably, then, he thinks that 'this change would produce more wealth' is not a value judgement but is about something more or less 'objective', for example, satisfactions. But he surely would not say that there was necessarily more satisfaction because those who gained could overcompensate those who lost. Yet he defines an increase of wealth in this way, for, as we have seen, he is only laying down a *definition* when he says 'when the production of wealth goes up, some income distribution could be found which makes some people better off, and no one worse off than before'. He insists that this is an important point, whereas, in fact, it is a definition. If it were not a definition, one should be able to test whether it is true that, when the production of wealth increases, there is a distribution which could make some better off, and none worse off. For such a test to be conceivable, some independent definition of 'increase of wealth' would have to be provided.

The quarrel with Mr. Kaldor is not that he lays down a definition, but that he lays down a persuasive definition where none seems really to be required. Mr. Kaldor goes on to say that he suggested a *test* by which the 'elements' of income distribution and production efficiency could be separated. But he suggested not a test, but a definition, which certainly separated out income distribution, but only by ignoring it. What Mr. Kaldor did, in fact, was to propose a definition of 'increase of wealth' which ignored

[1] W. J. Baumol, 'Community Indifference', *R.E.S.* (1946–7).
[2] N. Kaldor, 'A Comment', ibid.   [3] *E.J.*, Sept. 1939, p. 549.

distribution. This is just what the quarrel is about. We do not believe that any definition of an increase of wealth, welfare, efficiency, or real social income which excludes income distribution is acceptable.

In an article entitled 'The Foundations of Welfare Economics',[1] Professor Hicks gave his blessing to Mr. Kaldor's contribution. Later, in 'The Rehabilitation of Consumer's Surplus',[2] Professor Hicks wrote:

> How are we to say whether a reorganization of production, which makes A better off, but B worse off, marks an improvement in efficiency? The sceptics declare that it is impossible to do so in an objective manner. The satisfactions of one person cannot be added to those of another, so that all we can say is that there is an improvement from the point of view of A, but not from that of B. In fact, there is a simple way of overcoming this defeatism, a perfectly objective test which enables us to discriminate between those reorganizations which improve productive efficiency and those which do not. If A is made so much better off by the change that he could compensate B for his loss, and still have something left over, then the reorganization is an *unequivocal improvement*.[3] . . . Further, this criterion is more useful than any other as a basis on which to establish maxims of sound economic policy.

It should be noted that Professor Hicks here says that there is a '*perfectly objective test*'[3] of productive efficiency. He also calls this 'perfectly objective test' a 'criterion'. One can only have a test for something which is otherwise recognizable, or which has other defining characteristics. The presence of one thing may be a test of another if there is an empirical relation between the two. But it is surely not suggested that there is an empirical relation between productive efficiency and the possibility of overcompensation. This could only be established if productive efficiency is otherwise recognizable. How is it recognized? Since there is no answer given, we must suppose that Professor Hicks was not lending his support to a test, but to a definition or criterion of the phrase 'an increase in productive efficiency', just as we must suppose that Mr. Kaldor was proposing not a test but a definition of 'an increase in productive efficiency', 'an increase in the sum total of wealth', &c. For 'perfectly objective test' we may thus read 'definition' or 'criterion'. In Chapter V we have seen that 'the well-being of the community'

---

[1] *E.J.*, Dec. 1939, p. 696.
[2] *R.E.S.* (1940–1), p. 108.   [3] My italics.

or 'the happiness of the community' are not names for something, or some emotion or feeling, for which one can have tests in the same way as one can and does have tests for the happiness of individuals, the presence of acid, or the speed of an aeroplane.

It is not, however, necessary to define the phrase 'increase in general economic welfare' in order to arrive at the usual welfare conclusions. All one needs is a *sufficient* criterion. Thus all that needed to be proposed was that whenever one could say 'this would enable the gainers to overcompensate the losers' then one could also say 'this would increase general economic welfare'. The muddle between a sufficient criterion and a test has to a certain extent persisted, suggesting that some economists are still utilitarians at heart, and believe that the general welfare is some homogeneous kind of emotion which one can measure. Witness the following quotation: 'Modern economists have now developed a method of "compensation" by which it is possible to find out whether society as a whole is better off or worse off by a given change even if this change involved changes in the distribution of income. . . .'[1] This should read: 'Modern economists have asserted that, by definition, society as a whole is better off or worse off according to whether the gainers could, or could not, overcompensate the losers'. One cannot easily find out about the welfare of society, and hypothetical compensation is not a method of finding anything out.

It is, perhaps, needless to add that the proposed criterion, whether it is to be a criterion of wealth, efficiency, welfare, or real social income, contains an implicit value judgement. Indeed, Professor Hicks speaks of an unequivocal improvement and holds that this criterion is a basis for sound economic policy. Conclusions based on such a criterion must either be moralizing conclusions, or they must be stated as deductions from explicit ethical premises. But scarcely anyone would want to say that all changes, such that the gainers could overcompensate the losers, must be good. For most people it would all depend on who the uncompensated losers were. However, in a passage immediately following the above quotation, Professor Hicks seeks to justify the proposed criterion. To quote:

If the economic activities of a community were organized on the principle of making no alterations in the organization of production which were not improvements in this sense, and making all alterations which

[1] Dr. Hla Myint, *Theories of Welfare Economics*, p. 104, n. 1.

were improvements that it could possibly find, then, although we could not say that all the inhabitants of that community would be necessarily better off than they would have been if the community had been organized on some different principle, nevertheless there would be a strong probability that almost all of them would be better off after the lapse of a sufficient length of time.[1]

Professor Hicks is here envisaging a long series of changes, each of which would have only a small effect on real income distribution. He assumes that these effects would be more or less random, so that they would cancel out. But if the sufficient length of time is a long time, most of the inhabitants would be dead (even if better off). It is clear that if we are considering the welfare of a changing group of real people over a long period, then we cannot literally deal with individuals. It becomes a question of whether we are better off than our fathers, or grandfathers. Interpersonal comparisons are clearly involved.

We must also ask about the criterion for an increase in individual welfare. Is it the 'on a higher behaviour line' criterion? If so, we have seen reason to believe that, over a long period of time, this criterion is very liable to be quite meaningless. To put it briefly, the tastes of even average individuals are likely to have changed considerably. Many new goods will have been introduced. Quality changes will be great, making the concept 'the same good' very difficult or impossible to apply, except, perhaps, over a narrow range of necessities.

Finally, some of the changes which might pass the Kaldor–Hicks criterion (as it may be called) will have quite significant real income distribution effects, so that it would be, at best, wishful thinking to suppose that they would cancel out with the effects of other changes. There does not seem to be any justification for saying that there would be a strong probability that almost everyone would be better off in the end—even supposing they didn't die, and remained perfectly consistent people to whom the behaviour-line analysis would apply.

We may now ask whether, in view of this kind of difficulty, Professor Hicks's justification of the criterion is a reasonable one. We may, I think, safely say that almost everyone would accept a

[1] Loc. cit., p. 111. Professor Hotelling proposed the same justification in his article 'The General Welfare in relation to problems of Taxation and of Railway and Utility rates', *Econometrica*, July 1938.

policy, based on this criterion, as a good policy if it were true that it would make almost every small social group (consisting of an ever-changing collection of actual individuals) better off in the long run[1] than they would have been otherwise—meaning by 'better off' not 'on a higher behaviour line', but better off as judged by ordinary observation on the part of most people. But is it true, or reasonably likely to be true? The answer to this question depends on the applicability of the behaviour-line analysis; on the acceptability of the choice criterion as a criterion of increased economic welfare over a long period; and on the randomness of the distribution effects and their magnitude. It must be observed that what we are trying to do is to discover whether there is even a prima-facie case in favour of an analysis based on such a criterion. There is quite certainly no case for its general application, without examining the dynamic effects and the extra-economic effects which might result. We are at present only taking into account a limited number of difficulties, to wit, the applicability of the theory of consumer's behaviour to a changing population of changing tastes, and the question of real income distribution.

We could make Professor Hicks's justification somewhat more secure on the matter of distribution, by suggesting that only those changes which would have small distributional effects should be justified on this kind of basis; or by suggesting that large losers should actually be compensated. This would make it much more likely that distributional effects would cancel out. This raises the question: 'Why not compensate all losers?' This is easily answered. We could not, in practice, find out who had lost and how much would be required to compensate them. A complete knowledge of everyone's behaviour map would be required, because exactly to compensate someone is, theoretically, to raise him on to the same behaviour line as before. But we know nothing of anyone's behaviour maps, and, in any case, we have seen that most people have not the deep-seated habits required for us to be able to say that they have a behaviour map. All that would ever be practical would be the rough compensation of a few large losers. 'Welfare' conclusions never tell us that the gainers could actually over-compensate the losers. They only tell us that they could conceivably overcompensate them, if everyone was an economic man.

This question of actual compensation raises further difficulties

[1] But it would not have to be too long. The losers might get impatient.

of a philosophical rather than a technical kind. It has been suggested that the advocation of actual compensation 'betrays a conservative bias'.[1] This suggestion does not seem to be formally correct, if the Kaldor–Hicks criterion plus actual compensation is put forward as a sufficient criterion only. Thus it is sufficient that everyone should gain, for a change to be an improvement. It is not denied that a change may be an improvement although some lose. In particular, it is not denied that redistribution could improve welfare. Nevertheless, it must be admitted that it would be rather absurdly schizophrenic to say (a) this change ought to be carried out, and compensation ought to be paid, for then everyone would gain, and (b) but the compensation ought to be paid back again because that would increase welfare as well. If the Kaldor–Hicks criterion was satisfied, and the new distribution was regarded as better than the old, this would have to be said. It seems quite clear that few people would want to say that the change would increase or decrease welfare without attending to the distribution effects, and if these were favourable the advocation of actual compensation would be rather absurd, even if it did not 'betray a conservative bias'.[2] Income distribution must, then, be admitted as an ethical variable, to which the values, favourable or unfavourable, are given, and we must have a criterion which includes this variable.

Before, however, we attempt to develop the above line of thought,[3] it is necessary to attend to a criticism of the Kaldor–Hicks criterion, which has been made by Professor Scitovsky.[4] He has shown that the Kaldor–Hicks criterion may give rise to a contradiction. If a change which passes the Kaldor–Hicks criterion is made, and compensation is not actually paid, then there will be a different distribution of real income before and after the change. It is, then, possible that the reverse movement would also be

[1] Cf. T. Scitovsky, 'A Note on Welfare Propositions in Economics', *R.E.S.*, Nov. 1941. (The powerful emotive effect of the expression should be discounted.)

[2] If, however, we bring in wider considerations of justice or equity, it is not so absurd. Equity may demand that some individuals must be compensated, even though their losses shift income distribution in the right direction. One might not object to a whole social group being made poorer although one would object to a few members of the group becoming poorer as the result of a particular change.

[3] Much of the argument of the next few pages has appeared in my 'Welfare and Tariffs', *R.E.S.*, vol. xvi, no. 2, and in my 'Foundations of Welfare Economics', *O.E.P.*, N.S., no. 2, June 1949.

[4] Op. cit., *supra*.

sanctioned by the Kaldor-Hicks criterion. Thus the two situations
would each be said to be better than the other. This contradiction
can most easily be understood with the aid of a diagram.

FIG. VI

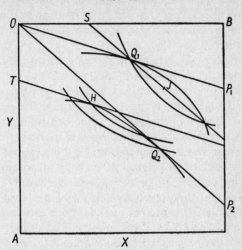

In Fig. VI A and B trade in the goods X and Y. Behaviour lines
are drawn for both, but A is a monopolist who takes into account
his influence on price, and sees that he may do better for himself
by not trying to reach the highest possible behaviour line at any
particular price. Thus he sets the price OP_1, and allows B, who is
assumed to take that price as given, to trade as he pleases. Q_1 is the
first equilibrium position, at which point B reaches the highest
behaviour line open to him.

The question now arises as to whether economic welfare would
be improved by making A allow B to trade at the price OP_2. If this
was done, the Kaldor–Hicks criterion would be fulfilled, because,
if A was compensated with OS of X, the new equilibrium position
would be within the upper ellipse, and both A and B would be on
higher behaviour lines (SQ_1 is parallel to OP_2, representing the
same rate of exchange between X and Y as is represented by OP_2).[1]

---

[1] It is not generally true that there must be an equilibrium point with price
OP_2 within the upper ellipse. There may not be more than one equilibrium
point, given the price OP_2. We suppose that there is, only to illustrate the
working of the criterion. See p. 110 below.

But compensation is hypothetical, and so the actual second position is Q_2 with price OP_2. But if the price was changed back to OP_1, and if B was compensated with OT of Y, then the position H would be reached where A is on a higher behaviour line than he was at Q_2, and B is on the same behaviour line as at Q_2. Therefore the Kaldor–Hicks criterion would be fulfilled, and Q_1 would have to be said to be better than Q_2. Each position would thus be better than the other.

Professor Scitovsky gets round this contradiction by proposing that a change should be said to 'increase welfare' only if (a) the Kaldor–Hicks criterion is satisfied, and if (b) 'the people who are against the change would be incapable of bribing those in favour to vote against it, without thereby losing more than they would if the change was carried'.[1] (Essentially, this is only another way of saying that the gainers should not also be able to compensate the losers for a change back to the original position; but it was important to see that if the distribution of welfare was significantly different in the two positions then compensation might be possible in both directions). Thus in the present case A, who is against the change, could bribe B, with OT of Y, not to vote for the change. Therefore condition (b) is not satisfied. If both (a) and (b) are satisfied the change is said to increase welfare. If either is satisfied, and the other fails, the result is said to be indeterminate. If both fail, the change is said to decrease welfare. The illustrated case is thus indeterminate, and the contradiction is removed.

Professor Scitovsky is, of course, considering only cases where compensation is not paid (if compensation is paid the contradiction cannot arise). Comparing therefore Q_2 with Q_1, we see that B has gained and A lost (assuming for the sake of argument that 'on a higher (lower) behaviour line' is acceptable as a criterion of 'gain' ('loss')). Therefore, if we set no valuation on their respective gains and losses, we can say only that the price OP_2 is *potentially* better than the price OP_1, whether or not the second part of the criterion ((b) above) is satisfied. We can say OP_2 is *potentially* better than OP_1 because compensating A with OS of X would make both better off (we assume for the sake of argument that the situation can be said to be better if both A and B are better off, or if either is better off and the other no worse off). But the price

---

[1] T. Scitovsky, 'A Reconsideration of the Theory of Tariffs', *R.E.S.*, vol. ix, no. 2.

OP_2 would only be actually better if compensation was really paid, and both ended up on higher behaviour lines within the upper ellipse (say, at the point $\mathcal{J}$). By exactly the same argument, OP_1 is also potentially better than OP_2. But it is not a contradiction to say that OP_2 is potentially better and potentially worse than OP_1. The contradiction thus only arises as a result of ignoring income distribution, and calling something actually better when it should only be called potentially better.

Professor Scitovsky, on the other hand, says that the position Q_2 is actually better than Q_1 so long as A could *not* bribe B to accept the price OP_1, and also says that Q_2 is actually neither better nor worse than Q_1, if A could thus bribe B. But what is the justification for this? In Q_2, A would be actually worse off than before, and B actually better off, whether the bribe could be paid or not. How can one say anything about an actual change in welfare, if B's actual gain is not weighed up against A's actual loss? If the second part of the criterion (b) is satisfied, then OP_2 is potentially better than OP_1, and OP_1 is potentially worse than OP_2. If (b) is not satisfied, then each price is potentially better than the other.

To say that one situation is potentially better than another is no reason for moving to it. If nothing more can be said, we have not arrived at any useful conclusion. We might say that compensation ought to be paid, when, with the price OP_2, we would arrive at an equilibrium position $\mathcal{J}$ within the upper ellipse. But we have seen that compensation might be impossible, because we could not find out the correct amount OS, which A ought to be paid. Also the position Q_2 might easily be considered to be better than any position, such as $\mathcal{J}$, within the upper ellipse (this would be a case of a Pareto sub-optimum position being 'better than' a Pareto optimum position). In other words, if the *contract curve* is defined as the locus of all points at which A's and B's behaviour lines are tangential, then it might be a case of some point off the contract curve Q_2 being better than some point $\mathcal{J}$ on it. We are still at sea.

Before we try to clear up the above difficulty we must examine the impact of Professor Scitovsky's contradiction on the Kaldor–Hicks criterion, and on Professor Hicks's justification. The latter proposed the policy of putting into effect all changes which passed the Kaldor–Hicks criterion. We now see that this might lead to 'reforms' which, by the same criterion, would have to be revoked, and then made again, and so on. This would obviously not be good policy. The above situation is, however, unlikely to arise if the shift in income distribution is small. Therefore we can say that the Hicksian policy can, at best, be justified only in respect of those proposed changes in which the real income distribution effect is likely to be small. We have also seen that the Hicksian justification for the proposed policy is, at best, only plausible for such changes, because, if distribution effects are large, it is not plausible to say that they would cancel out. It is evident that the Kaldor–Hicks criterion is quite inadequate for changes which involve large distributional effects. For these, some judgement is required as to whether the real income redistribution would be good or bad.[1] We might suggest that such a change be recommended if it passes the Kaldor–Hicks criterion, and if any change in distribution is not bad. If it is bad, but compensation would make it good, then compensation should be paid.

But we have not yet removed all the difficulties, since, even if the change causes a good shift in real income distribution, and passes the Kaldor–Hicks criterion, a reverse change might still be recommended by the latter. One might say that the reverse change is now ruled out because it would be, *ex hypothesi*, a change towards a worse real income distribution. This, however, is still not the solution, because, if the Kaldor–Hicks criterion recommends the reverse change, that indicates that the better distribution of real income might have been better brought about by simply redistributing purchasing power, rather than by making the proposed change (assuming that the redistribution of purchasing power could be effected without violating any 'optimum' conditions). This can be seen by reference to Fig. VI. Imagine that Q_2 represents a better distribution of real income between A and B than Q_1. But without changing the price from OP_1 the position H, which represents (approximately) the same distribution[2] as Q_2,

[1] This does not, of course, mean that the economist must either himself judge whether the change in distribution would be good, or wait for someone else to make the required judgement. He can always qualify his conclusion, and say that such and such a change would be a good thing if it does not lead to a redistribution of real income which would be regarded as bad. Every reader of the economist's conclusions can decide this issue for himself.

[2] A situation in which some people are only a little better off and some no worse off than in another situation can quite reasonably be said to have the same distribution of real income as that other situation. As we saw in Chapter IV, the distribution of real income is not a precise concept, and it is ridiculous to try to be pedantic about it. For instance, if two people are judged to be economic-

could be reached, and A would be better off and B no worse off than if the redistribution had been effected by changing the price from OP_1 to OP_2. Therefore Professor Scitovsky's test still seems to be required, but the interpretation of it is altered; it now tells us whether a good change in distribution would be better effected by the change under consideration, or by simply redistributing money. We thus have a threefold criterion:

(a) Is the Kaldor–Hicks criterion satisfied?
(b) Is the Scitovsky criterion satisfied?
(c) Is any redistribution good or bad?

All the possible combinations of answers may be set out in a table thus:

TABLE I

Case No.	1	2	3	4	5	6	7	8
CRITERIA								
Kaldor–Hicks criterion satisfied? . . .	Yes	Yes	Yes	Yes	No	No	No	No
Scitovsky criterion satisfied? . . .	Yes	Yes	No	No	No	No	Yes	Yes
Any redistribution good?	Yes	No	Yes	No	No	Yes	No	Yes

Before examining the inferences to be drawn from the eight possible combinations of these criteria some further discussion of the meaning of a good and bad redistribution is needed. If we say that a move from Q_1 to Q_2 (in Fig. VI) would be a good redistribution, what exactly do we mean? We mean that any purely distributional change (by which is meant the direct transfer from one individual to the other of sums of money or sets of goods) which would produce a point which is distributionally indifferent to Q_2 would be a good thing. It is assumed that there is at least one point attainable by direct transfers from Q_1 which is regarded as distributionally indifferent to Q_2, and in which everyone is better off, or no worse off, than in Q_2, or in which everyone is worse off, or no better off. In the discussion above it has been assumed that H is such a point—so that to say that Q_2 is distributionally better than Q_1 is to say that H is better than Q_1. Similarly to say that Q_1 is distributionally better than Q_2 is to say that J (or some similar

ally equal, and then one gets £5 per annum more and the other stays the same, it need not be wrong to say that they are still economically equal. But this would, of course, soon cease to be the case if there were a cumulation of such shifts.

point within the upper ellipse) is better than Q_2. For consistency, it is required that if H is better than Q_1, then J is worse than Q_2.

At this stage it may be helpful to introduce the device of a 'utility possibility' diagram (Fig. VII consists of four such diagrams). On each axis the utility of an individual is measured on an arbitrary ordinal scale. The curves drawn show the maximum utility which can be attained by one individual given the utility level of the other. This maximum utility level depends upon what we assume remains fixed. If the set of goods, *and* the prices, remain fixed then the utility possibility curve traces out the utility levels attained by each person as direct transfers of goods are made from one to the other. A different curve will correspond to each relative price. This is the case of Fig. VI. But much broader interpretations are possible. If the prices are allowed to vary as one moves *along* the curves, then they trace out the maximum utility level possible for one person given that of the other, on the assumption that each point corresponds to a point on the contract curve as defined above. The curves then represent the maximum utility possibilities of a given set of goods. A movement along the curve results from direct transfers of money between the individuals. A different curve then corresponds to each different set of goods. On a still broader interpretation, both prices and production, and hence the set of goods, can be allowed to vary as one moves along the curve by means of direct transfers of money. A curve then represents the utility possibilities of a given endowment of factors of production: and a different curve corresponds to each different endowment. In this case various assumptions can be made about the allocation of the factors of production. It can be assumed that the 'optimum' conditions of production and exchange are satisfied, in which case the curve represents the *maximum* utility possibilities. Alternatively one might take the curve to represent what would actually happen as money was shifted between the individuals, the points being determined by the actual price and output policies which would be followed by the productive units in the economy.

Which interpretation is relevant depends upon the problem being analysed. For instance, when dealing with the valuation of the national income it may be convenient to inquire into the utility possibilities of a fixed set of goods. But this is rather a special case. For any practical application one would normally be interested in the utility levels which would actually result from shifting money about—in which case it is the set of factors of production, and price and output policies, which are assumed constant as a move along the curve takes place.

Whichever interpretation is used the formal properties of the diagrams remain the same. No significance attaches to the shape of the curves (this is because the utility scales are arbitrary), except that they must slope down from left to right, if they are used to analyse problems in which it is impossible to make one man better off without making another worse off. But, while the formal properties are unchanged, the meaning attached to the redistributive element of a change varies according to the determination of the utility possibility curves. Thus if it is said that distribution would be improved by moving from Q_1 to Q_2, that has to be taken to mean that a point on the utility possibility curve of Q_1, which is either south-west or north-east of Q_2, is better than Q_1. The location of this point and hence the exact sense attached to 'redistribution being good' depends upon what is assumed to remain constant as one moves along the utility possibility curve. The closest approximation to the ordinary meaning would seem to be when the curve represents the utility possibilities of the factors of production under given price and output policies. For then we are assuming that if someone says that a change from Q_1 to Q_2 would be distributionally good, he means that a point which would *actually* have been reached by shifting money, and where everyone would be worse off, or everyone be better off, than at Q_2, is better than Q_1.

Each diagram is applicable to one of the four possible combinations of the Kaldor–Hicks and Scitovsky criteria, the relevant case numbers of Table I being shown in the bottom left-hand corner. In each case if the curve through Q_2 passes north-east of Q_1, the Kaldor–Hicks criterion is satisfied: and if the curve through Q_1 passes south-west of Q_2 then the Scitovsky criterion is also satisfied. In addition, if redistribution is good (as in cases 1, 3, 6, and 8), the left-hand point on any line is better than the right-hand; and vice versa if redistribution is bad. It must be remembered that H now stands for any point in the south-west or north-east quadrants of Q_2 which would be judged distributionally indifferent to Q_2, and similarly for J in relation to Q_1. In what follows, any movement along the curve through the initial point Q_1 will be referred to as a 'redistribution', while any movement along the curve through Q_2 will be referred to as a 'compensation'.

The question which we now seek to answer is whether a change from one line to the other is a good thing. (According to the interpretation of the curves the change might be merely a change of price, as in Fig. VI, or a change involving a new set of goods.)[1] This cannot be clearly answered until it has been decided how free one is to move along each curve, i.e. make purely distributional changes. One can assume that no distributional changes are possible, i.e. that one cannot move from Q_1 to H, or from Q_2 to J.

FIG. VII

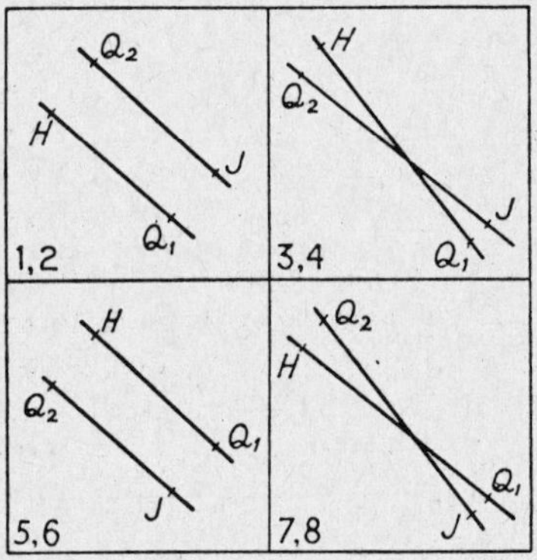

This needs some elaboration. It has been argued that, in the real world, complete compensation, so that no one would be left hurt by a change, would rarely if ever be possible. But if it is *not* possible to reach a point like J (in the north-east or south-west quadrant of Q_1) from Q_2, then the formal argument is unaltered by saying that no compensation is possible, for Q_2 can, where necessary, always be regarded as the point which would be reached after all practical compensation had been paid, if it was desirable to pay it. Similarly it might normally be quite impractical to find a point like H which was attainable from Q_1, and Q_1 can then be regarded as the point reached after all practical redistribution had been allowed for. Sometimes, therefore, the most realistic assumption to take would be that only the two points Q_1 and Q_2 are actually attainable. Let us call this Assumption A. But the most general case is certainly where all four points are attainable (Assumption B).

[1] See p. 102.

Take first the assumption that only Q_2 and Q_1 are attainable (Assumption A). Where only two points are attainable the question whether the change should be made is of course the same as the question whether welfare would be increased. Inspection of Fig. VII shows that the answers to the question of whether the change should be made are as shown in Table II, which gives the eight possible combinations of the criteria, and the inferences to be drawn.

TABLE II

Case No.	1	2	3	4	5	6	7	8
CRITERIA								
Kaldor–Hicks criterion satisfied? . . .	Yes	Yes	Yes	Yes	No	No	No	No
Scitovsky criterion satisfied? . . .	Yes	Yes	No	No	No	No	Yes	Yes
Any redistribution good?	Yes	No	Yes	No	No	Yes	No	Yes
INFERENCE								
Should the change be made? . . .								
Assumption A . .	Yes	?	Yes	No	No	?	No	Yes
Assumption B . .	Yes	Yes	No	Yes	No	No	No	Yes

In cases 1, 3, and 8, Q_2 is shown to be better than Q_1. In cases 1 and 8, Q_2 is the best of the four points: in case 3, H is better than Q_2, but *ex hypothesi* is unattainable. In cases 4, 5, and 7, Q_1 is better than Q_2, although, in case 4, J is better than Q_1. In cases 2 and 6, the result is indeterminate. Thus, in case 2, Q_1 and Q_2 are both better than H and worse than J, and vice versa in case 6, there thus being in neither case a relation established between them.

The table shows clearly that neither the Kaldor–Hicks nor the Scitovsky criterion are, alone or together, sufficient for an increase in welfare. In case 4 the Kaldor–Hicks criterion is satisfied, but the change would decrease welfare. The same is true of the Scitovsky criterion in case 7. Used together they indicate a change in case 2, which could result in a decrease in welfare. Nor is either of them alone, or together, a necessary criterion. On the other hand, both the combination of the Kaldor–Hicks and the redistribution criteria, and the combination of the Scitovsky and the redistribution criteria, are sufficient (but not necessary) for an increase in welfare.

But the question still arises as to whether these criteria (which, in this case, are welfare criteria) have any point to them at all. It has been argued that where no compensation or redistribution is possible, i.e. where the criteria are criteria of welfare, they are useless on the following grounds.[1] They require that someone should make the judgement that Q_2 is distributionally better (or worse) than Q_1—which is to be taken to mean that H is better (or worse) than Q_1. But, it is argued, if this someone, whoever he may be, can make judgements of this kind, then he can say directly whether Q_2 is better or worse than Q_1. Hence the criteria are redundant.[2] There is no doubt that this criticism would be overwhelming if it were true that our 'someone' already had well-ordered preferences between all configurations of the economic system, and if one could describe to him exactly the configuration which would result from the change under discussion. In fact, of course, people do not have such well-ordered preferences: nor would it be possible to describe exactly what goods, &c., every individual would be getting after the change; still less can we say *how much* utility or welfare each individual would be getting after the change. Given that one cannot describe the state each or every individual would be in after the change, the best one can probably do is to say that the situation would be much the same as would result from, say, transferring £100 of net income from one to the other, except that both (or all) would be better off than if this was actually what was done. If this is accepted, then even though the actual question asked is in terms of a comparison of Q_1 and Q_2, a point like H comes in as an essential intermediary: and it cannot be said that the Scitovsky part of the criterion is redundant.

Now take the second assumption B[3]—that all four points are attainable. This is more involved because the question whether welfare would be increased by a move from one point to another ceases

---

[1] C. Kennedy, 'The Economic Welfare Function and Dr. Little's Criterion', *R.E.S.*, 1952/3, no. 52.

[2] The same criticism arises when we come to consider the 'Valuation of Social Income' in Ch. XII—where it will be further discussed.

[3] These, A and B, are not the only two possible assumptions. In the first edition of this book the only set of inferences drawn from the eight cases was based on the assumption that redistribution before the event was possible—but not compensation after it. This produces for the eight cases the following answers. Yes, ?, No, No, No, No, No, Yes—as in Table I of the first edition. It now seems to me that this was a rather arbitrary assumption, as various critics have pointed out.

to be the pertinent question when more than two points are involved. Consequently the criticism discussed above does not arise, since one needs to know which is the best point, and how to reach it. The diagrams show that in cases 1, 2, 4, and 8 the best point is on the curve through Q_2, and that in the remaining cases it is on the curve through Q_1. In cases 1 and 8 the change should be made without compensation; in 2 and 4 it should be made with compensation. In cases 5 and 7 the *status quo* should be preserved, while in 3 and 6 there should be only redistribution. Table II again shows that neither the Kaldor–Hicks nor the Scitovsky criterion are by themselves sufficient or necessary. The combination of the Scitovsky criterion with either the redistribution or the Kaldor–Hicks criterion *is* sufficient—but the same is not true of the combination of the Kaldor–Hicks and the redistribution criterion.

For both assumptions only the combination of the Scitovsky criterion and the redistribution is 'reliable' (in the sense that if both are satisfied then welfare is increased, and the change should be made, whichever set of assumptions is taken). The combination remains reliable if it is assumed that compensation alone is possible, or if it is assumed that redistribution alone is possible: but it is not 'efficient' in the sense that it picks up all cases in which a change should be made.

This seems to be as far as one can take the subject of the 'welfare criteria'. Before discussing their value, if any, one important limitation must be noticed. If the Kaldor–Hicks and the Scitovsky criteria conflict, that indicates that the utility possibility curves cut between the two points under consideration—and if they agree, then the utility possibility curves do not cut between the two points. But no indication is given either way as to whether the curves cut elsewhere. So long as the subject under discussion is limited to the question whether a particular change should be made, and if so whether compensation should be paid or not, or if the change is not made whether there should be some redistribution in lieu, this does not matter. But if wider questions are raised, it may matter very much. Take, for instance, Assumption B, case 4. The diagram shows that the change should be made and compensation paid, in order to reach the point J. But now imagine the curves extended to the right and cutting again. It was held to be a good thing that transfers should be made from Mr. A to Mr. B—so as to travel from Q_2 to J—and it might well be considered a good thing that

Mr. *A* should pay over still more to Mr. *B*, so moving farther to the right along the curve. But by then another intersection with the Q_1 curve could have taken place: in which case the change should never have been made.

It is very necessary to bear this limitation in mind. But equally one should not be too heartbroken, for the human mind cannot in practice contemplate all the possibilities. In practice, economic policy very largely presents itself as a series of choices as to whether certain changes should be made or not. Sometimes the change is mooted for its distributional effects, in which case it is usually relevant to consider whether there are other ways of redistributing wealth so as to produce what would be regarded by the supporters of the change as an equally good distributional effect—but which might make almost everyone better off than if the change were made (as in cases 3 and 6). Or, the change may be mooted because it is thought to be in line with some vaguely conceived general economic policy; in which case its distributional effects will also almost invariably enter as an argument—and all our cases become in principle relevant. What in practice is not usually very helpful in either of the above cases is to suggest that what is really being aimed at may be some more radical redistribution of wealth, in which case any decision on the mooted change should be deferred. The truth is that economic change proceeds largely by considering suggested improvements one at a time. If, as a result, some changes are made which, in the light of subsequent decisions, should not have been made, that is too bad. But it cannot always be helped.

Let us now try to sum up this discussion so far as we have got. First, neither the Kaldor–Hicks nor the Scitovsky criterion, either alone or together, can possibly be taken to be a criterion of welfare. Either, taken in conjunction with a judgement that the redistribution involved is good, can be taken as a sufficient (but not necessary) criterion of an increase in economic welfare. But, where full compensation and redistribution are possible, then criteria for an increase in welfare are not pertinent, for what is then required is a criterion for whether the proposed change is desirable having regard to the possibilities of compensation and redistribution. Where redistribution and compensation are possible, but where wider redistributions than those involved in the change are not in question, then the Scitovsky criterion is sufficient (but not necessary) for the change to be desirable if the redistribution involved is also good—

while the Kaldor–Hicks criterion is not sufficient even combined with a judgement that the redistribution is good. We can thus say that an economic change is desirable (and increases welfare) if it causes a good redistribution of wealth, and if the potential losers could not profitably bribe the potential gainers to oppose it—always assuming that no still better change is therefore prejudiced.

FIG. VIII[1]

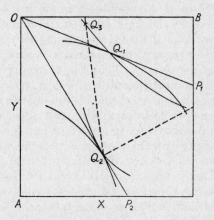

The next step is to discuss the question of when one can know whether either the Scitovsky or the Kaldor–Hicks criterion is satisfied. Now economic theory tells us nothing except when the change is from a 'sub-optimum' to an 'optimum' position.[2] Only in that case can one know on *a priori* grounds that the behaviour line or plane to which one moves is anywhere higher than that from which one starts. Let us therefore ask, first, whether the Kaldor–Hicks criterion is always satisfied for any movement to a Pareto 'optimum'. This requires rather a careful answer. Consider Fig. VIII. Q_1 is the initial position where A behaves as a monopolist setting a high price (OP_1), but with an obligation to let B trade freely at that price (as in Fig. VI). Q_1 is not on the contract curve, i.e. is not a Pareto 'optimum' position. Q_2 is on the contract curve; we may suppose it to be reached by the government dictating the price

---

[1] The broken lines give the loci of the points which A and B would select as the price line OP_2 was shifted to the right.

[2] Some theorists have thought otherwise. The question is discussed in Ch. IX and in App. IV.

OP_2, so that it is in both A's and B's interest to trade freely. Now can B overcompensate A while free trade and the price OP_2 is preserved? The answer may well be 'No', for as the price line OP_2 is shifted to the north-east (as B hands over compensation), no other point may be found where both persons' desire to trade can be satisfied. In other words, no equilibrium point other than Q_2 may exist within the box given the price OP_2. In the diagram the two broken lines represent paths A and B might take as OP_2 was shifted parallelwise to the north-east. In the case depicted there would be excess demand for Y relative to X. If B were forced to exchange as much as A wanted after having paid compensation, then the transfer required to compensate A could well leave B worse off—e.g. the point Q_3. Thus the payment of compensation may either be incompatible with equilibrium, or, if an additional condition is introduced, which yields a determinate solution, then there may be no possibility of compensation. In general, it is true that the Kaldor–Hicks criterion is satisfied for a movement to an 'optimum' position only if it is supposed that the compensation is to be paid in a manner which does not itself upset the 'optimum' conditions. Thus, if the Kaldor–Hicks criterion is to be satisfied, the change must not be merely a change of price—but a change to a variable price which neither party can influence monopolistically. A more general example of this is where the movement to an 'optimum' position results in a change in the collection of goods produced. Where this happens then it is not necessarily true that the new collection of goods could be distributed in such a way as to make everyone better off, or no worse off. This is because, as compensation is paid, the said collection of goods ceases to be the collection appropriate to the changed distribution: or, in other words, the 'optimum' conditions of production and exchange would be violated unless the collection of goods was allowed to change as compensation was paid. What can be said is that if the change is described merely as a change which brings all the optimum conditions into play, and keeps them in play, then the Kaldor–Hicks criterion is satisfied. If the change is described in any other way (such as a change of price, or a change in the collection of goods produced) then the criterion may not be satisfied.

Discussion of whether the Scitovsky criterion is satisfied is much simpler. It is always satisfied for a change to an 'optimum' position, however the change is described. This is because no question of redistribution *from* the 'optimum' position arises. In the Scitovsky criterion, the hypothetical redistribution considered is from the 'sub-optimum' position. Thus in Fig. VIII it is obvious that A, the potential loser from the change of price OP_1 to OP_2, could not bribe B to oppose the change, because, since Q_2 is an 'optimum' point, any other point on the behaviour line of B which passes through Q_2 necessarily lies on a lower behaviour line of A than that passing through Q_2. Thus if it is a change of price which results in an 'optimum' position, then the Scitovsky criterion is satisfied for that change of price. If a change in the collection of goods is entailed, then it is true that the old collection would not be sufficient to make everyone as well off as he is in the new situation.

We have said that *a priori* economic theory can tell us that the Scitovsky and Kaldor–Hicks criteria are satisfied only if the change is a change to a position in which *all* the optimum conditions of production and exchange are satisfied. But, of course, that does not mean that one can never form the judgement that a change to a non-optimal position would not in fact satisfy one or both the criteria.

We show in Chapter XII that an increase in the national income as measured by the prices reigning after the change ($\sum P_2 Q_2 \geqslant \sum P_2 Q_1$) ensures that the Scitovsky criterion is satisfied,[1] in that the output of goods prior to the change could not have sufficed, however distributed, to make everyone as well off as they actually are after the change. Now one may sometimes be able to tell, with fair confidence, before the event, that a certain change in production would increase the national income in this sense. Unfortunately, unless one can tell more than this, one has not found a very good reason for making the change. For what is required in order that the Scitovsky criterion be fulfilled *in the relevant sense* is that without the change the given factors of production could not have produced *any* set of goods which would have made everyone as well off as after the change. This does not mean that a considerable increase in the national income cannot be taken as evidence that the change should be made on our criterion: but it cannot prove it to be fulfilled.

It is shown in the same chapter that an increase in the national

[1] Subject, of course, to many comparatively unrealistic assumptions, such as that all individuals are consistent, all goods are chosen by individuals, that the national income has been correctly added up, &c.

income never proves that the Kaldor–Hicks criterion is satisfied.[1] This does not mean of course that one could never guess that it would be satisfied. But it does not follow that because a change would increase the national income before compensation, it would still do so after compensation. This is especially likely to be the case in view of the fact that in practice it is impossible to shift money about without disturbing the 'optimum' conditions. This fact, contrariwise, makes it easier to be sure that the Scitovsky criterion is satisfied—since the more 'inefficient' the means of redistribution the easier it is to know that mere redistribution could not have produced a position in which everyone would be as well off as they would be if the change under consideration were made.

To sum up the above discussion, any change which brings one to an 'optimum' position is sufficient to ensure that the Scitovsky criterion is fulfilled for that change: and the fulfilment of that criterion is sufficient to ensure that welfare is increased, provided that the distribution of wealth is not adversely affected, and to ensure that a redistribution of money income could not have made everyone as well off as they would have been after the change. Comparing non-optimum positions (which in practice is all that ever can be done), we saw that economic theory cannot tell us whether either the Scitovsky or the Kaldor–Hicks criterion would be fulfilled for a move from one to the other; but from empirical evidence it may be possible to tell, although an increase in the national income is not sufficient evidence.

So far as any kind of change is concerned, if the Scitovsky criterion would be satisfied and wealth would be more favourably distributed as a result of the change, there is no need to worry about the Kaldor–Hicks criterion. But, secondly, if redistribution without the change were impossible, and that caused by the change were favourable, then the change should be made if the Kaldor–Hicks criterion were satisfied, even if the Scitovsky criterion were not. Thirdly, if wealth would be less favourably distributed as a result of the change, one should look to see whether the change-plus-compensation could not make everyone better off: finally all this is subject to the overriding consideration, that it is unwise to make good changes if still better ones are thereby prejudiced.

We have already discussed the value judgements which underlie the above analysis. On the whole, I think, one can fairly safely

[1] See pp. 220–1.

assume that they would be acceptable to a vast majority of people. But certain factual assumptions are also presupposed, and, in discussing these, for more practical purposes, it is useful to make a distinction between a *policy* of putting into operation all changes which satisfy the Scitovsky (or Kaldor–Hicks) criterion and which have only an insignificant effect on distribution, and putting into effect changes which also pass the criterion, but do have a significant, but not bad, effect on distribution. The policy might be an acceptable one, and, indeed, a possible one, because there are probably many changes such that very few people would worry about the income redistribution which they would cause. Where the redistribution would only be small, it would be difficult to say how it would alter, and for this reason a majority of people would very likely be prepared to judge that it would be as likely to be good as bad; in which case a change which passed the criterion would probably be good in most people's opinion. But, nevertheless, the policy rests on the factual assumption that these small shifts in distribution would not be cumulative in some particular direction. This may be a dangerous assumption, and therefore the policy might be a bad one, if we did not have good reason to suppose that the distribution effects of those changes, which we chose to include under the policy, would be random. In fact, one cannot really ever ignore distribution. Even if shifts in distribution are small, and therefore judged not to be bad, one wants to have some reason to suppose that they would be random. If the distribution effects were not random, then, after the policy had been in operation some time, we would have a significant redistribution of income which might be good or bad. If it proved to be bad, it might or might not be possible to compensate. If the redistribution were good, we might still find that the policy had been economically wrong, and that it would have been better simply to redistribute money.

The goodness of such a policy also, of course, rests on the assumption that individuals are sufficiently consistent. As we saw in Chapter III, it is obvious that they are not likely to be very consistent. Moreover, since it is a policy we are judging, the period of time in question is a fairly long period, in which case the consistency of even average individuals becomes very doubtful.

Given all these doubts, it seems eminently clear that we could not have much confidence in such a policy unless it only included changes such that, in theory, the gainers would be able greatly to overcompensate the losers. If the potential gains were great enough, most people would be prepared to tolerate losses, so long as they did not last for long. Almost anyone would, for instance, agree that it would be a mistake to suppress important inventions. On the other hand, where the potential gains are large, it is unlikely that real income distribution would not be significantly affected. Thus many people would hold that the industrial revolution decreased economic welfare for a considerable period of time. My conclusion is that one could have little confidence in the sort of policy suggested by Professor Hicks.[1]

Turning now to changes which do affect income distribution significantly, we have the same fundamental value judgements, and we still, of course, require the assumption that individuals are consistent. We do not, however, require the assumption that income redistribution effects would be random. Also, since we are now dealing with isolated changes, and not with a policy, a rather shorter period of time may be relevant, in which case the consistency assumption is not so unplausible. Nevertheless, given that I accepted the fundamental value judgements, and thought that the change would shift real income distribution in a good direction, I would certainly require that the potential gains should be fairly large before I could say with any confidence that the change would be better than a policy of income redistribution alone.

On the other hand, as already noted, in practice a policy of redistributing income by shifting money is impossible without violating the 'optimum' conditions. This means that often one might want to recommend changes which would cause a good redistribution, even although the Scitovsky criterion was not satisfied. In which case, *a fortiori*, one would want to recommend them if it were. What this all adds up to is that the question whether income redistribution would be definitely good, or could be made good by compensation, is a more important part of the criterion than the Scitovsky part, unless it is obvious that the magnitude of the theoretical gains (the amount by which the gainers could conceivably overcompensate the losers if everyone was an economic

[1] A. M. Henderson has suggested ('The Pricing of Public Utility Undertakings', *Manchester School*, Sept. 1947, p. 230) that the randomness of distribution effects is an assumption which has been presupposed in economic doctrine ever since Adam Smith. This seems to me to be an inadequate reason for continuing to make such a dangerous assumption.

man) is great. This is most likely to arise where the change is one which might have a cumulative effect, as opposed to a once-and-for-all effect, on the output of goods. I certainly do not want to suggest that it is necessarily wrong to accept bad redistributions, or not press for good ones, in the name of economic growth.

In the latter part of this chapter we have rather loosely spoken of 'recommending', and used the word 'should', and so on. These phrases are justified in so far as we have introduced ethical premises, but it is important to remember that we have ruled out all ethical considerations which do not relate to the amount of goods and services consumed by individuals. Thus our recommendatory conclusions must not be regarded as absolute recommendations, or unqualified value judgements; we also require that all non-economic effects of the change should be neutral, or beneficial; or, if bad, they must be outweighed by the good economic effects.

Finally, we must make one very important point. When discussing a good economic policy, we tried to aim at general acceptability; but that does not, of course, imply that what is generally acceptable is good. We only aim at general acceptability in order that the analysis should be of interest to as many people as possible. We are not thereby absolved from making our value premises explicit if we want to avoid the charge of moralizing. Since value judgements are presupposed, it follows that, in the last analysis, whether a policy would be a good one, or a change increase economic welfare, is purely a matter of personal opinion. This is particularly obvious in the case of changes which affect income distribution significantly. Each person must answer for himself the question 'Would this change affect real income distribution favourably or unfavourably?' This does not mean that welfare economics must be useless. It only means that people who differ on the subject of distribution will seldom agree on the desirability of economic changes. This is simply a fact which we have to accept. Even so, welfare economics may still help people who disagree on the subject of distribution to agree on the best way of bringing about any given redistribution.

It may be useful to conclude this chapter by briefly tracing the relation which the above exposition of the foundations of welfare economics bears to utilitarian welfare economics. The first important point is that it makes the ethical implications of the subject perfectly explicit. Secondly, it does not beg the question in favour of any particular ethical creed. It provides therefore a more general framework than utilitarian economics, which can be fitted into it by suitable translations. Thus a utilitarian may, if he wishes, always interpret 'on a higher behaviour line' as 'more satisfaction'. Likewise, he may interpret 'a good redistribution of income' as 'a redistribution which would increase happiness'. But if one does not believe that the view, that economics is about satisfactions, is sufficiently plausible, one can merely judge that it is a good thing that a person be in a preferred position. Also, since the above schema is explicitly ethical, it follows that the notorious question of whether interpersonal comparisons are value judgements ceases to be of any importance. In order to reach our ethical conclusions, we have to judge that a certain redistribution would be *good*, and not merely that it would increase happiness. But interpersonal comparisons are not, in fact, merely value judgements, and people will generally use these factual comparisons to help them decide the value question whether a certain redistribution would be good or bad.

Since we believe that the essential purpose of the economics of wealth, happiness, or welfare is to make recommendations, and to influence people, it follows that it should be put on an explicit, and not merely an implicit, value basis. We therefore prefer the above schema to that of utilitarian economics. But, having said this, we must add that the utilitarian scheme of things was more logical, more acceptable, and less misleading than that version of the New Welfare Economics which was based merely on conceivable overcompensation.

CHAPTER VII

THE NEW WELFARE ECONOMICS (2): THE ECONOMIC WELFARE FUNCTION

THERE remains for consideration the system of welfare economics favoured by the first school of thought mentioned in the previous chapter. This system was first worked out by Professor A. Bergson in his article 'A Reformulation of Certain Aspects of Welfare Economics'.[1] On this formulation the 'optimum' conditions of production and exchange are derived as *necessary* conditions for 'maximum welfare'. In the last chapter we developed a *sufficient* criterion for a desirable economic change, and no such concept as 'maximum welfare' was used. It follows that if the 'optimum' conditions are deduced from this later kind of basis, they must be deduced as *sufficient* conditions for an economic improvement, and not as *necessary* conditions for achieving 'the maximum'. This is one of the distinctive differences of emphasis between the two systems.

The Bergson–Samuelson system proceeds by way of a 'social welfare function'.[2] In other words it is postulated that all possible configurations of the social system are arranged in order of value. This means that, if the system is ever to be applied, we require someone—let us, for the moment, call him 'superman'—to answer the question 'Is X better or worse than Y?' for all conceivable values of X and Y. The value judgements of this 'superman' must be consistent in the same sense as an 'economic man' must be consistent, i.e. if he says A is better than B, and B better than C, he must say that A is better than C.

But no conclusions about the real world can be reached if one tries to talk about everything at once. So let us replace the 'social welfare function' by an 'economic welfare function'.[3] This means that it is proposed to take into account only the economic differences between each pair of possible situations. The word 'economic' is defined as in Chapter I. The order in which the situations are arranged on the economic welfare scale may, of course, differ from the order in which they are arranged on the social welfare scale. We cannot therefore say that a situation of greater economic

[1] *Q.J.E.* (1937–8), pp. 310–34.
[2] Cf. Samuelson, op. cit., pp. 219–28.
[3] Cf. Bergson, op. cit.

welfare is a better situation in the eyes of 'superman'. But, for the sake of brevity, we shall use such words as 'good', 'bad', and 'ought'. The resultant value judgements must therefore always be regarded as qualified by the condition that the non-economic differences between the two situations must be a matter of ethical indifference, or they must support the value judgements made as a result of a consideration only of the economic differences. The phrase 'in the opinion of "superman"' ought also to qualify the value judgements.

To make any progress some assumptions must be made about the form of the 'economic welfare function'. In other words, we require some value postulates. Let us, then, postulate that 'welfare' is an increasing function of the 'well-being' of 'individuals', i.e. whether we move up or down the scale of 'economic welfare' depends on whether 'individuals' become 'better off' or 'worse off' (if this is not postulated, there is no problem of how 'goods' ought to be allocated to 'individuals', and therefore the 'optimum' exchange conditions could not be derived). We also postulate that 'economic welfare' is greater if one 'individual' is 'better off', and no 'individual' is 'worse off'. Then, in order to relate 'better off' and 'worse off' to economic theory, it must be stipulated that an 'individual' is 'better off' if he is 'on a higher behaviour line', and similarly for 'worse off'.[1]

It follows that 'economic welfare' is greater if some 'individual' is 'on a higher behaviour line', and if no other 'individual' is affected at all. This suffices for the deduction of the 'optimum' conditions of production and exchange as *necessary* conditions for attaining the highest possible value of the economic welfare function.[2] It can be shown that if any one of these conditions is not fulfilled, then it is conceivable that some 'individual' should be made 'better off', without any other 'individual' being made 'worse off'. But the fulfilment of all these 'optimum' conditions of production and exchange is still not sufficient to ensure that the highest conceivable value is attained. They suffice only for the attainment of a Pareto optimum.[3] The final condition for achieving

[1] This last postulate will be slightly modified later.
[2] In Appendix III we throw some doubt on whether these conditions should be regarded as necessary for a Pareto optimum: if these doubts are accepted, then it follows that they are not necessary for *the* optimum. But, in conjunction with an ideal distribution of welfare, they would remain *sufficient* for the optimum.
[3] See p. 84 above.

the 'optimum' (among all the Pareto 'optima') is that there should be an ideal distribution of 'welfare' among the 'individuals'. It thus has to be imagined that 'superman', besides laying down the value postulates already shown to be required, also defines an ideal distribution of 'welfare'.

As has been said, the exponents of the above approach to 'welfare' economics have neglected to define sufficient conditions for an improvement in 'welfare'.[1] But one sufficient condition is, of course, implied, i.e. that all the 'optimum' conditions, including the ideal distribution of welfare condition, be put into operation at once. Thus the neglect of sufficient conditions for an increase in 'welfare' tends to turn the system into the theory of socialist economics.[2] This assimilation of welfare economics to socialism is evidently suggested by the lack of any discussion of when it might be a good thing to put one 'optimum' condition into operation, even if some of the others were not fulfilled, thereby suggesting that it is a case of all or nothing. To a certain extent this emphasis on the 'optimum' conditions as each being necessary for *the* 'optimum', but not sufficient for an 'improvement', is undoubtedly an accident of the mathematical analysis employed. But, whether accident or not, the implication of all or nothing is there, unless the author takes care to let it be understood that he does not intend to imply anything at all.

Nevertheless the conclusions which were reached in Chapter VI could have been derived from an economic welfare function defined by means of the value postulates proposed above. If one has the same premises one can, naturally, reach the same conclusions. The difference between the two approaches is as follows. To speak of an economic welfare function implies that every situation can be said to be 'better than', 'worse than', or 'in different to' every other situation;[3] this implies that there is a best or a number of 'equally best' situations; which, in turn, implies an ideal distribution of welfare. On the other hand, the situational analysis, developed in Chapter VI, presupposes only that a limited number of points

[1] It is not quite true that sufficient conditions for an improvement were altogether neglected. Professor Bergson (*Q.J.E.* article, p. 333) in effect concludes that increases in the 'national dividend' would increase economic welfare if they were positively correlated with good changes in welfare distribution.

[2] It is noteworthy that the article on welfare economics by Professor Bergson, in *A Survey of Contemporary Economics*, is entitled 'Socialist Economics'.

[3] Cf. Samuelson, op. cit., p. 221.

(four) are, necessarily, thus orderable.[1] The situational analysis is derivable from an economic welfare function, and, since the reverse does not hold, the economic welfare function can be said to be more general. But the advantages of increased generality are very dubious—except from the mathematician's point of view—if the economic welfare function cannot be applied. It seems to me that the functional terminology is advantageous only if one can significantly speak of maximizing economic welfare, using the term in its ordinary sense. Therefore since the maximization of welfare implies the possibility of an ideal distribution, let us pretend that we are starting off with an ideal distribution, as defined by 'superman' whoever 'he' may be. It follows that one cannot deduce that any change should be made unless, after compensation, it makes someone better off, and no one worse off.

But we have already seen that, if the actual compensation of all losers is required before any economic change can be said to be good, then probably no good economic changes can occur. No change of any significance in the real world could ever be made without harming some people. Also compensation can never be more than rough and ready, partly because the behaviour maps of individuals (even supposing them perfectly consistent) are not known, and partly because the effects of any important economic change may be extremely widespread, and the number of individuals involved very great.

It will be remembered that the payment of compensation was also criticized on the ground that it betrayed a conservative bias. But the present case is very different, for an ideal distribution has been presupposed. If we start with an ideal, conservatism is, by definition, the best policy. But what does this concept of an ideal distribution really mean? We have seen that the ideal distribution was to be defined by 'superman'. But nobody could *say* what distribution of real income, or welfare, would be ideal. We have no terminology for describing welfare distributions. The definition, therefore, must be ostensive. We have to suppose that 'superman' would point to a certain configuration of the economic system, and say '*that* represents the ideal welfare distribution'.

It is time that something was said about the interpretation of

[1] It may be suggested that we have a partial economic welfare function even if only two situations are assumed to be orderable. If one is determined to use mathematical language, at whatever cost in clarity, this can, of course, be said.

this word 'superman'. Could 'superman' be interpreted, for in-stance, as public opinion? It is difficult to imagine how public opinion could define an ideal distribution. Take a more or less democratic country such as England. Some might consider the distribution of welfare in England now to be ideal, but many more would not. Howsoever it was altered, there would still be many who would not find it ideal. Indeed, it seems doubtful whether it would ever be possible to get two people, let alone a majority, to vote 'Yes' in answer to the question 'Is the present distribution of welfare ideal?', no matter how welfare was distributed. Thus, in a democratic state, it seems absurd to suppose that public opinion could define an ideal distribution.

Could 'superman' be interpreted as Parliament or the Cabinet? This idea leads to the suggestion that economists, in a state with a democratic government, must always take the prevailing distri-bution as ideal, because the government would have changed the distribution if it had wanted to. This suggestion rests on two fallacies. It is certainly a fallacy to suppose that the government must approve of the prevailing distribution, merely because it has the power to alter it. This is like saying that one must always want to be in the place where one is, even if one happens to be motoring through it. But the present suggestion also rests on the highly undemocratic idea that the government always knows what is best —or that it alone can say what is in the public interest. Those economists who are not civil servants are permitted to criticize the aims, policies, and opinions of the government.

It thus appears that the 'ideal welfare distribution' could at best be defined only in a totalitarian state, where economists, or other subjects, never question the value judgements of their rulers. But even in such a state it might not be safe to assume that the distri-bution of welfare was always just what the rulers wanted. In the real world, the redistribution of welfare is a slow and difficult business. And, even if economists in such a state could assume that distribution was ideal, there would still be great difficulty in making changes which did not upset that distribution. The difficulties in-volved in the idea of trying actually to compensate all losers would not be removed. The distribution of welfare would inevitably shift, in which case it would still be necessary to inquire whether the resultant redistribution was good or bad. We can only conclude that the 'economic welfare function' would be inapplicable even in an absolutist state, and doubly so in a democratic one, where there would be as many (vague) welfare functions as there are individuals. It can be regarded only as a formal device necessary to a perfectly general abstract system of 'welfare', which bears no relation to practical policy.

Now the third school of thought—the Kaldor–Hicks–Scitovsky school—concentrated not on developing the necessary conditions for Utopia, but on providing a sufficient criterion for an economic improvement. It is clear that this kind of approach is suggestive of reform rather than revolution; of patching up rather than tearing down and building anew. But the criteria developed were not acceptable because they ignored income distribution. It was also not clear that the ethical, recommendatory, nature of welfare economics was recognized. We therefore introduced value judgements into the analysis. The two fundamental value judgements were (a) that welfare is an increasing function of the well-being of individuals, and (b) that an individual is better off if in a chosen position. These two value judgements are identical with those which must be used by the exponents of the 'economic welfare function', if all the traditional 'optimum' conditions are to be deduced.

But there the resemblance ends. The Kaldor–Hicks school of thought made welfare independent of distribution. We refused to accept this latter stipulation, and introduced a new sufficient criterion for a desirable economic change. The use of the phrase 'increase of economic welfare' is made dependent on the judgement that the resultant redistribution would not be bad. This means that, in our system, unqualified conclusions can never be reached, if it is desired to remain neutral on matters of welfare distribution. But, by leaving open the question of whether any shift in distribution would be good or bad, we avoid having to make the useless presupposition of an 'ideal welfare distribution'. The application of the theory therefore becomes more general.[1] Anyone can decide for himself whether the projected redistribution would be good or bad, and therefore whether (in theory) the change ought to be made or not. One of the least tolerable features of the ideal distribution concept is that it limits the use of the theory to those who happen to believe that the distribution of welfare is ideal.

---

[1] In welfare function terminology people who would define widely different functions may agree on the desirability, or otherwise, of a given change. People need not agree about everything to agree about one thing.

The other important difference is that the 'optimum' conditions need not be derived as necessary conditions for 'maximum welfare'. 'The maximum' is a concept without any possible empirical significance, and therefore it seems preferable not to use it. It is more meaningful to derive the 'optimum' conditions as sufficient conditions for an improvement, without attempting to define a maximum position. The 'economic welfare function' is the basis of a perfectly valid system. It has been criticized, not on logical grounds, but on the ground that it cannot be applied. We prefer the less highly formalized, less comprehensively rationalistic, situational kind of analysis. Of course, we may be forced to decide that even this kind of analysis is hopelessly inapplicable. But at least it seems to offer more hope of application.

Let us review the progress made so far in this book. We have developed a formal sufficient criterion for deciding when a change is economically desirable. It is desirable if (a) it results in a good redistribution of welfare, and if (b) the potential losers could not bribe the potential gainers to vote against the change. This criterion may be expressed, in other words, as follows: *A change is economically desirable if it results in a good redistribution of welfare, and if a policy of redistributing money by lump-sum transfers could not make everyone as well off as they would be if the change were made.* It is important to remember that this is a sufficient criterion only: it is not suggested that changes which do not satisfy it may not also be desirable. Secondly, it is conceivable that some changes which satisfied it might prejudice still better changes: so the qualification 'so long as it is judged that still better changes are not thereby prejudiced' should be made. One thing that the criterion does, is, as it were, not to give the green light to all changes which increase welfare: a change which would increase economic welfare, but can be shown to prejudice a still better position attainable merely by redistribution, is not given the green light. So one important kind of alternative policy, i.e. redistribution is partly taken account of —but the criterion cannot ensure that yet other kinds of policy, which would result in still better positions, might not be prejudiced by a change which it permits.

With this qualification the criterion is an adequate basis for welfare economics, because, as we shall see in the following chapter, it permits the deduction of the traditional 'optimum' conditions, as sufficient conditions for a desirable change, given that the fulfilment of the condition would not have an unfavourable effect on distribution. Whether a certain economic change would be good, or not, thus depends on a value judgement about income distribution. It is a matter of opinion whether any given shift in distribution would be good or bad, and therefore always a matter of opinion as to whether some economic change is desirable or not. This does not in the least imply that welfare economics must be useless. It may enable people who largely agree on matters of distribution to agree on the desirability of certain specific changes. And even if an economist thinks that some suggested change would affect distribution unfavourably he can still make some recommendation. He can, for instance, say that if the government is determined to shift distribution in that way, then it would be better to do it by making the suggested change rather than by some other means. But this does not, of course, imply that he would be prepared to say that the change would increase welfare.

The above analysis presupposes only two value judgements, both of which we believe to be widely acceptable. The first is that the welfare of the community is an increasing function of the welfare of individuals. The second is that an individual is better off if he is in a chosen position. We found that value premises are essential to welfare economics because welfare conclusions *are* value judgements, and because value conclusions require value premises. Our criterion for a desirable economic change thus resulted from the introduction of a value judgement about welfare distribution into the Kaldor–Hicks–Scitovsky 'situational', or 'partial', analysis.

We believe that anyone who accepts the two fundamental value judgements, and our definition of the word 'economic', must accept the above criterion. This completes our discussion of the foundations of welfare economics. These foundations are, in our opinion, sound. If welfare economics is found to be useless, it is not because there is anything shifty about the philosophical or logical foundations. We claim to have stated the required postulates in a clear, precise manner. It only remains to accept or reject them. It will be presumed, in what follows, that they are accepted.

The criticisms of welfare economics which will occupy us in subsequent chapters will be neither logical, nor linguistic, nor philosophical. We shall be concerned with the realism of the theory, i.e. with the question of how far the defining characteristics of our concepts are realized in practice. We have already, to a limited extent, been concerned with this question of realism. It has been seen that the exact application of the 'in a chosen position' criterion to the real world, in a form which is theoretically useful, demands that individuals should be perfectly consistent 'economic men'. But any exact application was obviously out of the question. We therefore asked ourselves whether the behaviour-line analysis of individual economic behaviour was *sufficiently* realistic for us to have a reasonable degree of confidence in the deductions made from such a basis.[1]

A tentative answer to the above question was given in Chapter III. It was decided that the behaviour-line analysis applied very badly to actual individuals. On the other hand we believe that most people would still be prepared to accept the two fundamental value judgements, even given that the word 'individual' is not to be taken absolutely strictly. It was concluded that if 'individual' is interpreted in a vague way as referring to average men, or small homogeneous groups, then it would be very rash to conclude that the facts of inconsistent behaviour, taken alone, render all prescriptive economics useless.

The above discussion of the reality of one of our essential factual assumptions has been rather tentative. We have spoken vaguely of an analysis applying 'well' or 'badly', and talked of 'a reasonable degree of confidence'. Why do we have to make such vague judgements? Why cannot the question, whether the theory applies well enough, be definitely answered? What are the usual scientific tests for when an assumption, or a hypothesis, is good enough?

In science the above sort of question is answered pragmatically. Assumptions are good enough if they yield conclusions which can be tested, and are found to be true—or, if not precisely true, are better than nothing, and better than results yielded by any other hypothesis. Evidently, in order to answer such a question as 'Does the behaviour-line analysis apply well enough?' the conclusions which result from its application to the real world should be tested. But the conclusions are welfare conclusions. Are such conclusions testable? In principle, 'Yes'. Having selected an individual who

[1] The applicability of the behaviour-line analysis does not depend only on the degree of consistency displayed by individuals. It also depends on how far economic goods are divisible. The problems arising from the unreality of the assumption of perfect divisibility will be discussed later, in Chapter X.

approved of our value judgements, we could then make changes which satisfied the criterion of desirability, and ask him whether the resultant situation was better or worse than the initial one. But from this description of how the conclusions could be tested in principle it becomes fairly obvious that they could not be tested in practice. The reasons are (*a*) that no controlled experiment is possible. Even if our guinea-pig said that an improvement had resulted, we should be unable to rule out the possibility that the improvement was the result, not of the changes deliberately made, but of concomitant changes—and (*b*) the canvas is too large for any individual to be able to observe it all, and so make a reasonable judgement.

Physicists do not have to worry about whether the concepts of the deductive systems, which they use, have any recognizable interpretation. In physics, it does not, for instance, matter in the least whether or not electrons are identifiable objects which behave in the postulated manner. What are important are the conclusions in terms of physical objects, which can be verified or falsified. But social scientists, in lieu of readily testable conclusions, must concern themselves with the extent to which the defining characteristics of their concepts realize themselves.[1]

Thus the question of whether the assumptions of welfare economics are good enough (when they are obviously not very good) is a matter of individual judgement—and never a matter of proof. Since, in subsequent chapters, we shall be questioning many of the factual assumptions, implied by any application of welfare economics to practical policy, this fact should be borne in mind. So far we have been concerned only with one assumption, that of con-

---

[1] The fact that our theoretical conclusions cannot be tested, and that we therefore have to fall back on testing our postulates, marks an important difference between welfare economics (and, I think, all the social sciences) and the physical sciences. This has been well put by F. S. C. Northrop in his article 'The Impossibility of a Theoretical Science of Economic Dynamics', *Q.J.E.* lvi, 1941–2, as follows: 'the difference in scientific method is marked. Physics tests its deductive theory indirectly by empirically checking its theorems; Economics, directly by empirically confirming its postulates. In Physics one believes in the validity of its postulates because their deductive consequences, the theorems, are experimentally confirmed; in Economics, one believes in the validity of its theorems because they are the logical consequences of the immediately confirmed postulates.' As comment we may add that this passage seems to apply perfectly to welfare economics, but not to positive macroeconomics. We must also add that our postulates are not, in fact, confirmed—at best they are confirmed to have a grain of truth—and so we may, or may not, believe in the truth of the theorems.

sistency of choice. Whereas my judgement is that we cannot simply dismiss welfare economics on the ground that this is an absurd assumption, nevertheless I think that its obvious unreality is alone sufficient to make it foolish to be concerned with minutiae. Before applying our formal criterion we should at least require that the losers would appear to be, in theory, incapable of bribing the winners to oppose the change by a fairly handsome margin.

The fact that it is a matter of judgement whether the abstract welfare theory applies well enough to the real world to justify its application to live issues, implies, I think, that welfare economists cannot, even if they wish to, avoid all responsibility for deciding questions of value. Since welfare judgements about the real world are value judgements, it follows that the question whether the abstract theory applies well enough for us to risk such conclusions is a value question. When an economist says 'If you accept such and such premises, then these conclusions follow' he must remember that the given premises will be understood to run in terms of real individuals, &c. But the economist himself works in terms of rather unreal abstractions; he must accordingly remember that his practical conclusions are suspect. The non-economist should be warned of the assumptions which the economist slips in in order to be able to deduce his practical conclusions from the given premises. In practice, to warn the non-economist of all the assumptions made, would be to teach him a lot of economic theory. Thus economists themselves have largely to decide whether the theory is good enough. They cannot free themselves from all responsibility. The distinction sometimes drawn between economist *qua* economist, and economist *qua* moralist, is an unreal one.

In the next chapter the 'optimum' conditions of production and exchange will be developed, both as necessary conditions for a maximum, and as sufficient conditions for a desirable economic change. From what has been said above, however, it is clear that the latter sense of the word 'optimum' is the only one which is regarded as being of any possible practical significance.[1] We shall also show under what conditions these 'optimum' conditions would, in theory, be fulfilled. We shall endeavour to present the theory as applied theory. Even so we shall only take the unreality

[1] It is also shown in Appendix III that considerably weaker assumptions about individual behaviour are required if we are content to derive the 'optimum' conditions solely as sufficient conditions for an improvement.

of a limited number of assumptions into account—to wit (*a*) the assumption that individuals are independent and free to choose between different collections of goods, and that they make consistent choices, and (*b*) the assumption that production units are independent. We shall, in fact, try to show with what degree of plausibility it can be said that these 'optimum' conditions are based on individual preferences. In later chapters the applicability of welfare theory will be discussed from a wider viewpoint.

CHAPTER VIII

THE 'OPTIMUM' CONDITIONS OF PRODUCTION AND EXCHANGE (1)

I. THE 'OPTIMUM' CONDITIONS OF EXCHANGE

WE postulate a fixed stock of 'goods' to be distributed between a number of 'individuals'.

1 (a) *The marginal rate of substitution between any two 'goods' must be the same for every 'individual' who consumes them both.*

For two 'goods' and two 'individuals' this can be proved with the aid of a box-diagram of behaviour lines. Thus, in Fig. IX, *A*'s

FIG. IX

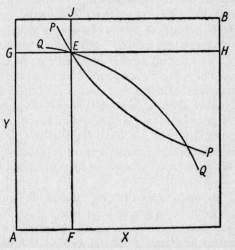

behaviour lines are convex to the origin *A*, and *B*'s to the origin *B*. Adjacent sides of the box represent the total amounts of the two goods *X* and *Y* to be divided between *A* and *B*, and thus every point represents a certain division of the goods between them. At the point *E*, for instance, *A* gets *AF* and *AG* of *X* and *Y* respectively, and, similarly, *B* gets *BJ* and *BH*. The point *E* is one at which the slopes of *A*'s and *B*'s respective behaviour lines (*PP* and *QQ*) are different. Whenever this is the case, it can be seen by inspection that it must be possible for one to reach a higher curve, while the other remains on the same curve, or also reaches a higher one. It follows that equality of the marginal rate of substitution is a necessary condition of 'maximum welfare'.[1] This two-person, two-good case can be generalized to apply to n persons, and n goods. The proof of this, and of all similar generalizations of the other 'optimum' conditions, is left to the mathematical economists.[2]

Putting the above condition into operation, when it is not already fulfilled, is, in theory, a sufficient condition for an increase in welfare, so long as the distribution of welfare is not thereby made worse. This follows because any movement to a position of tangency of behaviour lines is a movement which satisfies the Scitovsky criterion. Once such a position is reached, as a result of some change, it is impossible that the Kaldor–Hicks criterion should be satisfied for the reverse change away from the tangency position. This is the same as to say that the Scitovsky criterion must be satisfied for any change to a point of tangency of behaviour lines.

In what circumstances is this 'optimum' condition fulfilled? In Chapter II we saw that a behaviour line must be tangential to any fixed price line at the chosen point. This condition is therefore satisfied if individuals are free to choose, and if there is only one price in the market, because, then, all behaviour lines must be tangential to the same price line, and therefore have the same slope. The fixed price must, of course, be such that all the goods are sold. This requirement is not necessary when it is assumed, as in Fig. IX, that all the goods have already been distributed before exchange takes place.

Earlier we promised to modify the postulate 'an "individual" is "better off" if he is "on a higher behaviour line"'. The modified postulate is as follows: 'an "individual" is "better off" if he is "on a higher behaviour line" and if his well-being is not unfavourably

---

[1] Sometimes the only positions in the box which satisfy the condition that it must not be possible for one to reach a higher line without the other falling to a lower one will be on the boundaries of the box. In such a case it cannot be said that equality of the marginal rates of substitution is necessary for an 'optimum'. The same also applies if behaviour lines are permitted to be kinked. The modifications which need to be made to the 'optimum' conditions in these cases are dealt with in Appendix III.

[2] Reference may be made to Bergson, op. cit.; Lange, 'Foundations of Welfare Economics', *Econometrica*, July–Oct. 1942; Samuelson, op. cit., pp. 229–40.

affected by changes in the well-being of other "individuals"'. The object of this modification is to remove the assumption that individuals' welfares are completely independent. Professor Bergson has shown that the 'optimum' conditions do not require this assumption of independence. To quote:

> In so far as Marshall and Pigou conceive of welfare as the sum of the utilities of different households, their formulation involves an additional decision on ends, namely one to the effect that the interrelations in the utilities of the different households have a zero social value. The magnitude of the change in the community's welfare, resulting from a change in the budget position of any one family, does not depend at all on the living standards enjoyed by other households.

For purposes of analyzing the optimum allocation, however, it is unnecessary to refer to this special and obviously very dubious case; it has been shown that all propositions of interest can be deduced from the more general function in the formula given above.[1] The demonstration of this point would seem to be one of the more interesting doctrinal gains resulting from the introduction of the welfare function[2] into the analysis.[3]

It must be noticed that Professor Bergson does not merely claim to dispense with the independence assumption in arriving at the barren truism that the ratio of the marginal social values ought to be the same for any two goods whichever individual consumes them, but also in arriving at the condition that the marginal rate of substitution ought to be the same. How is this possible, in view of the fact that, if the independence assumption is not made, one cannot say that economic welfare is increased if some 'individuals' are 'on higher behaviour lines', and none are on lower ones? The answer is that if, say, A and B (as in Fig. IX) could be raised to 'higher behaviour lines', then, even if their increased welfare has such external diseconomies of consumption[4] that the

[1] The 'formula given above' is the economic welfare function, $W = F(U_1, U_2, U_3 \ldots)$, where U_1, U_2, U_3 represent the utilities of the different households as they see them, and W, the welfare of the community, is understood to be an increasing function of these utilities.

[2] Yet the hedonistic calculus formulation can very easily be modified to take account of economies and diseconomies of consumption, as Professor Bergson himself, in effect, showed (cf. his Q.J.E. article, p. 313, n. 9). The 'doctrinal gain' may have resulted from the introduction of the welfare function, but it is not inconsistent with utilitarian economics.

[3] A. Bergson, 'Socialist Economics' in *A Survey of Contemporary Economics*, ed. Ellis. See also Bergson, loc. cit., Q.J.E. (1937–8), p. 313, n. 9.

[4] See Ch. III.

general welfare would be reduced, it would still be possible to increase general welfare, in that one could reduce A and B to their
former welfare level by removing purchasing power, and then distribute the potential benefit to those individuals whose external
diseconomies of consumption, if any, do not completely offset that
benefit. Thus, unless all individual increases in welfare have more
than offsetting external effects, which would obviously prohibit
any increase in general welfare, this 'optimum' condition of exchange is deducible without the use of a postulate which implies
independence. In fact, given an 'economic welfare function', we
do not require to translate 'benefit' as 'on a higher behaviour line'
in order to use the behaviour-line analysis in the deduction of the
'optimum' conditions as necessary conditions of 'maximum welfare'. We may notice that Professor Bergson's criticism of Marshall
and Professor Pigou applies better to the subsequently developed
Kaldor–Hicks analysis, in which independence is required, because
no economic welfare function is introduced, and income distribution is ignored.

From the above it follows that there is only a potential increase
in welfare if we put A 'on a higher behaviour line' and no other
'individual' on a lower one. To make the potential 'increase' actual,
it is necessary to ensure that the potential 'gain' is distributed to
the right 'individuals'. But, although one can thus deduce this
'optimum' exchange condition as a necessary condition of 'maximum welfare', how can one ever know that putting it into operation would be a sufficient condition for an increase in welfare? Now
the magnitude of external consumption effects varies with the distribution of welfare. Therefore they will be taken into account in
deciding whether the fulfilment of the condition would cause a not
unfavourable redistribution. The condition that the distribution
of welfare must not be adversely affected *includes* the condition that
the potential 'gains' resulting from putting this 'optimum' exchange condition into operation must be distributed to the right
'individuals'. This can be seen as follows. The redistribution which
the change would cause, even allowing for the external consumption effects, would not, in itself, decrease welfare. Therefore a
change which would result in this redistribution, and be such that,
from the point of view of the new redistribution of welfare, those
who had gained could overcompensate those who had lost, must
increase welfare.

We have, however, dealt only with one kind of interdependence, the kind which makes a man worse off because his neighbours get better off, without altering his consumption pattern. But a change in the welfare of others may also alter a man's consumption pattern, and this difficulty cannot be removed in the formal analysis. Also, there is yet another kind of external consumption-effect which attaches to the consumption of a particular good, whoever consumes it, and not to the welfare level of particular consumers. Thus the consumption of Rolls Royces, whoever owns them, may give considerable displeasure to some people who do not own them, and considerable pleasure to others. Again, a beautiful house may have important external economies of consumption. This kind of interdependence does not upset the 'optimum' conditions of exchange, but it may, as we shall see, upset some of the 'optimum' conditions of production. That this is so is intuitively clear. Even if Rolls Royces are displeasing (or pleasing) to those who do not own them, it still follows that those who want them most should own them. But if they cause displeasure, or pleasure, to others their production should be curbed or encouraged as the case may be.

But, finally, the external effects may depend upon who consumes the goods. Radios cause displeasure to others in the hands of owners who live in crowded places and play them loudly: but not in other hands. The presence of such external effects upsets the 'optimum' conditions of exchange, and it ceases to follow that a fixed stock of goods is 'ideally' distributed if sold at a single price which equates supply and demand: moreover, no conceivable system of indirect taxes or subsidies would meet the case; in fact, some restriction of individuals' freedom of choice is usually the only possible manner in which such anti-social behaviour can be restrained.

If we include 'leisure' as a 'good' in the behaviour-line analysis, we can express another 'optimum' condition of exchange:

1 (b) *There must be equality of the marginal rate of substitution between 'leisure' and any given consumption 'good' for all 'individuals' who 'work' and consume that 'good'.*

As before, if this condition does not hold for every pair of 'individuals', it would be possible for one of them to reach 'a higher behaviour line' without the other falling to 'a lower behaviour line'.

But, as we saw in Chapter III, there is a great difficulty about fitting leisure into a behaviour-line analysis, because it is not, in general, the case that the amount of work which a man does is his free choice. It may be true that, if a man has to work eight hours or not at all, he may take his leisure in the form of slackness, and thus try to adjust his subjective marginal rate of substitution of leisure for the good in question to their relative prices, as determined by the price of the good and his marginal earnings. Where a man is paid by time, and where he cannot, for reasons of production technique, be allowed to vary his working time as he chooses, this 'optimum' condition could only be brought about in this way. It cannot reasonably be claimed that the consistency which a man shows in his working time is a sign that he has constant preferences. It is rather a sign of lack of choice at the margin.

There is also the difficulty that there are many different kinds of work of varying degrees of unpleasantness. A man cannot normally split his work up between many different jobs, in the way that a consumer can split up his consumption. The rate at which he would be willing to exchange leisure for the given good would, of course, depend on the relative pleasantness of the job he was doing. We really need a different leisure corresponding to every different kind of work. Taking into consideration the different kinds of work means that we require another 'optimum' condition, to wit:

1 (c) *The marginal rate of substitution of one kind of 'work' for another must be equal for all 'individuals' who do both kinds of 'work'.*

The unreality of this condition is manifest. It is, however, true, in a sense, that both working time and relative wage-rates are partly determined by individual preferences. But the preferences are usually collective rather than individual. To put it in another way, the trade union seems to be the relevant 'individual' in the case of choices about work, while actual or typical individual workers, or their families, are more relevant to the consumption of ordinary goods. Yet, in condition 1 (b), the same interpretation of 'individual' is required, whether he is consuming or working. The marginal rate of substitution referred to cannot therefore be precisely determined by observing the free choices of any real individuals.

Thus the value postulate 'an individual benefits if he reaches a higher behaviour line' leaves us rather in the dark. Ought hours of work to be removed from collective bargaining, and become again the object of more individual choice? Ought the decline in production, which would probably occur as a result of the increased difficulty of factory organization, to be tolerated? The theory cannot give us much help here, unless we make a number of *ad hoc* value judgements to cover the points raised. Moreover, these difficulties are far from being trivial. It is not very consistent to lay great emphasis on individual choice in the consumption-good market, and very little emphasis on individual choice in the labour market. But that is what economic theory seems to have done.[1] Yet most individuals spend far more time working and being leisurely than they do consuming objects which can be 'brought into line with the measuring rod of money'.

But, in order to be able to progress with our analysis, we must assume these difficulties solved, for the remaining 'optimum' conditions depend on the fulfilment of those already discussed. We can suppose that certain *ad hoc* value judgements are given. It may, for instance, be laid down that a man's welfare is greatest if he works a forty-hour week. The relative diswelfare of different jobs may be considered to be in line with relative wages determined in some given way. We come now to the 'optimum' conditions of production.

II. THE 'OPTIMUM' CONDITIONS OF PRODUCTION

We must now give up the postulation of a fixed stock of goods. But all the following 'optimum' conditions depend on the behaviour-line analysis of 'individual' behaviour, if it is assumed that welfare is a function of the well-being of individuals. This assumption, which is, of course, implicit or explicit in almost the whole of the theory of economic welfare, will be made throughout. Consumption, although there is no longer a fixed stock of goods, can now be thought of as split up into periods, in which a fixed stock of goods, which was produced in the preceding period, is allocated to individuals. For the present we ignore savings and investment, and we assume constant technique, and constant managerial

[1] Cf. E. H. Phelps-Brown, 'Prospects of Labour', *Economica*, Feb. 1949, p. 7.

and workmen's ability and zeal. The first 'optimum' condition of production is, then, as follows:

II (a) *The ratio of the marginal products of any two 'factors of production' must be the same for every 'good' in the production of which they both co-operate.*

In other words, the rate at which one 'factor' can be substituted for another, without altering the amount of 'goods' produced, must be the same in all lines of production. The validity of this condition can be shown by reference to Fig. IX. The lines PP and QQ must be reinterpreted as iso-product curves. A and B are now 'goods', not 'individuals'. X and Y are 'factors', not 'goods'. Thus, the point E now represents a situation in which AF of factor X, and AG of factor Y, are devoted to the production of A. Similarly, BH of Y, and BJ of X, are devoted to the production of B. The slope of an iso-product curve at any point represents, for a given distribution of the factors, the rate at which X can be substituted for Y in the production of A (or B) without altering the amount of A (or B) produced. Iso-product curves are, like behaviour lines, assumed to be convex to their respective origins, which implies that the rate at which one factor can be substituted for the other decreases as the substitution goes on (i.e. more and more Y (X) is required to compensate for the loss of a given amount of X (Y) as the amount of X (Y) used is reduced). If an iso-product curve failed to be convex over part of its length, then, if the price ratio of the factors remained constant, no combination of factors represented by any point on the concave part of the curve would ever be chosen, since a higher output could, in that case, be obtained at the same cost. If the iso-product curves were nowhere convex to the origin, only one of the two factors would be employed, and the 'optimum' conditions for their best usage would, then, be irrelevant. The condition of equal marginal substitutability is therefore an 'optimum' and not a 'pessimum' condition of production. As before, it can be seen, by inspection of Fig. IX, that, if we are not at a point of tangency of iso-product curves, then the production of A, or B, or both, could be increased without increasing the total amount of any factor used.

Now, if the production of one good can be increased, without that of any other declining, then it must (by the definition of a behaviour line) be possible to raise some 'individual' or 'individuals'

to higher behaviour lines, without affecting any other unfavourably, so long as we choose the right 'individuals' and the right
'goods'.[1] Therefore this is a necessary condition of 'maximum
welfare'.

We must remember, however, that we have extended the behaviour-line analysis to include 'leisures'. Therefore 'factors' cannot be interpreted as human factors of production. Formally, we
require the value premise that economic welfare is not affected by
shifting 'factors' between jobs. This premise cannot apply to human
factors if we include, as we do, work or leisure in the behaviour-
line analysis.

Now the above analysis requires that 'production units' be independent, i.e. there must be no external economies or diseconomies
of production. We saw that if the iso-product lines in the diagram
were not tangential, then more of both 'goods' A and B could be
produced without withdrawing 'factors' from other uses. It was for
this reason that it was said that the production of A and B could be
increased without any decrease in the production of any other good.
But this does not necessarily follow, if we do not assume independence, because, analogous to external diseconomies of consumption, there might be external diseconomies of production.
Thus an increase in the production of A and B might cause a
decrease in the production of C, even though C still retained the
same 'factors' of production. If *everything* which a 'firm' actually
produced could be accounted to it as part of its 'product' (positive
or negative), and if everything it consumed could be accounted
to it as a 'factor', then every 'firm' must, by definition, be independent. But, in the real world, such perfect accounting is not
possible, and therefore we have to reckon with external economies
and diseconomies in applying our analysis. If, given a uniform
system of accounting, we knew which firms had external economies
and diseconomies, we could ensure that production would be
increased by making marginal factor substitutabilities equal, for,
if they were unequal for two firms which had external diseconomies
of production, then, at the same time as we made them equal, we
could withdraw factors of production, so that only the products of
other firms with no external diseconomies of either production or

---

[1] We must choose the right 'individuals' and 'goods', because, as we have seen
(p. 132), both individuals and goods may give rise to external diseconomies of
consumption.

consumption would actually be increased. But how are we to estimate these external effects? Given a 'superman' who could fill these otherwise empty boxes,[1] and set values on the external economies and diseconomies, then, and only then, could we say that putting the above 'optimum' condition into operation, even given that the distribution of real income is not unfavourably affected, would increase economic welfare. Without such a series of *ad hoc* valuations, we can only know that, if the above condition is not satisfied, then it must be possible to increase economic welfare, but we cannot be sure that putting the condition into operation will not actually make matters worse. In other words, such external economies and diseconomies of production and consumption are irrelevant to the deduction of this condition as a *necessary* condition of 'maximum welfare'. But necessary conditions are not very interesting. It is *sufficient* conditions for improvements that we really want; and those external economies and diseconomies, which may attach either to the production or the consumption of a particular good, prevent us deducing the present condition as sufficient for an increase in economic welfare. They must therefore be assumed to be absent.

There is another kind of external economy and diseconomy which we must notice. It is possible that the production of some 'good' could be increased without there being less of any other 'good', and still it might not be possible to increase general welfare, if the firm whose production was increased also produced 'nuisances' which were not counted in the analysis. Formally, one can get round this difficulty by postulating that the concept 'good' covers everything produced. But, again, in practice, we cannot rely on ideal accounting, and anyway 'nuisances' are not normally objects of individual consumption, for, if they were, they would be charged to the firm; therefore they cannot be very well fitted into the behaviour-line analysis. The traditional examples of these 'nuisances' are smoke, noise, and smells. Uncharged-for benefits may also occur, but are not so obvious. One might suggest those entertaining advertisements which at least do something to offset the ugly ones. It is clear that these effects help to destroy the precision of our analysis. Ideally we require that they should all be valued, and charged to the firms.

Ignoring the external effects mentioned above, we may ask in

[1] Cf. J. H. Clapham, 'On Empty Economic Boxes', *E.J.* (1922).

what circumstances the present 'optimum' condition would be fulfilled. If a producer can exchange one inanimate factor for another at a fixed price, which he cannot influence, then, if he is to produce any given output at the minimum possible cost, he must make the marginal substitutabilities of the factors equal to their relative prices. Therefore, if each producer has to pay the same relative prices for factors, then the 'optimum' condition is fulfilled. This marginal analysis can only be applied to divisible factors of production, and obviously can never be precisely fulfilled in a world in which demand, technique, and factor prices may be all changing. One can say, however, that, in order to give producers the best chance of getting as near to this static ideal as ignorance of the future permits (or makes desirable), one ought to see that every producer is faced with the same relative factor prices.

To include animate factors in this condition would be to demand that, for instance, a man and a machine should be paid the same relative wages on a farm, and in a coal-mine. Since we have excluded this, a valuation must be put on the relative diswelfare of work under various conditions. We have already seen that this valuation cannot be very plausibly extracted from a behaviour-line analysis of free choices on the part of actual individuals. Nevertheless, our 'superman' may want us to take 'individual preferences' into account in some sense. How could we best interpret this requirement?

We might take relative wages, as determined by collective bargaining. But 'superman' might want us to try to get nearer to real individuals' preferences than that. One possibility would be to set relative wages at the point at which there is no tendency for either line of production to grow at the expense of the other. But should we take the short or the long run? There are large costs involved in labour movement in the short run which are avoided in the long run through expansion by juvenile intake, and contraction by retirement; the long run avoids the actual movement of individuals. It would appear, then, that we should take the short run if we want to get as close to actual individuals' preferences as possible. But, then, these would only be the preferences of the marginal men, and would take into account movement costs, which should presumably be excluded when we are simply considering the relative disutilities of the two jobs. There is no reason to suppose that they are representative of the relative preferences of intra-marginal men. In fact, these, if human nature does not change very much, are much more likely to be represented by the wage-rate which would result in an absence of long-run labour movements.

The alternative is, of course, that 'superman' would cut through these difficulties by setting his own valuation on the relative real costs of different occupations. In any case, we must suppose that this question is settled in the best way. Then the relative prices between men and other factors are determined for each industry, and each producer ought to bring, as before, these relative prices into line with his iso-product curves.

It may be noticed that the present 'optimum' condition is the only one of the 'optimum' conditions in which the word 'optimum' need not refer to welfare. If this condition is not fulfilled for all factors of production, including workers, then *production* could, in theory, be increased. The production of the whole economy consists of a heterogeneous collection of things and services. One such heterogeneous collection can be strictly said to be greater than another only if there is more of at least one kind of thing, and no less of any kind. Thus, we can say that production could be increased, without any increase in resources, or in the number of hours worked, if the 'optimum' condition is not fulfilled for all factors of production (we ignore the production of nuisances). We should, however, avoid saying that production is inefficient if the above condition is not fulfilled, even for non-human factors. To say 'production is inefficient' strongly implies that it would be a good thing if production were made efficient. This is not necessarily the case. To make this condition operative would not necessarily be an improvement, because a higher level of production (even with no change in the amount or kind of work done by any worker) may entail less welfare. To sum up, as with the 'optimum' exchange conditions, the present condition is a necessary condition of 'maximum welfare', but it is only a sufficient condition for an improvement if (a) the 'optimum' exchange conditions 1 (a), 1 (b), 1 (c), are not disturbed, (b) if the distribution of real income condition is not adversely affected, (c) if there are no external diseconomies of production, and (d) if there are no external diseconomies of consumption (of the kind which attaches to the consumption of a particular product). We come now to the second of the 'optimum' production conditions.

II (b) *The marginal rate at which one 'good' can be transformed into another must be equal to the 'individuals'' common marginal rate of substitution of one for the other.*

This condition can, again, be illustrated by reference to Fig. IX if we reinterpret it. The line QQ must now be thought of as the locus of all those collections of the two 'goods' X and Y which, with a given set of 'factors', could just be produced if the 'factors' were always combined in the production of both X and Y according to the 'optimum' condition II (a) above. This line is usually known as a transformation curve. Its concavity towards the origin A implies a diminishing rate of transformation of one 'good' into the other. The line PP now stands for one of the behaviour lines of any one of the 'individuals' who consumes both X and Y. (If the 'optimum' exchange conditions are satisfied, then the slope of the behaviour line at the point E must, since E is supposed to be a point of equilibrium, be the same for all 'individuals'.) It can now be seen by inspection that, if the slope of the transformation curve is not equal to the slope of the behaviour line, then the relative production of X and Y could be altered in such a way as to enable A, and all other 'individuals', to reach higher behaviour lines.[1]

The above 'optimum' condition is not valid as a sufficient condition for an increase in welfare unless all the exchange conditions, and the production condition II (a), are also satisfied (or unless some other value judgements have been introduced to take the place of 'individual preferences' as a value criterion). These other 'optimum' conditions are necessary conditions of the 'optimum' on their own account, but require that distribution is not thereby made worse if it is to be sufficient for an increase in economic welfare to put them into operation. The present 'optimum' condition requires, however, that all the preceding 'optimum' conditions should already be satisfied if it is to be necessarily a good thing to put it into operation.[2] It is therefore more shaky than any of the others. The difficulties engendered by external economies and diseconomies are also present, but in a more acute form. The previous

---

[1] The modifications required if individuals' equilibrium positions are boundary ones, or if behaviour lines are kinked at the equilibrium point, are explained in Appendix III.

[2] But it requires more than this: it cannot really be considered as a separable sufficient condition from the next condition to be discussed, II (c). Neither of the two taken alone can be regarded as a sufficient condition even if all the remainder are satisfied. This is shown to be the case on page 163.

'optimum' condition of production was a necessary condition for an 'optimum', even if external diseconomies were present. These external effects only came in when we were considering whether it would be a good thing to put the condition into operation. In the present case, however, the presence of external production and consumption effects, or nuisances, means that this condition would not even be a necessary condition for an 'optimum' at all. It would, then, at best be an approximation to such a condition.

The problem of the valuation of labour also becomes more serious. Let us suppose that the fulfilment of this 'optimum' requires firm A to expand at the expense of firm B, which expansion necessitates the movement of labour, if the optimum condition II (a) is to remain undisturbed. Suppose that the value judgement is given that wages should be determined in accordance with workers' preferences, and that our best interpretation of this rather vague judgement is that relative wages ought to be such as to result in a long-run equilibrium in the supply of labour to different firms. It follows that labour would not be induced to move in the short run. The fulfilment of the present 'optimum' would, then, be impossible in the short run. But, if the wage-rate was allowed to rise in the short run, that would mean revising our previous decision. If wages are such as to induce the marginal worker to move in the short run, then they are not in accordance with the average worker's preferences. (We may add that, if wages are allowed to rise in the short run, then 'price everywhere in the same proportion to marginal cost' does not fulfil the present 'optimum' condition—see below.) Perhaps the best way of preserving this 'optimum', and keeping in line with individual preferences would be to pay the marginal workers a lump sum in order to induce them to shift, not charging this to the expanding firm, and keeping wages in line with the long-run equilibrium relative wage (if that could be discovered). But the truth of the matter is that the instruction, to take individual preferences into account, cannot be at all precisely interpreted in the matter of the supply of labour.

Assuming that all previous 'optimum' conditions are satisfied, we may now ask in what circumstances the present 'optimum' would be fulfilled. The usual answer is that it is satisfied if marginal costs are everywhere proportional to prices. This follows only if the ratio of marginal costs is equal to the rate of transformation. Rents which might accrue to the factors as a result of the transformation should be excluded. Suppose that wages rise in the expanding industry as the transformation is made. If relative wages were in line with individual preferences before, they can no longer reflect individual preferences for the intra-marginal men, who must now earn rents. Since we have decided that it is relative individual preferences which are relevant to transformation rates, these rents should be excluded. If wages rise in the expanding industry, and marginal costs include only wages, then marginal cost will equal marginal wage-cost, and not the cost of the marginal men. In these circumstances equiproportionality of marginal cost and price is not a correct deduction from the above 'optimum' condition. The Lerner 'Rule' may be substituted,[1] i.e. the price of each factor ought to be everywhere in the same proportion (or equal) to the value of its marginal product. Even this will only be correct for labour (in the short run) if it has been decided that the relative wage-rate which will just induce the marginal men to move is what we mean by 'the rate which reflects individual preferences'. We have seen that this is not an altogether plausible interpretation.

We come now to the last 'optimum' production condition, which may be expressed as follows:

II (c) *The rate at which 'work' can be transformed into any given 'good' must equal the marginal 'individual' rate of substitution of 'leisure' for consumption of that 'good'.*

Granted that there are 'individuals' who have this common rate of substitution between some given 'leisure' (corresponding to a given kind of 'work') and the consumption of some given good, then this 'optimum' may also be illustrated by means of Fig. IX, if we again reinterpret it. The line *PP* now maps *A*'s behaviour with respect to some given 'leisure' *X*, and some given 'good' *Y*. *QQ* represents the different additional quantities of *Y* (measured from *A*) which could be produced with varying amounts of 'work' on the part of *A*, combined with given quantities of all the other 'factors'. Thus, at the point *E*, *A* has *AF* hours of leisure and consumes *AG* of *Y*. *AG* is also the additional amount of *Y* produced as a result of *A*'s working for *EH* hours. The concavity, towards the origin *A*, of the work–good transformation line *QQ* implies that *A*'s work is subject to the law of diminishing marginal productivity. It can be seen, by inspection, that if these two rates are not equal,

---

[1] Cf. A. P. Lerner, *Economics of Control*, p. 64.

then *A* or some other individual could reach a higher behaviour line, without anyone else suffering, if the amount of work he did was altered. If, for instance, he worked less, consuming only enough of *Y* to keep him on the same behaviour line *PP*, then an increased amount of *Y* would be available for consumption by other individuals.

The validity of the above condition depends upon the fulfilment of all the 'optimum' conditions of exchange, including the two rather shaky ones associated with the supply of labour. In what circumstances will it be fulfilled? It has to be assumed that the individual makes the rate at which he is willing to substitute leisure for the given good equal to the rate at which it is possible for him to make the substitution, i.e. to the net marginal earnings per unit of time derived from his work, expressed in terms of the given good. Therefore it follows from the 'optimum' condition that the rate at which his work can be transformed into the given good (his marginal physical productivity) should be made equal to his net marginal earnings in terms of that good. In terms of money, his net earnings ought to be equal to the value of his marginal product. From condition II (*b*) it followed that the price of the factor ought to be everywhere in the same proportion to the value of the marginal product. We now see that *if there is no marginal taxation levied on the individual's earnings*, then it follows that, in the case of labour, this proportion ought to be equality.

But it can be shown that if the business man minimizes costs, then marginal cost is equal to the price of each factor divided by its marginal physical productivity.[1] Condition II (*a*) is satisfied by the policy of cost minimization provided that the factors of production are in perfectly elastic supply. It therefore follows, in conditions in which marginal costs ought to be made equiproportionate to price, that this equiproportionality should be unity. In other words, marginal cost should be brought into equality with price. This condition depends upon there being no marginal taxation, so that one can also conclude that no one who works, and can vary the amount of work he does, ought to pay income tax, or any indirect tax (indirect taxation is also, of course, 'ruled out' by the previous 'optimum' condition).

We have already seen that the validity of the 'optimum' condition, from which these conclusions are deduced, depends on the

[1] See P. A. Samuelson, *Foundations of Economic Analysis*, p. 66.

'optimum' conditions of exchange being satisfied. But they also require the satisfaction of the 'optimum' condition of production II (b) (from which we deduce, if the supply of factors is perfectly elastic, that prices should stand everywhere in the same proportion to marginal costs). The 'optimum' condition II (b) itself requires the fulfilment of the optimum production condition II (a). We may conclude that if it is to be proved to be a good thing to make price equal to marginal cost, given the value judgements on which this analysis rests, we require:

1. that *all* the other 'optimum' conditions of production and exchange be satisfied;
2. that factors are in perfectly elastic supply;
3. that there is no income tax, and no indirect taxes or subsidies;
4. that it could be put into effect without adversely affecting the distribution of real income;
5. that there are no external diseconomies of production or consumption.

These are rather formidable requirements.

III. THE 'OPTIMUM' CONDITIONS OF SAVING AND INVESTMENT

Up to this point we have ignored savings and investment. We will now deal with the 'optimum' conditions which may be developed in respect of them. They all follow from the same value premises as those which we have already introduced. We shall first deal with the two 'optimum' savings conditions, which are analogous to the 'optimum' exchange conditions. They are, in fact, exchange conditions, but the 'goods' to be exchanged are peculiar. The first savings 'optimum' condition is as follows:

III (a) *There ought to be the same marginal rate of substitution between money and any given bond or share for every individual who 'consumes' both.*

This is obviously the same as the first exchange condition, except that we here include money and bonds as 'goods'. It is, in theory, satisfied if the prices of shares, bonds, &c., are the same for all individuals.

It is, however, more unlikely that an individual will have a consistent consumption pattern with respect to bonds than with respect to consumption goods, because the expected price of bonds is liable to govern his behaviour to a considerable extent. The fulfilment of this condition is therefore more shaky, as a sufficient condition for an increase in economic welfare, than is the corresponding exchange condition.

The second savings 'optimum' condition may be stated thus:

III (b) *There ought to be the same marginal rate of substitution between money and any given good for all individuals who 'consume' both.*

Whether a man holds money or spends it, is also governed, to a considerable extent, by expected price movements. Exactly the same remarks therefore apply to this condition as applied to III (a) above.

IV. *The rate at which any given present good can be transformed into the same good, at some given future date, ought to be equal to the common marginal rate at which individuals are willing to substitute one for the other.*

In order to arrive at this 'optimum' investment condition, we have to make some assumptions about psychology. The purely behaviouristic analysis so far adopted fails us. We have to assume that, when individuals save, they are, in effect, exchanging present money for future money.[1] It then follows, by definition, that the common marginal rate at which they forgo present in favour of future purchasing power (money in favour of bonds, &c.) is equal to their present *time preference*.[2] If we assume that there is no taxation on savings (i.e. no income tax), then this is also, by the definition of behaviour lines, necessarily equal to the rate of interest. Next we must assume that all individuals have the same expectations as to the future price movements of every good which they expect to buy. Then, if we know this expected price change of any given good, we know every individual's time preference with

[1] But it must also be assumed (unrealistically) that would-be dissavers can freely exchange future money for present money by borrowing.

[2] I here use 'time preference' to express the rate at which an individual is willing to exchange money now for money at some given future date. This is not the usual sense, which is the rate at which an individual would be willing to exchange money now for money at some given future date *if he expected that the marginal utility of money would be the same for him at both dates.* No doubt time preference in this latter sense may play some part in determining the rate of interest—but it does not seem possible to discover very easily what anyone's time preference is in this sense. It is, perhaps, not a very useful concept, and I have therefore borrowed the expression to describe something different.

respect to that good (i.e. that particular expected commodity-rate of interest) for every future period. We know, for instance, that every individual would be willing to exchange one watch now for two next year, eight the next, or whatever it is.

Given similar assumptions to those made under II (b) and II (c) above, it follows that the discounted expected value of the marginal product of an investment good ought to equal the present price of that good, on the further assumption that producers have the same price expectations as consumers. Similarly, it follows that investment for the future production of a good ought to be carried to the point at which the discounted expected marginal cost is equal to the discounted expected price. It is obvious, however, that this is even more shaky than the condition that output ought to be adjusted until present marginal cost is equal to the present price. It assumes everything the latter assumes, and much more besides. If individuals are mistaken about future prices, which they will be if they do not correctly foresee distributional and technological changes, then the condition is upset. It can, of course, be argued that ignorance of the future is inevitable, and will constitute a difficulty whatever investment principles one adopts. But, on the other hand, it may be argued that individuals are not the best judges of what the future will hold.

There are further difficulties. The present 'optimum' is derived by including money and bonds in the behaviour-line analysis, which makes that analysis even more dubious than otherwise. We also had to assume that individuals save in order to spend in the future. But, to a certain extent, it is true that savings have an intangible yield in the shape of imagined security. It is also not the case that people save mainly to spend themselves. They save (or used to save) largely for their legatees, whose preferences may be quite different to their own. We also have to assume that all individuals expect the same price changes, which is very unrealistic. When risk enters in, we have to assume that investors and speculators are the best judges of the riskiness of different shares. This assumption may also be considered dubious. Moreover, the interpretation of 'individual preferences' itself becomes rather difficult when we consider that almost all private saving is now done by corporations. Perhaps this should be prohibited? Finally, these difficulties are in addition to the formidable ones which arise in connexion with the 'optimum' production conditions.

Given the 'optimum' savings and investment conditions, it follows that, when there is full employment, we should not interfere with the supply of money in such a way as to influence the rate of interest. Full employment of all inanimate factors[1] is, of course, prescribed by the value premises which we have introduced. It has, however, been thought by some writers that determination of the rate of interest by individual preferences may be inconsistent with the maintenance of full employment. It has been said that the decision as to what the rate of interest ought to be is 'unavoidably political'[2] (which, on our formulation, means that another value judgement must be introduced). Recently, however, it has been shown that full employment is not theoretically inconsistent with the determination of the rate of interest by individual preferences.[3] Once given full employment, it may be preserved by ensuring that planned savings are equal to the supply of loans. This could be done (in an ideal system) by ensuring that the rate of interest rises or falls far enough to cause a variation in investment sufficient to offset any change in planned savings.

A decline in spending may, for instance, be taken as a sign that time preference has shifted in favour of the future. If there is no effect on the rate of interest, because of an increase of hoarding, this does not mean that it can no longer be maintained that every individual makes his time preference equal to the rate of interest. It is, in fact, this adjustment which causes the decline in present spending. It does mean, however, that we can no longer say that time preference is, by the defined method of constructing behaviour maps, *necessarily* equal to the rate of interest. We must here introduce a psychological explanation of behaviour if we wish to say that the decline in spending is caused by an increased preference for future goods, and to say that the supply of loans ought to be kept equal to planned savings. This is because we are here dealing with a shift in behaviour lines, and, as we maintained in Chapter II, it is only when we have to consider shifts in behaviour patterns that psychological explanations enter into economics.

Suppose, however, that we are not at a position of full employment. Would it interfere with individual time preferences if, say, the government borrowed from the banks and spent the money on

---

[1] The employment of human factors is determined by condition 1 (*b*).
[2] Cf. A. Lerner, *Economics of Control*, p. 262.
[3] F. J. Atkinson, 'Saving and Investment in a Socialist State', *R.E.S.* (1947–8).

providing free consumption goods? Would this be 'forced' consumption? Alternatively, if the government spent the money on
public works, would this be 'forced' saving? The answer is clearly
'No'. It cannot be said that such action would be interfering with
individual preferences as to how the production of the economy
should be divided between investment goods and consumption
goods, because, at best, it is only true that the interaction of individual preferences can determine such an 'ideal' division for a
given level of production. Thus 'forced' saving or consumption
can only occur when there is inflation. If people continue to try to
spend more than the value, in a preceding period, of the national
output of consumption goods, then the only thing which prevents
a runaway inflation is 'forced' or unintended saving on the part of
individuals. Suppose, then, that the government decides to increase
investment when there is already full employment. This must be
financed by unintended savings, or preferably by non-marginal
taxation (preferably because unintended saving implies a hap-
hazard redistribution of real income which may very well be dis-
approved of). Should we now say that individual preferences as to
the correct amount of investment have been interfered with? The
answer is, in theory, 'Yes'. The 'optimum' conditions of production, and investment, together, in theory, determine the 'optimum'
amount of every good to be produced, both now and at every
future date. Thus, to stimulate the production of future goods
(given full employment) by lowering the rate of interest, or in any
other way, is, in theory, to interfere with the 'optimum' conditions
in just the same way as subsidizing the production of a present good
out of taxation (even non-marginal taxation) is interfering with the
'optimum' conditions. We must remember, however, that the
concept of an 'optimum' rate of interest depends on the validity
of the optimum savings and investment conditions above; and we
have seen reason to believe that they can only be deduced from the
value premises we have postulated by making a number of most
unrealistic assumptions.

To conclude this chapter, it may be worth noticing that some of
these 'optimum' conditions can be deduced from quite different
value premises to those which we have postulated. The ones which
we postulated were used for various reasons: (a) because they alone
suffice to deduce all the 'optimum' conditions developed above,
and (b) because all the above conditions are more or less tradi-

tional in economic theory, and therefore we can say that the value postulates we have made are implicit in much economic theory, and finally (c) because we think that they would be generally acceptable in any liberal society. This is not, of course, to say that the system which has been somewhat precariously based on them would be acceptable. That is very much more doubtful.

Let us, then, briefly consider some other set of value premises, as follows:

> The relative value of different products is to be determined by some schedule drawn up by the government. Welfare is maximized when the value of the national output, thus determined, is greatest.

What 'optimum' conditions can we now develop? It is clear that all the exchange conditions vanish, as well as the 'ideal' income distribution condition, unless we find that income distribution and exchange conditions affect the value of the national output by causing people to vary the intensity of their work. If such variations could not be overcome by force, it would be a matter of empirical investigation to find out which method of allocation and distribution was best, from the point of view of maximizing the value of the output, according to the fixed value coefficients. If organization was not valued as an end in itself, i.e. was not accounted part of the product, the price mechanism might be left in being as requiring least organization. The 'optimum' production condition II (a) would remain, and be applied to all factors. This would require the direction of labour. Men would be required to work until their marginal productivity fell to zero. Whether this would be short- or long-run marginal productivity would depend on the relative scheduled values of products over time. Real wages would depend on the relative valuation given to the various wage-goods, which would, presumably, be such that workers did not starve, but which would otherwise depend on governmental decision. The 'optimum' production condition II (b) would remain, with the difference that the marginal rate of transformation must now equal the relative scheduled values; but it would still be subject to the difficulty of external economies and diseconomies of production. The savings conditions would likewise vanish. The investment condition IV would remain, but with the difference that the government's relative scheduled values for future products over present products would determine each commodity-rate of interest, and replace the precarious combination of expected price movement plus rate of interest, which determined the expected commodity-rate of interest in the first system discussed.

The 'optimum' conditions which remain, II (*a*), II (*b*) modified, and IV modified, rest, however, on a very much more secure basis than do the corresponding conditions in the previous system; because we no longer rely on a behaviour-line analysis, with all the doubt about whether it applies to real individuals; because we no longer have to wonder how the word 'individual' can be interpreted in some of the conditions; because we have postulated that the distribution of real income is irrelevant.

Welfare economics may thus be fairly simple in a collectivist state. Its conclusions could be applied with some degree of confidence. But, of course, many people will want to say that it is quite ridiculous to maintain that the brief sketch made above has anything to do with welfare economics. I would agree. But, in saying that, I doubt we would be saying anything more than that we do not find its value premises acceptable. To call such a sketch a sketch of welfare economics might not be a misnomer. But it would definitely be persuasive naming.

CHAPTER IX

THE 'OPTIMUM' CONDITIONS OF PRODUCTION AND EXCHANGE (2)

IN the last chapter it was shown that the 'optimum' conditions rest with varying degrees of plausibility on 'individual preferences'. We also showed, for each 'optimum' condition, what prior conditions require to be satisfied if it is to be a good thing to put it into operation. The circumstances under which each 'optimum' condition would be fulfilled in the real world were also stated. Whether or not it would be a good thing to reproduce these circumstances is a question the answer to which depends partly on the plausibility of the theoretical deductions, but also on wider considerations which must now be discussed.

Let us begin with the 'optimum' condition of exchange I (*a*), from which it was deduced that all individuals should be faced with the same set of prices, and be free to choose. It is clear that this precludes rationing, which is the most important way in which this condition is upset in the modern world. Rationing is introduced when the price of certain necessities and semi-necessities would otherwise rise so much that there would be a considerable redistribution of real income. Thus it is tempting to say that rationing is only necessary because the distribution of real income is not 'ideal'. This is, however, only true if the 'ideal' distribution of income is held to be represented by an equal distribution of money—and probably no one in the world who is in a position of responsibility holds that. But if some other distribution of money is 'ideal', then a rise in the price of necessities (necessities are, roughly speaking, all goods regularly consumed by the poorest section of the community) must always result in a shift of real income away from those with lower money-incomes. Now rationing would fall under case 6 of Table II, and therefore it would be correct, according to the theory, not to introduce it, but rather to redistribute income by taxation. This would, however, upset another 'optimum' condition. Therefore what is required is to redistribute income by non-marginal taxation. Quite apart from the fact that such taxation would upset people's ideas of equity very much more than rationing, this is not a practical suggestion. Redistribution by capital taxation is a slow and cumbersome process. In the meantime, the rise in the cost of living for the working classes might provoke a wage inflation, which would itself cause a shift in the distribution of real income which might well be regarded as undesirable. Here, the chief reason why welfare theory fails us is that it is static, and pays no attention to the time-lags which occur in the real world.

Quite apart from the question of inflation, there is wide agreement that rationing is the right policy when important shortages occur. This seems to show that real income distribution effects would generally be held to be of considerably greater importance than the fulfilment or non-fulfilment of the theoretical 'optimum', supported as the latter is, in this case, by a wide belief in the intrinsic value of freedom of choice. Yet this particular 'optimum' condition is the most securely based of them all, since (a) it does not depend on the fulfilment of any of the other 'optima', and (b) because we can here deal with a very short period, since we can abstract from production changes, whence the application of the phrase 'economic man' presents least difficulty. There is no reason to suppose that rationing would not sometimes be the best policy in a fully socialized but individualistic economy. Finally, where such shortages do not occur, and with reference to things and individuals for which and whom freedom of choice is commonly regarded as good (e.g. excluding children and lunatics on the one hand, and such things as dangerous drugs on the other), then there is no disagreement about whether this condition ought to be satisfied or not.

We have already seen that the two remaining 'optimum' conditions of exchange (1 (b) and 1 (c)) are much less securely based. The balancing of work against leisure, and of one job against another, cannot, in any normal system, be very plausibly made the subject of a marginal analysis of the free choices of actual individuals. Nor can we simply say that the system ought to be altered to make the reign of individual preferences more secure in this field, because individual workers are far from being independent, and therefore changes in the amount and kind of work done by one worker are liable to have considerable diseconomies of production. To put it in another way, variations in the amount and kind of work that Smith does cannot necessarily be made a matter of indifference to Jones. With regard to these two conditions, it is clear from what was said in the last chapter that 'individual' can only be reasonably interpreted to apply to average individuals, taken over a fairly long period of time. This is not, of course, to say that actual individuals ought to be made to shift their jobs, if so required. That question clearly cannot be considered in the light of economics alone; we can only say that, given our value judgements, it must decrease the economic welfare of a particular individual if we force him to work where he does not want to, or if we give him an all-or-nothing choice as to the amount of work he does. The balancing of the claims of free choice for actual workers against the advantages of increased production is a matter towards the decision of which the static theory of welfare seems to give us little help. The 'optimum' conditions under discussion are formally independent of the 'optimum' production conditions, but it seems clear that, in practice, any attempt to increase the degree of their realization would not necessarily result in an improved state of affairs.

It seems remarkable that economic welfare arguments have not been pressed against such movements as the 'closed shop' when marginal-cost pricing in public utilities, the arguments for which depend, among many other things, on the realization of these conditions, has been suggested. This is not to say that economic welfare arguments can be plausibly used in this connexion. Decisions on such questions, where it might at first sight be thought that the theory of economic welfare would have something to say, are liable to be influenced by important ethical considerations, which are independent of economic welfare, and which dwarf into insignificance the rather shaky deductions which the latter theory offers for our guidance. That this is so does not seem to be merely an accident of the system, or the time. It arises from the fact that (a) the phrase 'individual preferences' cannot be very clearly or precisely interpreted, and because (b) work gives rise to external economies and diseconomies.

Thus there is no reason to suppose that an absolutist government, which accepted an individualistic 'welfare function', would be right, according to its own lights, if it attempted to increase the freedom of choice of workers; nor is there any reason to suppose that such a government would actually try to do this. There is no clear-cut line of division on this point between utopians and the rest.

We come now to the first production condition II (a), which implies that different firms ought to be free to buy material factors of production at the same price, and human factors at price differentials depending on relative individual preferences for the different jobs. As far as the material factors are concerned, to put this condition into operation is a sufficient condition for an increase in welfare if any redistribution of income is not unfavourable. Probably discrimination between firms in the matter of supply of raw materials and power is not very common, except as the result of governmental control. Nor is it very likely that there would be a significant redistributional effect consequent on putting the condition into operation where it does not already hold. It thus appears to be one of the best cases for applying our criterion that we are likely to find. The condition is, in normal times, probably the least controversial of all. It is widely accepted that discrimination in the supply of factors to firms is a bad thing,[1] and any discriminating monopolistic supplier of a factor would probably get little sympathy if he were harmed as a result of putting the present condition into operation.

We have also noticed that this 'optimum' condition is strictly only a sufficient condition for an improvement if there are no external economies and diseconomies. The best method of dealing with these external effects is agreed. They ought, if possible, to be charged to firms, or, if the external effect is a 'nuisance' which could be easily avoided, controlling legislation may be more appropriate. In either case there is little point in discussing how much confidence we would have that, as the result, the gainers could overcompensate the losers, because the answer would depend entirely on the particular case and the magnitude of the external effects, and because this is not a controversial matter. As far as the human factors of production are concerned, the condition implies that firms ought to be free to employ what labour they want at the prevailing market price of labour. Again, in normal times, this condition is not controversial.

But, in abnormal times, as, for instance, when a country is suffering from an adverse balance of foreign trade, a choice of evils may have to be made. Both financial and physical controls, designed to correct the adverse balance, may, if they are to be

[1] This wide acceptance is, however, almost certainly based on the belief that such discrimination is unfair, rather than on considerations of (static) welfare theory.

effective, imply that one or other of the 'optimum' conditions must
be broken. Thus we may, for instance, be faced with a choice
between deflation and physical controls as means of shifting factors of production from home to export industries. The former
method is liable to result in unemployment, and the latter may
result in an infringement of several of the 'optimum' conditions,
including the present one. Controls on either materials or labour
alone will tend to upset the 'optimum' factor proportions. The
preservation of 'optimum' proportions may then well be impossible
without control of labour. We have already seen the difficulties
which arise in trying to reconcile a rapid shift of labour in the short
run with the preservation of relative wage-rates determined by
individual preferences.

The upshot is that welfare theory does not assist us materially
in deciding what is the best way of resolving 'abnormal' difficulties.
And 'abnormalities' are, perhaps, not so very uncommon. On the
other hand, when there is no particular pressing reason for upsetting the 'optimum' factor use condition, then whether it should
or should not be fulfilled is not a point at issue.

The next 'optimum' condition, II (b), requires that output
should always be adjusted, given a perfectly elastic supply of
factors, until price is everywhere in the same proportion to marginal cost. We can best deal with this condition in conjunction
with the final production condition, II (c), which requires that
human factors (and all other factors which are also consumption
goods) should be paid, given that there is no marginal taxation, the
value of their marginal products. Together, the two conditions
require that output should always be adjusted until, if possible,
price is equal to marginal cost.

Let us first be clear what 'marginal cost' means in this connexion. It has been suggested that 'marginal cost' is vague. There
are short-run and long-run marginal costs. In fact, there may be a
different marginal cost for every different length of time which we
may choose to allow for the marginal adjustment of output to be
made. To which marginal cost ought price to be equated? The
ambiguity of 'marginal cost' has allowed some writers to suppose
that the theory says that price ought to be equated to long-run
marginal cost. But it might be argued that all costs are marginal
in the end, so that marginal cost pricing and average cost pricing
are one and the same thing.

The above suggestion is, of course, fallacious. First, the theory does not claim that price ought always to be equal to marginal cost. It maintains that output ought always, if possible, to be adjusted until price is equal to marginal cost. One of the two points of so adjusting output is that the rate of transformation between any two goods ought always to be made, if possible, equal to the individuals' common marginal rate of substitution between the two. Thus, take the case of a bridge for which the marginal cost of a crossing is zero, i.e. a crossing cannot be transformed into anything else, because it uses up no factors of production. Therefore the output of crossings ought to be expanded until the price is zero. But, suppose that the bridge reaches full capacity at some positive price. Then, if price was lowered to zero, queues would form to cross the bridge. Demand would then be greater than supply, and the first exchange condition would not be satisfied. The 'optimum' pricing policy is always such as to equate supply and demand.

Thus output ought, if possible, to be adjusted until marginal cost equals price. Let us now suppose that short- and long-run marginal costs diverge. Ought output to be adjusted until short-run marginal cost or long-run marginal cost equals price? The theoretical answer is that output ought, in the short run, to be adjusted until short-run marginal cost equals price, and it ought, in the long run, to be adjusted until long-run marginal cost equals price. Once having reached the long-run position, i.e. once the supposedly 'optimum' plant is laid down, then, whatever happens to price, the short-run output with this plant ought theoretically to be adjusted so that short-run marginal cost equals price. The equality of both short-run and long-run marginal cost with price may, of course, be impossible. This does not matter. At any given moment, it is theoretically correct that short-run marginal cost should, if possible, be made equal to price. It may happen that such an output policy will prevent the firm earning enough to be able to make, without assistance, the long-run adjustment required of it. There is no logical difficulty here, since the firm can be subsidized.

Before we discuss the theoretical validity of this output criterion, there is one more possible source of confusion with which we must deal. What is the unit of output with which we are dealing when we speak of marginal cost? Are we, for instance, to take a passenger train or a passenger's seat on the train as the unit? The answer to this depends entirely on the nature of the 'individuals' with which we are concerned. To see this, we have only to remember that the rate at which one product can be transformed into another is, theoretically, to be made equal to the 'individual's' rate of substitution between the two. Thus, in the case of the train, if the 'individual' is to be interpreted as the ordinary single passenger, then we are concerned with the marginal cost of carrying an extra passenger. This may be taken as being approximately equal to zero. In other words, a particular individual railway journey cannot be transformed into anything else. It follows that price should be lowered until either the train is full, or price is zero.

On the other hand, an 'individual' may be differently interpreted. If a school decides to hire a train for an outing, we must treat the school as a collective, and the train should be run only if the school pays the whole cost of running it. Normally, of course, it would not be plausible to treat the collection of people who happened to be assembled on a certain train as a collective. Nor would it, for instance, be plausible to treat all users of a certain park as a collective. The theory requires that no charge, or next to no charge, should be made for the use of most of these objects, parks, trains, &c., which are too big to be consumed by one person.

Let us now consider the conditions under which an output policy based on marginal costs would be valid. We saw in the last chapter that all the 'optimum' conditions of exchange, and the production conditions II (a) and II (b), would first require to be satisfied. Quite apart from the difficulties involved in supposing that individuals are perfectly consistent, we have in this chapter seen reason to believe that none of the conditions of exchange (except perhaps I (a) in 'normal' times) is likely to be very closely satisfied. This goes for a utopian society, set up with the 'optimum' conditions as its Bible, as much as for a society which knows no economic theory. The same is true, except when times are 'normal', for the production condition II (a). In the last chapter we saw that production condition II (b) is particularly shaky. We have to presuppose that actual individuals are free to choose the amount and kind of work they do, and that these can be varied at the margin. But this condition also requires that there be no taxation on the margin of effort, because, if there is such taxation, then the rate at which the individual is willing to exchange work for leisure will not be equal to the rate at which such exchange results in greater production. This question of taxation must be examined at greater length.

It is evident that the 'optimum' conditions rule out both direct and indirect taxation. If there is direct taxation, then a worker will, if he behaves as an economic man, equate his marginal net earnings to the rate at which he is willing to substitute leisure for work. In which case his *net* earnings ought to equal the value of his marginal product. If price equals marginal cost, his net earnings will be less than this. But indirect taxation affects a man's net earnings in real terms in just the same way. Each man is assumed to bring his rate of substitution of leisure for work into line with the rate at which supplying more work enables him to consume more of the good he helps to produce. If this good is taxed, then this latter rate must be less than his marginal physical productivity. If it is some other good that is taxed, we have the same effect, because the purchasing power of the good he helps to produce in terms of the taxed good is reduced. Therefore the only permissible tax is a poll tax. It follows at once that the condition that marginal cost equals price is invalid in a country such as England, where marginal rates of taxation are far from negligible.

It may, however, be argued that there is no reason why, in a properly designed society, there should be any marginal taxation. This is a very dubious argument. In such a society some 'ideal' distribution of real income must be preserved. At the same time, everyone's net earnings must equal the value of their marginal product. But there is no reason to suppose that there would be anything 'ideal' about a distribution in which people received the value of their marginal products. The higher earners might still be considered to be too rich. If so, some of their real income must be removed by a poll tax. But to preserve the 'ideal', this so-called poll tax would have to vary with income earned. In which case it would not, of course, be a poll tax, and would offend against the 'optimum' conditions! It follows that the economic Utopia presupposes that it is considered that the 'ideal' distribution of real income is determined by marginal productivities.

The above is not the only difficulty. It is also exceedingly difficult to imagine a modern society where there would be no taxation, and where everyone was paid the value of their marginal products. Rents, where they could be collected, must cover all government expenditure, the 'ideal' living standards of all those who do not work, and, perhaps, a budget surplus as well. There is a tendency to think that a social dividend, rather than taxation, would be the order of the day. This appears to be optimistic when we remember that many firms would be operated at a loss. Indeed, when we bring in dynamic elements and allow for the possibility of change, it is evident that a society which called itself 'ideal' would have to allow for a considerable degree of flexibility. Flexibility implies surplus capacity, and surplus capacity implies that marginal costs are less than average costs. Perhaps, then, all firms would be operated at a loss, in which case taxation might have to be very high. I think we can reasonably conclude that an ideal society must have taxation. But only a poll tax is permissible. Is there any reason why poll taxation should not be used? It seems quite obvious that it would be impossible to assess individuals' liability to such a tax in a manner which would be considered reasonable and fair. It would inevitably give rise to such grave injustices that it would be considered intolerable. Furthermore, the maintenance of full employment requires a very flexible tax system which can operate with rapidity, and a system of poll taxes would be very inflexible. It seems a trifle absurd to consider such a tax, the impracticability of which scarcely needs pointing out. We consider it only because some welfare economists have gaily bandied about the idea of 'lump-sum payments'.[1] It is abundantly clear that lump-sum confiscations and compensations cannot become a matter of routine policy. They can be used only occasionally, when exceptional changes are made.

We can thus conclude that it is impossible to envisage a society in which all the 'optimum' conditions, presupposed by the idea that price ought to equal marginal cost, are fulfilled. If for no other reason, the inevitable presence of marginal taxation would require that price be somewhat lower than marginal cost. Furthermore, the 'optimum' condition II (b) would require that the extent to which marginal cost was greater than price would depend on the capital : labour ratio. In which case, the 'optimum' condition which

[1] The significance of the payments being 'lump-sum' is that they must be uncorrelated with any economic category, correlation with which would upset the 'optimum' conditions. Even capital taxation, unless it is each time believed to be 'once and for all', is ruled out, because it would affect people's behaviour in respect of both saving and working. It would, in Professor Pigou's terminology, have 'announcement' effects.

lays it down that prices ought to be at least proportional to marginal costs could not be fulfilled. These conditions might thus, in practice, be inconsistent. Furthermore, the lower prices are made, in the endeavour to attain the 'ideal' output, the greater taxation may have to be.

There seems to be some evidence for the view that, over a wide field of manufacturing industry, marginal costs are fairly constant until absolute full capacity is reached. But absolute full capacity can surely only be an 'ideal' on paper. If output falls only a little short of full capacity, average cost may be considerably higher than marginal cost. Thus, the fact that price (if equal to average cost) may be considerably greater than marginal cost cannot be taken to be an indication that output is considerably below the so-called 'optimum'. This sort of consideration leads us into the theory of monopoly and monopolistic competition, the discussion of which we must defer to a later chapter.

We may sum up the present discussion by asking (as we have asked for the other 'optimum' conditions) what is required for it to be sufficient for an improvement in welfare always to adjust output wherever and whenever possible until price is equal to marginal cost. Formally the answer is that it can be proved to be sufficient only if all the 'optimum' conditions are put into operation at once, and if the resultant redistribution of income is considered to be not unfavourable, and if all external effects are absent. But we have seen that it is manifestly impossible to put all the conditions into operation. Indeed, with regard to all the 'optimum' conditions, except II (b), we have shown that there is no very good reason to suppose that a government determined to 'improve economic welfare', according to our criteria, would be justified in trying to see that they were at all closely satisfied. It therefore becomes highly unlikely that economists would be justified in informing such a government that output ought always to be adjusted until marginal cost was equal to price. They surely could not have any very great confidence in believing that, as a result, the gainers would be able to overcompensate the losers.

How can one begin to estimate the extent of the conceivable gains, even on the impossible assumption that all the other conditions were satisfied? There is clearly no way of measuring such potential gains. All that one could do would be to give the reader some rough idea of the adjustments in output that would result.

Presumably the output of some public utilities would be rather greater. The output of those industries where competition was 'purest' would be reduced, notably agriculture and other primary products. There might be certain adjustments within manufacturing industry. The size of such adjustments could not be estimated without large-scale research into costs. My guess is that it would be rare for the resultant adjustment to be more than a very small percentage of total output. Against the gains, which the reader may think could conceivably result, must be set (a) the fact that some of the presupposed 'optimum' conditions are rather meaningless, since the behaviour-line analysis applies, at best, only very roughly; (b) the fact that it would seldom be at all clear that, according to our criteria, they ought to be satisfied, even if they could be.

In order to make price everywhere equal to marginal cost we would also need to alter the whole order of society. The whole of manufacturing industry would have to be socialized, since pure competition does not exist within this sphere. If this has to be done, then it is clear that dynamic arguments, taking into account the possible improvement or deterioration in such things as industrial relations, and managerial ability and zeal, and the effects on inventions and techniques, are vastly more important than the static arguments of economic welfare theory. Also, it is clear that the political and social changes, which would be involved, might have effects on welfare, for good or ill, which would dwarf the comparatively minor adjustments of output into utter insignificance.

If the idea of making marginal cost everywhere equal to price is abandoned, the question arises as to whether a more easily achieved part fulfilment of the 'optimum' conditions would not be a good thing. The thesis that it would be was advanced by Professor R. F. Kahn in his article 'Some Notes on Ideal Output'.[1] The idea is, essentially, to equalize marginal rates of transformation and substitution by getting prices everywhere in the same proportion to marginal costs—i.e. fulfil optimum condition II (b) and forget II (c). The argument is simply that if the ratio of price to marginal cost is greater in one productive unit A than in another B then a shift of factors of production from B to A will increase the national income.[2] This is because the ratio price : marginal cost is

---

[1] R. F. Kahn, 'Some Notes on Ideal Output', E.J., Mar. 1935.
[2] It will be shown in Ch. XII that an increase in the national income measured

equal to the ratio of the value of the marginal physical product of a factor to its price: consequently a shift of a pound's worth of any factor from B to A must increase the value of the product.

This thesis cannot be theoretically valid unless it is assumed that the change will not affect the supply of original productive factors (work and saving). If it does affect it, then there is no guarantee that the national income will be increased. In general one must assume that the supply of productive factors may be changed, since the pattern of the outputs and prices of goods will be changed, and this may affect the supply of, e.g. leisure, through the relations of complementarity and substitutability which exist between leisure and each of the goods.

This thesis that even if price cannot be made equal to marginal cost it should at least be equiproportional to it, is formally identical to the case for direct versus indirect taxes, which is examined in Appendix IV, to which the reader is invited to turn for further discussion of this point. But here it may be noted that the proportionality thesis, as it may be called, is a particular case of the thesis that it is better to have some optimum conditions satisfied rather than none, or more than fewer. There is no theoretical warrant for this (it is rather like saying one must be higher up a hill if one is on a ridge, where there is at least one direction which takes one downhill, than if one is not on a ridge), unless special assumptions are made. For instance, one can say that the validity of the exchange conditions does not depend upon the satisfaction of the production conditions: but this is valid only for a fixed set of goods. Similarly the proportionality thesis cannot be valid unless there is a fixed supply of factors of production.

Another difficulty inherent in the proportionality thesis is that some goods are both final consumers' goods and intermediate productive services, e.g. coal. If the price of electricity were greater than its marginal cost, and that of coal equal to its marginal cost, then the rate at which coal was transformed into electricity could not be equal to the rate at which the consumer was willing to substitute one for the other.

at prices prevailing after the change shows that the Scitovsky criterion is satisfied—but not satisfied in a sense which proves that the change causing the increase is a desirable change in our sense. The increase in national income here referred to in the text is in terms of prices reigning before the change, but so long as the planned shift in factors is small there is a high probability that such a change would also result in an increase at subsequent prices.

But Professor L. W. McKenzie has shown that the proportion-ality thesis would be invalid even if it were assumed that factor supply would be unaffected, and even if no goods were both final goods and factors of production.[1]

In effect the thesis assumes that all goods are produced in pro-ductive units whose inputs consist only of original factors of pro-duction. If, as is always the case, a firm uses both original factors and intermediate products, then its relative usage of them will be 'distorted', since, if the price of the intermediate product is greater than its marginal cost, then the relative prices of these factors will not equal the rate at which more of the intermediate product could be obtained by devoting more of the original factor to its production. There will be a bias operating against inter-mediate products, which will be greater the greater the number of different productive units (in which price exceeds marginal cost equiproportionately) through which the intermediate product passes. Thus, although by shifting factors from a productive unit A in which price : marginal cost is lower to one B where the ratio is higher, one ensures that the value of the new goods pro-duced in B exceeds the value of those no longer produced in A, it does not follow that the value of the *final* goods produced in the economy is thereby increased.

All this is overwhelming against the proportionality thesis, viewed as a general theoretical proposition. But this is not the same as saying that it can have no practical value. Most detailed and partial applications of welfare theory will be via examining in particular cases whether a change in output or price policy would be likely to increase the national income. In making such an examination one may sometimes be justified in judging that certain *ad hoc* simplifying assumptions can be safely made, e.g. that the supply of original factors would be unchanged. Such predictions of an increase in national income must rest on comparisons of prices and (marginal) costs. Where, for some pair of goods, the relative marginal costs are greatly out of line with relative prices, there is a prima facie case for investigation. In making the investiga-tion one will be aware of the fact that any change in the outputs of the two goods in question will affect not only their own relative prices and costs, but possibly those of many other goods. One will

[1] L. W. McKenzie, 'Ideal Output and the Interdependence of Firms', *E.J.*, Dec. 1951.

also be aware of the fact that marginal costs may be partly in respect of goods whose price is already 'distorted': and one must keep one's eyes open for external economies and diseconomies, &c. Even given these elaborate complications, one may nevertheless sometimes be justified in the view that the national income could be increased by a change. Only if one is prepared to accept the thesis that costs have no bearing on what and how much should be produced can one really deny this. But, it should be noted, that even after arrival at this point one still has not got a theoretical warrant for the change.[1]

[1] See pp. 231–2.

CHAPTER X

INDIVISIBILITIES AND CONSUMERS' SURPLUS

THE 'optimum' conditions of exchange and production which were developed in Chapter VIII, and discussed in Chapter IX, apply only to marginal changes. That is sufficiently obvious. The whole analysis was conducted in terms of rates of exchange or transformation; and wherever it makes sense to speak of rates, there, by definition, the marginal analysis is applicable. Where, however, the amount of a thing bought or produced can only be varied in jumps, i.e. where there are 'indivisibilities', there, again by definition, the marginal analysis cannot apply.

Thus, to say that some indivisibility occurs is only another way of saying that a marginal analysis cannot be applied. The problem remains of when it is legitimate to apply the calculus, and when not. It has been seen that, in the physical sciences, the way to answer this question would be to apply the calculus, and test the resultant conclusions. But, in practice, welfare conclusions about society cannot be tested. The only procedure left is to make some estimation of how well the defining characteristics of our concepts (e.g. if a marginal analysis is to be applied, 'goods' must be perfectly divisible) are realized. One's faith, or lack of faith, in the conclusions can be based only on this kind of estimation.

In discussing the theory of consumers' behaviour in Chapters II and III, it was presupposed that the objects of economic choice were perfectly divisible. A consequence of this assumption is that the individual would remain on the same behaviour line if one unit of a good were withdrawn and the money, which he paid for it, were given back. We can put this in another way by saying that it is assumed that there is no consumer's surplus on the marginal unit of consumption. If, in reality, consumption units are expensive, it may not be true that it is thus a matter of indifference to a man whether he consumes the nth unit or not. Or, again, to put the same point in another way, a consumer normally buys so few of such things as motor-cars, refrigerators, and wireless sets, that it does not really make much sense to speak of the rate at which he is willing to substitute one for the other. The case is even worse when we consider different jobs. One clearly cannot speak of the marginal rate at which a man is willing to exchange being a don for being a dustman.

We have already seen that the fact that jobs are not perfectly divisible is a good reason for not taking those 'optimum' conditions, which depend on this assumption, too seriously. The obvious indivisibility of many consumption goods is an additional reason, especially if one is concerned with the 'optimum' output of manufactured goods of a luxury or semi-luxury kind. Few consumers will ever buy more than a very few identical units of such goods. Thus, we cannot plausibly say that an individual brings the rate at which he is willing to exchange a car for a radiogram into line with their relative prices. If consumers really could, and did, do this with respect to all goods, it would follow that it would be impossible ever to raise the price of any superior good without every individual reducing his purchases. This is manifestly not the case. It could be true that no one man would ever own more than one radiogram, but it certainly would not then be true that a small rise in the price of radiograms would result in none being sold. Equally, it is not absolutely certain that one will get rid of an employee by reducing his wages a little.

The above paragraphs may help us to see which kind of changes can reasonably be said to be marginal, and which not. Strictly speaking, a change is marginal, for the purposes of welfare theory, only if it does not affect the consumption of any individual by more than a marginal amount. Thus, if we are to be strict, we cannot apply the marginal analysis to any change (however small) in the production of a good of which the individual does not consume many units. Even if 1,000 Bentleys are produced per annum, one extra Bentley cannot necessarily be considered to be a marginal unit, because no man consumes many Bentleys per annum. On the other hand, if 1,000 Bentleys are sold per annum, it is reasonably plausible to suppose that there would be some consumer who would scarcely be willing to pay any more than he in fact did. In which case there would be no loss of consumers' surplus on the withdrawal of the marginal (as we may therefore call it) car. On the other hand, if the minimum possible adjustment was, say, 100 Bentleys, it would be unplausible to suppose that no consumer would lose as a result of such a shift in production. A good test of whether an increase in production is marginal or not is to ask whether it would be possible to sell the increased number of units (or would have been possible to sell those units which are no longer produced) for significantly more than they in fact sell, if discrimination between customers were possible. If this would be possible, then the change is not marginal. Notice the presence of the word 'significantly'. It is there to indicate that, in the last analysis, whether a change can be considered to be marginal or not is a matter of personal judgement. There is no scientific test of when to apply the analysis, and when not. A marginal change must, for the purposes of welfare theory, also be marginal with respect to workers as well as to consumers. If an insignificantly small increase or reduction in wages would not cause a movement of workers sufficient to result in the required change of production, then that change cannot be considered to be marginal.

A particular, but important, case where the marginal analysis cannot be applied, is where the effective unit of production is so large that no single consumer would buy it—e.g. new roads, railway lines, parks, or museums. In such cases the good may be divisible in that consumption of it can be shared: though in such cases the application of behaviour-line analysis is often complicated by important external economies and diseconomies. But the unit of production is manifestly too large for the decision, whether to produce it or not, to be considered 'marginal'. In other words the price which would equate supply and demand for the good, would be such that many people would have been willing to pay far more than they in fact have to.

Since, by definition, consumers' surplus does not arise in respect of marginal changes, it was thus necessary to define the scope of marginal changes (that is also the range within which the 'optimum' marginal conditions of production and exchange are valid). We must now define the concept of consumers' surplus more carefully. With Marshall it was the difference between the sum of money actually paid by an individual for a given number of units of some consumption good, and the sum of money represented by the relevant area under his demand curve for that good. This difference was supposed to be a money measure of the excess satisfaction which the consumer derived from that product; so long as we do not take this idea too seriously, there is no doubt that it has a certain plausibility. As it stood with Marshall, the doctrine presupposed, in fact, a cardinal measure of 'utility'. Professor Hicks has, however, rehabilitated the theory in terms of an ordinal utility system,[1] and consumers' surplus has come to be regarded not as a money measure of excess satisfaction (though if one pleases one can still so regard it) but rather as the sum of money which would require to be paid to a consumer, or which he would be required to pay after some change was made, if it was desired to raise or reduce him to the same level of satisfaction (to the same behaviour line) as before the change.

FIG. X

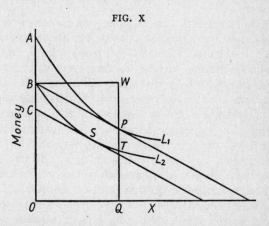

The changes to be considered may be (finite) changes of the quantity of goods or of the price. Let us consider quantity changes first.

In Fig. X money is measured along the vertical axis, and amounts of some good X along the horizontal axis. In the initial situation, let us suppose that the consumer has an income of OB, and that the slope of BP represents the price at which he is free to

[1] J. R. Hicks, 'The Rehabilitation of Consumers' Surplus', *R.E.S.*, vol. viii, 1940–1. See also among others: A. M. Henderson, 'Consumers' Surplus and the Compensating Variation', ibid.; J. R. Hicks, 'Consumers' Surplus and Index Numbers', ibid., vol. ix, no. 2; R. L. Bishop, 'Consumers' Surplus and Cardinal Utility', *Q.J.E.*, May 1943; J. R. Hicks, 'The Four Consumers' Surpluses', *R.E.S.*, vol. xi, 1943; F. Knight, 'Realism and Relevance in the Theory of Demand', *J.P.E.*, vol. lii, 1944; J. R. Hicks, 'The Generalized Theory of Consumers' Surplus', *R.E.S.*, vol. xiii, 1945–6; 'L'Économie de bien-être et la théorie des surplus du consommateur', and 'Quelques applications de la théorie des surplus du consommateur', *Bulletin de l'Institut de science économique appliquée*, numéro 2, Dec. 1946; E. J. Mishan, 'Realism and Relevance in Consumers' Surplus', *R.E.S.*, vol. xv, no. 37, 1947–8.

buy X. P therefore represents his equilibrium position where he reaches the behaviour line L_1.

How much money would it be necessary to pay the consumer in order to compensate him for the loss of the opportunity to buy X, i.e. how much is needed to compensate him if X is withdrawn from the market? He must still be able to reach the curve L_1. The amount is therefore AB. The natural name for this sum of money is the 'quantity-compensating variation', i.e. it is the sum of money required to compensate the consumer for the withdrawal of X from the market.[1]

Let us now ask what sum of money the consumer could relinquish, as a result of the introduction of X, without making himself worse off. Let our consumer's initial position be B, on the curve L_2, i.e. he has the same income, but there is no X. X could now be introduced to the market at the price BP, and, at the same time, the consumer's income be reduced by BC. His equilibrium position would then be S (CS being parallel to BP), at which point he would be on the same curve as before (L_2). This sum of money we propose to call the quantity-equilibrating variation[2] (in income).

What relation do these two sums of money, AB and BC, have to the sum of money which Marshall defined as consumers' surplus? The area under the demand curve corresponds, if there is no change in the marginal utility of money, to the sum of money which the consumer would give up in order to buy the quantity he in fact buys, rather than go without it altogether. This sum is represented by the length WT in Fig. X. Since he actually pays WP, consumers' surplus is PT. But, if the consumer was free to buy as much or as little of X as he pleased, he would not, in fact, continue to buy OQ if he was mulcted of PT. By reducing his purchases he would reach a higher curve. Thus he can be mulcted of BC, which is greater than PT, without suffering any loss. If, however, the behaviour lines are parallel (i.e. have parallel tangents) the sums represented by AB, BC, and PT are all equal. The assumption of a behaviour-line system having this property over the relevant range corresponds to Marshall's assumption of a

[1] This sum of money, AB, was, however, named the equilibrating variation by Professor Hicks. The name compensating variation was reserved for another use.
[2] This is what Professor Hicks named the quantity-compensating variation. But it is the sum of money which a consumer is able to give up without becoming worse off—and it seems misleading to call this a compensating variation.

constant marginal utility of money. And it is only on this assumption that PT is equal to the usual demand-curve definition of consumers' surplus. We thus have the result that the quantity-compensating and equilibrating variations are equal to the area under the demand curve, if the marginal utility of money is constant, or if (in Hicksian terminology) there is no income effect.

FIG. XI

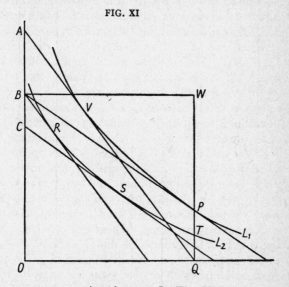

We may now turn to price changes. In Fig. XI we again give our consumer an income of OB. P is then the initial equilibrium position, with price represented by the slope of BP. Suppose the price is raised to BR. The consumer then settles at R, and is on the curve L_2 instead of on L_1 as before. If we now raise his income by AB, he will settle at V, which is again on L_1. Therefore AB is the increase in income which just compensates him for the increase in the price of X. We therefore (again reversing the Hicksian terminology) call this the price-compensating income variation.

If, however, BR had been the initial price line, the consumer would have been in the position R. A fall in price to BP would enable him to reach the curve L_1. If, however, his income is reduced by BC, he can only reach the position S on L_2. Therefore we call BC the price-equilibrating income variation.

Again, PT (assuming a constant marginal utility of money)

measures the extra amount which the consumer would be willing to pay in order to buy OQ of X, at the old price, rather than see the price raised to BR. As before, if the behaviour lines have parallel tangents within the relevant area of the map, the sum of money PT is equal both to AB and BC. In other words, if we neglect income effects, the compensating and equilibrating variations in income, whether in respect of price or quantity changes, are equal to the relevant area under the individual's demand curve. And the relevant area under the market demand curve, on the usual assumptions of 'perfect divisibility', 'economic men', and no 'income effects', shows the amount of compensation which individuals could pay, or would have to be paid, if they are neither to gain nor lose as a result of some change. It is, however, important to remember that the demand curve which is relevant is a Marshallian demand curve, it being assumed that all other prices are constant, and do not alter as a result of the change under consideration.[1]

We have said that the above theory is designed to provide a criterion for whether non-marginal adjustments of production ought to be made or not. Indeed, the theory tries to answer the same old question: 'Could those who gained by this change conceivably overcompensate the losers?', where the change referred to is a non-marginal jump. Whenever it cannot plausibly be assumed that all consumers of those goods which constitute a minimum addition to output (and similarly for a reduction) are marginal consumers, then it becomes necessary to invoke consumers' surplus in order to be able to find out whether overcompensation would be conceivable or not. Owing to technical indivisibilities, it is very likely that most changes in output which are the result of changes in plant, rather than changes in raw materials and labour, would theoretically require a consumers'-surplus analysis; thus, if a theoretical answer is to be given to the question whether some new investment (which will certainly always result in a non-marginal change if output with the new plant is extended until $MC = P$) should be made, then the answer can only be given in terms of consumers' surplus, unless we know the behaviour maps of all consumers—in which case we could, in theory, calculate whether the total of the equilibrating variations in income for each individual exceeded the total of the compensat-

[1] But there is some doubt about whether this really was Marshall's assumption. See R. F. G. Alford, 'Marshall's Demand Curve', *Economica*, Feb. 1956.

ing variations, i.e. whether overcompensation would be conceivable.

One of the more important of these non-marginal changes would be the introduction of a new good,[1] or the total withdrawal of some old good from production. We should also note that such changes may give rise to a gain or a loss in producers' surplus in the form of factor rents. There would, for instance, be a gain in producers' surplus if factors were withdrawn from uses in which their supply was perfectly elastic, in order to increase the output of some good in the production of which factors were not in perfectly elastic supply. This particular complication we shall in future ignore, it being assumed that costs are exclusive of workers' rents.

The traditional consumers'-surplus criterion is to the effect that a change should be made if the sum of money represented by the area under the relevant section of the demand curve is greater than the change in total cost; or, to put the same thing in another way, if a perfectly discriminating monopolist could cover costs. The theoretical justification for this criterion is clear. The consumers could pay exactly this sum of money, and be neither better

---

[1] Formally, a new good cannot be introduced into an old behaviour-line map. We can only guess whether the individual will be on a higher curve of his new map than he would be on the same map if he continued to have the present collection. The two situations are not strictly comparable. The best we can do is to imagine that the consumer knew all about the new good all the time, and that it had a definite place on his scale of likes and dislikes, and that he was simply prevented from buying it, because it had, let us say, an infinite price. This is, of course, unsatisfactory. The said good cannot, in fact, have been known to him, and its introduction might very well shift his rates of substitution between other goods. Some things make us develop a liking for or a dislike of other things. Much the same kind of difficulty occurs if we consider large price changes, which bring goods within the reach of those who could not afford them before. Many people know that caviar exists, but few know what it is like to eat it.

The index-number criterion for an increase in economic welfare remains formally valid. We can say, after the new good is introduced, that the consumer could, or could not, have bought his former collection of goods, and we know that in the former situation he certainly could not have bought the present collection, if it contains a new good. But the index-number criterion now fails us for a decrease in welfare. We can never say that in the earlier situation he could have bought the goods of the later situation. Thus, if we take our criteria too seriously, 'on a higher curve' becomes meaningless, while the index-number criterion can never show us that the introduction of a new good is wrong. In the text we ignore these difficulties; for which procedure the only defence can be that one has to swallow so many camels anyway that an additional one may be considered to be marginal.

off nor worse off—if they are 'economic men' and if there are no income effects. Also, since total costs represent the total sum of money paid to the productive factors, none of whom, it is assumed, earn any rents, then they also are neither better nor worse off as a result of the change—if they are all 'economic men', &c. Thus, given sufficient assumptions, we have the result that the gainers could overcompensate the losers if the sum of money represented by the area under the relevant section of the demand curve is greater than total costs. For the sake of brevity we will, for the rest of this chapter, speak of a change as 'correct' if the gainers could conceivably overcompensate the losers. There is perhaps, at this stage, no need to warn readers that 'correct' is only to be understood in this formal sense.

We may ask how this simple consumers'-surplus criterion compared with the profitability criterion. It is clear that the two are the same only if the change is marginal. Thus the 'correctness' of pure competition is only proved, given that the addition of a firm to a purely competitive industry in a purely competitive system results only in a marginal addition to output. This is obviously unrealistic. It is also clear that 'pure competition' is incompatible with the introduction of any new good. The *formal* validity of the profit criterion can thus only be demonstrated given the most unrealistic assumptions.

After the above digression let us turn back to the simple consumers'-surplus criterion. One of its chief demerits is that it is the result of a partial analysis only. It is assumed that, as a result of the change, there will be no significant change of price elsewhere. The demand curve is drawn up on this assumption. This is sometimes forgotten, and it is made to appear that the criterion has a wider validity than is really plausible. Under what conditions can it reasonably be assumed that prices elsewhere would not change? One possibility is to assume that the analysis is only intended to be long-run, and to assume that constancy of long-run costs is the rule. This is not very plausible, and the danger of introducing long-run considerations has already been pointed out. An alternative is to assume that the product under consideration is independent of all other goods, in the sense that an increase in its output would not shift the demand or supply curve, and therefore the price, of any other good by more than an insignificant amount. The increased supply of factors, which would permit the projected increase of production, would be drawn only from the margins of production elsewhere.

But, even when the good is independent in the above sense, it still requires to be assumed that price is equal to marginal cost elsewhere (either because pure competition prevails, which is impossible, or because a collectivist economy works in terms of the Lernerian rule, which is also impossible). If price is greater than marginal cost, then a small decrease in output elsewhere would result in a small decrease of profits, or producers' surplus, which would not be offset by any gain to consumers. This smallness would not be of the second order, and might therefore be significant. The consumers' surplus[1] resulting from the change must then be greater than the loss of producers' surplus (in the above sense) in other lines of production. The simple consumers'-surplus criterion therefore fails—even given independence—so soon as we remove the assumption that price is everywhere equal to marginal cost. Equally, the profit criterion is invalidated by imperfect competition. For instance, the profit which may accrue to any firm which sets up when price is generally greater than marginal cost, takes no account of the decrease in producers' surplus which it causes elsewhere. On the other hand, if a firm makes a profit without discrimination, there is almost certainly some gain in consumers' surplus, which also does not accrue to it; this may offset the loss of producers' surplus elsewhere. Thus, in an imperfectly competitive world, the profit criterion might well be more 'correct' than the simple consumers'-surplus criterion; it leaves out two factors of opposite sign, which may be better than simply leaving out one. But, of course, our present assumptions are very unreal. It should also be noted that we are certainly not considering the case of a new entrant to a monopolistic industry. Obviously, in that case, we could not reasonably assume independence.

Let us now reverse our assumptions, and suppose that price is everywhere equal to marginal cost, but the good with which we are concerned is not independent. For simplicity, we will assume that there is one close substitute, but that all other goods are independent of this pair of substitutes.[2] The introduction of the new

[1] For simplicity, 'consumers' surplus on A' will in future be taken to mean 'Area under demand curve less total costs' (rather than 'less amount paid').

[2] We cannot literally take a two-good or three-good case. Consumers' surplus would then become quite useless. See A. M. Henderson, 'The Pricing of Public Utility Undertakings', *Manchester School*, Sept. 1947, p. 247, n. 1.

good A will then shift the demand curve for the old good B to the left, and the output of B will fall. Let us also assume that marginal cost is constant for B, so that the price of B does not change. The area under the demand curve for A is then still relevant, because other prices are all constant. Consumers' surplus on B is, of course, reduced, but that is irrelevant to the problem. It would be wrong to suppose that we should take account of this reduction. That is not difficult to see. Some consumers of B will not buy any of the new good A, but their consumers' surplus may be reduced by the advent of A. Yet they clearly cannot be made worse off by this advent, since their consumption is entirely unaffected. On the other hand, those who do begin to consume A gain, whether or not they consumed B before. Their gain is 'correctly' measured by the consumers' surplus on A. Since marginal cost is assumed constant for B, there will be no loss of producers' surplus on B. But there may be on the other independent goods, depending on whether or not price is equal to marginal cost. Therefore we have the same criterion as for when the new good was independent, but price was not equal to marginal cost; to wit, the new good should be introduced if the consumers' surplus on it is greater than the loss of producers' surplus elsewhere. Once again, there is no reason to suppose that the profit criterion is less 'correct' than the simple consumers'-surplus criterion, which ignores the loss of producers' surplus elsewhere. If by the profit criterion we mean 'would an "ideal" output be profitable?', it is possible, but by no means certain, that this criterion would underestimate the 'advantages'[1] of introducing a new good. Wherever there is a large indivisibility, a loss would be made on the 'optimum' output. So long as consumers' surplus on A is greater than the loss of producers' surplus elsewhere, then some loss is theoretically tolerable. If by 'profitable' we mean 'a simple monopolist could cover costs', then, of course, it is less likely that profitability will underestimate the 'advantage'. Equally, it is possible that this latter criterion would overestimate the 'advantage', e.g. this is possible for the case of entry into a monopolistically competitive industry. Thus we have found that even if marginal costs are constant for any substitute one can be sure that the simple consumers'-surplus criterion is correct only if price is everywhere equal to marginal cost: and only in these

[1] By 'advantage' I here mean 'probability that the gainers could overcompensate the losers.

circumstances can one say that the profit criterion underestimates the advantages of introducing the new good. Otherwise one must allow for a loss of producers' surplus on the old goods.

The criterion—consumers' surplus less loss of producers' surplus elsewhere—ceases to have any meaning in terms of areas under Marshallian demand curves, when we remove the assumption of constant marginal cost for B: for the assumptions under which such a curve is drawn up are rendered invalid.

Professor Hicks has suggested[1] a means by which such a case could be reduced to terms of areas under demand curves and marginal-cost curves. He suggests that these curves should be drawn up step by step, assuming that at each step prices elsewhere are allowed to adjust themselves to each small increase in the output of the new good. For each small step, changes in output elsewhere would always be small, and also marginal, so long as price was equal to marginal cost, and therefore there would be no loss or gain of consumers' plus producers' surplus: for at each step price would alter infinitesimally, which would result in a finite gain or loss of producers' surplus at the expense of consumers' surplus, but the change in the sum of the two would be infinitesimal. This may formally solve the problem raised by the interdependence of prices, although it still relies on the assumption that price is everywhere equal to marginal cost.

However, the above ingenious construction is open to criticism. First, if price is everywhere equal to marginal cost, we must be considering either a 'purely competitive' system or a 'socialist blueprint' system. Let us take the first alternative. In a purely competitive system no indivisibilities occur, and therefore the step-by-step adjustment described by Professor Hicks really could (indeed would) occur. Therefore it appears that what Professor Hicks has done is to demonstrate the theoretical 'ideality' of purely competitive investment adjustments in terms of areas under demand curves—something which could not be done by means of a normal partial analysis, unless interdependence of prices was simply assumed away. But, of course, such a demonstration is not really required. Where no indivisibilities occur, and prices are treated as parameters, then the ordinary marginal analysis of Chapter VIII

[1] J. R. Hicks, 'Quelques applications de la théorie des surplus du consommateur', *Bulletin de l'Institut de science économique appliquée*, Dec. 1946, p. 24.

suffices to prove the point.[1] Let us, then, alternatively suppose that we are dealing, not with pure competition, but with a 'socialist blue-print' model in which large indivisibilities occur, but in which price is nevertheless kept equal to marginal cost, and that we are considering an indivisible change (since for no other change is any appeal to consumers'-surplus theory necessary). How, then, can the Hicksian demand curve be drawn? Its points show the prices at which various absurd 'non-optimum' outputs could be sold, given that prices elsewhere are those which would occur if these outputs were actually produced. If one guessed the area under such a demand curve, it is evident that no practical test could prove one wrong; nor yet does this construction appear to be of any assistance in aiding one to make an intelligent guess as to whether the gainers could compensate the losers. Finally, of course, we still have not accounted for the loss of producers' surplus, which would occur if price was not everywhere equal to marginal cost.

The above, rather intricate, discussion, which is not complete, but which I believe to have been already carried beyond the point of zero marginal value, now requires to be summed up. First, the simple consumers'-surplus criterion is valid only if the good is independent (or any substitutes are produced at constant marginal cost), and if price is everywhere equal to marginal cost. This implies that it would, at best, be valid only in an economy in which all the 'optimum' conditions of production and exchange were satisfied. Secondly, in such an economy, we could deal with goods which were not independent and whose substitutes were not produced at constant marginal cost, only by means of a Hicksian demand curve—which, as we have seen, is open at least to the same objection. Thus, unless price is equal to marginal cost everywhere, consumers'-surplus theory is useless, since there would result a multitude of small losses elsewhere, which could not possibly be estimated. The only exception might be if the increase in output were entirely at the expense of a strong substitute with constant

---

[1] In pure competition theory, we admittedly postulate one indivisible factor—the entrepreneur—in order to ensure that the long-run average cost of a firm always rises at some point. But, although the entrepreneur is indivisible in relation to the firm, entrepreneurship is regarded as perfectly divisible in relation to the industry. This dual nature of entrepreneurship is necessary because pure competition theory seeks to demonstrate the ideal output in relation both to firms, which are infinitesimal parts of an industry, and to industries.

marginal costs when, if price were greater than marginal cost, the loss of producers' surplus elsewhere might be estimated.

We do not propose to attempt to deal with cases of complementarity, nor with the elimination of a certain good, except to say that the latter appears to present worse problems than the introduction of a new good. Confining ourselves, then, to the cases of either the introduction of a new good or an indivisible expansion in the production of an old one, we may say that there appears to be a prima facie argument for the validity of some form of the consumers'-surplus criterion only in the following cases:

(a) when the good is independent, and price is everywhere equal to marginal cost;

(b) when there are one or two good substitutes with constant marginal costs, in which case losses of producers' surplus elsewhere might be estimated.

The case is, however, only a prima facie one. There is the obvious fact that areas under demand curves cannot be measured. Within very wide limits, it would be anyone's guess as to whether the consumers'-surplus criterion would be satisfied or not. It will, of course, be objected at this point that guesswork is, in any case, impossible to avoid. Before the event, profitability is only guesswork. Surely, it will be said, if consumers' surplus provides a correct criterion (which, of course, it does not, except in very special cases) it is better to guess at it, rather than at profitability. Let us, at least, guess at something which gives the right answer if we guess right. This defence[1] is plausible, but beside the point. Profitability is not, of course, 'ideal' (except, again, in very special cases), but, at least, one knows after the event whether one guessed right or not. The great trouble with any consumers'-surplus criterion is that one does not know, even after the event, whether the criterion was satisfied. In fact, the plain truth is that it does not yield us a criterion at all—or if it can be said to yield a criterion, then it is one which is open to anyone's interpretation within very wide limits.

To the above objections we may add that we have in this chapter been supposing that individuals are all 'economic', and never die; thus the great difficulties concerned with the application of the whole welfare system to the real world must be added to the

[1] Cf. A. P. Lerner, *Economics of Control*, p. 198.

G

particular difficulties associated with consumers' surplus. Even then, we have only been using the theory to estimate whether the 'gainers' could overcompensate the 'losers', ignoring the factor losses and rents (i.e. assuming that amounts and kinds of work are perfectly divisible), external economies and diseconomies, and the distribution of real income.

Our conclusion is that consumers' surplus is a totally useless theoretical toy. In this, we have to disagree with Professor Hicks's conclusion:

> But enough has been said to show that consumers' surplus is not a mere economic plaything, a *curiosum*. It is the foundation of an important branch of Economics, a branch cultivated with superb success by Marshall, Edgeworth and Pigou, shockingly neglected in the last twenty years, but urgently needing reconstruction on a broader basis. Beyond all doubt it is still capable of much further development; if economists are to play their part in shaping the canons of economic policy fit for a new age, they will have to build on the foundations of consumers' surplus.[1]

Professor Hicks has himself cultivated this branch of economics with superb success. But consumers' surplus is, nevertheless, a toy, in the sense that it cannot provide us with any practical objective criterion. We do not deny that, in the few theoretical cases in which we can contrast, say, gains in consumers' surplus on *A* (imagined as the area under the demand curve less the area of total cost) with losses of producers' surplus (imagined as profits) in another firm producing *B*—then the concept helps one towards an imaginative understanding of the nature of the problem. It is, in fact, to a limited extent, useful as a heuristic device—so long as its limitations, as such, are understood. It is also, admittedly, a useful phrase for referring to the fact that a person may be willing to pay more for something than he has to; and also for pointing out the fact that the amount someone pays for something cannot be taken as a measure of the satisfaction it gives him, and that the price of a good cannot be taken as a measure of its importance. But beyond that we cannot go.

Whereas Professor Hicks has 'rehabilitated' consumers' surplus, Professor Samuelson has gone to some trouble to prove it 'superfluous'. He argues its superfluity as follows:

> Should discriminating prices be allowed if a uniform price will not

[1] J. R. Hicks, 'Rehabilitation of Consumers' Surplus', *R.E.S.* (1940).

keep an activity in business? Should the number of firms producing differentiated products be reduced, and in what way? Should a particular small industry be expanded or contracted by means of tax or subsidy? etc. etc. Aside from their extraneous interpersonal aspects, all of these questions can more conveniently (and more honestly!) be answered in terms of the consumers' ordinal preference field.[1]

This is a rather surprising passage. It implies not only that all individuals are 'economic', but also that we have a copy of everyone's 'preference field' filed away. One must presume that Professor Samuelson is concerned only with whether to reduce the number of imaginary firms producing imaginary differentiated products in an imaginary society. Then the answer is indeed easy, to wit, 'Yes, if the imaginary gainers are imagined to overcompensate the imaginary losers'. We can readily agree that consumers' surplus is surplus in formal logic, but the point of the theory surely was to establish a practical criterion. At any rate, we have chosen to meet its claims at that level, and have argued that it fails completely. But that is a different matter.

Later Professor Samuelson argues somewhat differently:

. . . there arises the problem as to whether or not a commodity should be produced at all. If it is produced, the marginal costs conditions . . . should be realized, but there may be a better maximum where none is produced. Here the extreme position is of the corner type, and the conventional equalities must be replaced by inequalities. This involves decision-making at a distance; we cannot feel our way to the optimum, step by step, but must boldly experiment with diverse combinations. Where such 'all or none' phenomena are concerned, things often get worse before they get better, and so decisions *im kleinen* will not suffice. . . . In these cases involving finite decisions we must ask consumers (or Robinson Crusoe) whether a given abundance of fewer commodities is preferred to an alternative scarcity of a greater range of commodities.[2]

In a footnote to the above passage, Professor Samuelson adds:

In certain special cases consumers' surplus may be employed to describe finite inequalities. But these cases are rare, and, in any case, we are better off if we use direct methods.

Our analysis is in conformity with this footnote. There are few theoretical cases in which a consumers'-surplus criterion is valid. But the remark that we are better off if we use direct methods is

[1] *Foundations of Economic Analysis*, p. 197.
[2] Op. cit., p. 241.

mystifying. What direct methods are there? We can hardly hold a plebiscite to answer the question whether a certain firm should be closed. The above quotation brilliantly states the problem of indivisibilities. But sometimes it is a little difficult to decide whether Professor Samuelson is discussing the real world, or whether he is indulging himself in what he regards as a vice—translating mathematics into metaphor. For instance, when he says 'We cannot feel our way to the optimum, step by step, but must boldly experiment with diverse combinations', is he saying that the infinitesimal calculus cannot be applied to finite changes?—or is he suggesting that a proper procedure would be, for instance, boldly to close down, say, one quarter of all shops, and then see if the country had become happier—and if it had not, to put them back again? Many economic changes are irreversible except at great cost. Why, then, should we proceed boldly rather than cautiously? When he says we must 'ask consumers', does he really mean we should get consumers to vote on every indivisible move—or is he only saying that the formal answer can, in the theoretical calculus, be arrived at only by reference to 'indifference maps'? It seems probable that Professor Samuelson is translating mathematics into metaphor rather than trying to help towards any practical solution.

In contrast to any so-called consumers'-surplus criterion, profitability really is a criterion. If the aim is profits, and an enterprise is started with that in view, then we can, at least, tell whether its objective was achieved. Profitability is easy to test, and it is possible to gain experience in profit estimation. There remains the fact that the objective is not 'ideal', and also the fact that considerable monopoly power may have to be wielded in order to obtain the profit. This is not, in itself, an objection, because one can also estimate, and gain experience in estimating, the profit or loss that would accrue as a result of making the change and adopting a certain pricing policy. In extreme cases, as where the pricing policy is to charge nothing, then, of course, any such objective criterion ceases to be possible. We do not in this chapter wish to go into more practical matters, but merely to point out that if profitability (with or without certain conditions imposed) is abandoned, as a criterion for making finite changes, then there is no definite, generally applicable, rule which can replace it.

We should note that any criterion for making a finite change is formally independent of the so-called 'optimum' usage of the plant, the erection of which, say, constitutes the finite change. It is not, however, entirely independent in practice. Let us suppose that it has been decided that a change should be made if an intelligent business man estimated that profits could be made, given that he could use any output and price policy he chose. If we then make such a change, but impose a certain pricing policy, such as making the good free, we lose the test of whether the business man was right or not. The profits become hypothetical, and once more it is anyone's guess.

We shall, in the next chapter, deal further with the practical problems which have been raised above. Before leaving the subject of profitability, it may be worth while seeing whether there is much that can be (roughly) said in favour of, and against, profits as a criterion, at a theoretical level. An investment will be said to pass the test of profitability if a good business man could make profits without price discrimination, or with only a mild degree of price discrimination. We will again take the case of introducing a new good, and will first suppose that the good has no close substitutes; also, let us assume that it is the general rule that price is greater than marginal cost. We then have the case that the business man cannot tap some consumers' surplus, which is a 'gain', but also he ignores the 'loss' of producers' surplus elsewhere. Since these are factors which offset each other, it obviously cannot be proved that the business man's decision would be 'incorrect'. Equally obviously it cannot be proved 'correct'. As a second case, let us take the introduction of a new firm into a monopolistically, or oligopolistically, competitive industry. Price is everywhere (by definition) greater than marginal cost. In order to be able to talk in terms of consumers' surplus, we assume that there is a conventional price (or that there are constant marginal costs and a normal gross profit margin). We then again have the case that the business man fails to be able to tap some consumers' surplus, but also ignores the losses of producers' surplus caused elsewhere. Again, we cannot possibly say whether the introduction of the new firm is 'correct' or 'incorrect'. Indeed, only in the totally unrealistic and impossible case of the introduction of an independent good into a world where price is everywhere equal to marginal cost can it be proved that the profit criterion is 'incorrect'. Equally, it can, of course, never be proved to be 'correct'.

I think enough has now been said to show that there is no

general theoretical argument, which can be applied to the real world, either in favour of or against the criterion suggested above. Moreover, the same would be true of a host of alternative criteria. Our whole system is not only too unrealistic, but also involves us in the estimation of so many magnitudes which cannot be objectively measured, that it is quite senseless to suppose that it enables us to pick and choose, in any rational manner, between alternative criteria—unless one such criterion appears to be, at the theoretical level, fantastically wrong. The conclusion is clear. The best criterion for investment decisions must, within wide limits, be determined at dynamic and administrative levels—and not at the level of static welfare theory.

CHAPTER XI

OUTPUT AND PRICE POLICY IN PUBLIC ENTERPRISE

THIS chapter is an essay in applied welfare economics. We propose to review and discuss some of the contributions to the marginal-cost controversy. The suggestion of marginal-cost pricing in public utilities in a mixed economy appears to have been first made by Professor Hotelling in his article 'The General Welfare in relation to problems of Taxation and of Railway and Utility Rates'.[1] Professor Lerner, in his *Economics of Control*, also considers a mixed economy, but assumes that pure, or nearly pure, competition prevails in the private sector. Apparently inspired by these contributions, there was, in the post war years, an extensive discussion of the problem.[2]

It was not always quite clear whether the contributors were trying to decide on the best price and output policy for public enterprises in England (or in England in normal times, given a mixed economy), or for socialized firms in a fully collectivist economy. We shall assume that the problem relates to a relatively small number of public enterprises in a predominantly private enterprise economy, and in particular to the British economy, under present conditions of taxation.

Two obvious facts spring to mind at once. First, price is not equal to marginal cost elsewhere, and, second, there is heavy marginal taxation. We have already seen that, in such circumstances, pure theory offers no guidance.[3] The supposedly optimal character of marginal-cost pricing depends upon all the 'optimum' conditions being satisfied everywhere. There is a tendency to

---

[1] *Econometrica*, July 1938. The practice of marginal-cost pricing in a socialist economy was advocated earlier, chiefly by A. P. Lerner. Cf. 'Status and Dynamics in Socialist Economics', *E.J.*, June 1937.

[2] The following is a select list of the contributions. (There is no need to name titles, since all the articles mentioned below are on the same topic.) J. E. Meade and J. M. Fleming, *E.J.*, Dec. 1944; T. Wilson, *E.J.*, Dec. 1945; R. H. Coase, *Economica*, Aug. 1946; W. A. Lewis, *Economica*, Nov. 1946; H. Norris, *Economica*, Feb. 1947; A. M. Henderson, *Manchester School*, Sept. 1947, and *R.E.S.*, vol. xvi (1), no. 39, 1948–9. The latter two articles will be later referred to as Henderson (*M.S.*) and Henderson (*R.E.S.*).

[3] See pp. 162 ff.

suggest that the correct policy, when price can be assumed to be greater than marginal cost elsewhere, would be to make the price: marginal-cost ratio equal to the average prevailing elsewhere. But there is no theoretical warrant for this, even if one could safely assume that the supply of labour would not vary with any change in the price and output policy of the nationalized industries.[1] It is true, given this assumption, that if factors were moved out of production units with lower price : marginal-cost ratios and into production units with higher ones then the value of the extra goods would exceed those foregone. But this does not necessarily mean that the national income would be increased, except on the unreal assumption that all firms employ only original factors of production and produce only final goods.[2] But there would be no guarantee even that factors would on balance move where the price : marginal-cost ratio was higher as a result of moving the ratio in the nationalized industries from unity towards the average prevailing in the economy. This is because the directions of the factor flows would be governed by the substitutabilities of the various goods. Only if a certain price : marginal-cost ratio were the lowest in the economy does it follow that raising it a little would have this effect. Equally, pure theory does not suggest that it would *not* be a good thing to make the ratio equal to the average. All this is, in any case, rather academic, since no one knows what the average ratio in the economy is.

Almost all the contributors to the controversy failed to notice that the theory did *not*, in general, conclude that price ought to equal marginal cost. Even such opponents of marginal-cost pricing as Professor Lewis and Mr. Coase seem to have assumed that the output, which would be the effect of marginal-cost pricing, would be, in some sense, ideal. The exception was A. M. Henderson,[3] who argued that price should (in theory) be greater than marginal cost, except in the case when marginal cost is zero. This special case of zero marginal cost will be dealt with later.

So much for orthodox theory. We have argued earlier that no welfare conclusion can be reached unless it is at least given that no unfavourable redistribution of income results. Professor Hotelling[4] and Mr. Coase[5] appear to have been the only contributors who seriously considered real income distribution. Professor Hotelling

---

[1] See p. 163.   [2] See p. 164.   [3] *M.S.*, p. 242.
[4] Loc. cit., p. 259.   [5] Loc. cit., pp. 176–7.

evidently believed that a policy of marginal-cost pricing, combined with covering overheads by general taxation, would not have a significant effect on distribution. Thus he argued that a great variety of public works would be undertaken and 'a rough randomness in distribution would be ample to ensure such a distribution of benefits that most persons in every part of the country would be better off by reason of the programme as a whole'.[1] This argument is a (prior) application of what we have called the Hicksian justification for ignoring income distribution. Mr. Coase disagreed with the view that the resultant distribution ought to be neglected. It is certainly obvious that some people would pay more taxation, and get little or no benefit. Taking, however, a broad view, one could scarcely say that there would be what one might call an exciting change in distribution. But we must remember that the distributional effects must not merely be small; they must also be small in relation to the extent to which the gainers could overcompensate the losers. It is much more difficult to say that the distributional effects would be relatively small in this sense.

Mr. Coase implied that any redistributional effects will be bad, because he presupposed an 'ideal' distribution of income. We have argued above that this presupposition is meaningless and dangerous. The redistributional effects, if not negligible, will be regarded as either favourable or unfavourable, and can therefore be used as an argument for or against marginal-cost pricing. Mr. Coase also argued, against Professor Hotelling, that compensation could not be paid. Those who gain most would be those who consumed most public services; as Mr. Coase correctly argued, ordinary taxation procedures could not be used to redistribute income from consumers of goods produced under conditions of decreasing average costs to all other consumers.[2] He argued in favour of multi-part tariffs, because they would not produce any significant redistribution of income. Also, overheads would be covered out of consumers' surplus, and therefore the 'optimum' work–leisure condition would not be further disturbed by an increase in general taxation. The same argument may also, to a lesser extent, support the covering overheads out of local rates.[3]

[1] Loc. cit., p. 259.
[2] Loc. cit., p. 178. Of course, a lump-sum tax scheme could theoretically remove this difficulty. But, then, lump-sum taxes are neither ordinary, nor practical.
[3] See Henderson, M.S., p. 239.

A. M. Henderson also considered income distribution. He quoted the Hotelling–Hicks justification for ignoring it, but appeared to agree, in the main, with Mr. Coase. He wrote:

And, in fact, in most countries we find complaints that state help in this field has benefited some areas or some classes at the expense of extra taxation borne by the whole community. Such charges are almost incapable of disproof, and, whether they are justified or not, there is some objection to a policy which is almost certain to provoke them.[1]

This appears to introduce income distribution as something which is external to economic welfare, which has to be considered only as a matter of political expediency. But as we have emphasized, the question of income distribution is logically prior to the question of the ideal output. We should also notice that the sort of complaints to which A. M. Henderson referred may not be complaints so much about income distribution as complaints of inequality of treatment by the government; or they may result from the view that 'he who benefits ought to pay', an ethical view which is independent of views about income distribution and may well be inconsistent with them. It is, after all, quite possible to hold that *A* ought to pay on the ground that he benefits, but not pay on the ground that he is poor.

This brings us to Professor Lewis's article. It is particularly interesting because it introduces moral arguments, which are external to welfare economics, in the sense in which we defined the word 'economic'. By definition, under the heading of economic welfare, we have concerned ourselves only with the amount of things each individual got, and with how much of each he ought to have. Professor Lewis is, however, interested in the reasons why a man gets what he does. He appears to relate the amount an individual ought to have to the functions he plays in the economy. This is a view which has dropped out of fashion recently. Welfare theory admittedly tells us that a man ought to be paid the value of his marginal product, but it is not supposed to relate the amount he ought to be able to consume, ex tax, to his marginal productivity, or to anything else. Welfare economists, where they consider income distribution at all, usually seem to assume that the 'ideal' distribution is something which is quite independent of the amount of work individuals do, or the risks they take, &c.

[1] Henderson, *M.S.*, p. 230.

Professor Lewis argued that if price is not equal to short-run marginal cost, then specific equipment is used less than it ought to be. Thus, like most of the other contributors, he appears wrongly to have assumed that there is a strong prima facie case for an output at which marginal cost equals price. But against the advantages of an 'ideal' output there are, he maintained, certain disadvantages to be set. He argued that, if there is excess plant capacity, then setting price equal to 'immediately escapable' (short-run marginal) cost may mean that amortization quotas will not be earned on that part of the plant which has to be renewed. Thus short-run marginal cost may be less than long-run marginal cost. Only one reason, which is applicable to public concerns, is given as to why this would be a bad thing. He wrote:

This transfer of income to the consumer is a gift which he never expected, to which he has no particular right, and which he will receive only temporarily while the excess capacity lasts.[1]

It appears, then, that Professor Lewis considers that a consumer ought to pay the whole long-run average cost of anything he consumes. This is a kind of value judgement which is, by definition, extraneous to our concept of economic welfare. That does not in the least mean that such value judgements as these ought to be ignored. On the contrary, they may be very important. People undoubtedly do think in terms of 'Is X entitled to Y?', 'Has X a right to Y?', 'Is Z a fair price?', 'Why should I pay for Smith's wig?', and so on. These moral ideas may be connected with property, or the labour theory of value (which is itself, at root, a property concept. One has a right to, that is, a property right to, or right of ownership of, whatever one has 'mixed one's labour with'). Or they may not be amenable to any particular classification. But, in any case, they will always play a considerable part in any decision as to what policy is the right policy. They are welfare arguments, though not, by our definition, economic welfare arguments.

Apart from the long-run divisible and escapable cost (long-run marginal costs), it is also argued that escapable *indivisible* costs ought to be covered 'if the retention of these resources by the consumers is to be justified',[2] Again we have the same argument. It must be noticed that, although Professor Lewis, as well as Mr.

---

[1] Loc. cit., p. 237.   [2] Loc. cit., p. 239.

Coase, used this argument in support of multi-part tariffs, or discrimination, his argument had quite a different basis from that of Mr. Coase. The latter was concerned with an ideal real income distribution. As I have pointed out, Professor Lewis was concerned not so much with the amount consumers consume (he never mentioned real income distribution) but with their *right* to consume what they do. Although he advocated discrimination, he also recognized that, in some cases, discrimination would be regarded as unfair. For example:

The man who has to cross Dupuit's bridge to see his dying father is mulcted thoroughly; the man who wishes only to see the scenery on the other side gets off lightly. The public's attitude to price discrimination is not capable of rational exposition. Broadly speaking, it dislikes discrimination, but special cases are tolerated. Discrimination according to income is accepted from doctors, the Government, or electricity undertakings, and used to be accepted from shopkeepers, but would now probably be resented if tried by the baker or the 'bus conductor. On the railways it is freely accepted as between commodities, but not as between different parcels of the same commodity.[1]

Nevertheless, Professor Lewis went on:

Where there are escapable indivisible expenses to be covered, the case for discrimination is clear. It secures an output nearer the optimum, and levies the indivisible cost on those who get the greatest benefit (measured by their consumers' surplus) from retaining the indivisible resource in this line of production.

But why is the case so clear? There are two arguments in favour of it. First, the gainers could conceivably overcompensate the losers, and, secondly, those pay most who benefit most. But against it there is the argument 'people ought to be treated equally', i.e. 'there ought not to be discrimination'. The conclusion depends on the weight one attaches to these arguments. If, in general, it is true, as we have argued, that the conclusion that the gainers could overcompensate the losers is almost always an extremely shaky deduction, then perhaps one's dislike of discrimination might outweigh the pay-most-who-benefit-most argument.

There may also be inescapable costs. If price covers only escapable costs, the undertaking will show a loss. Professor Lewis argued that there is no reason why the mere fact that resources have been specialized (that certain costs are bygones) should

[1] Loc. cit., p. 7.

throw the cost on investors or anyone (e.g. taxpayers) but those consumers for whose benefit the resources have been put into their present form. Only if there is overcapacity due to mistaken foresight should the investors (or taxpayers) bear some loss; price should still cover the cost of that part of the permanent assets which is in use. Finally, the point is also made that the nuisance of rapidly fluctuating prices may outweigh the advantages of a moment-to-moment adjustment to supply and demand. Thus the conclusion is as follows:

. . . price should not fluctuate irregularly; should cover not only short-run but also long-run marginal cost; not only long-run marginal cost but also, preferably by way of price discrimination, escapable indivisible cost as well; and not only these, but as much of the non-renewable assets as can be extracted from consumers' surplus by price discrimination (but only to the extent to which such assets are actually used).[1]

But how did Professor Lewis weigh his different arguments in order to arrive at this conclusion? It seems that he thought that, even if discrimination is impossible, price should cover long-run marginal costs and escapable indivisible cost as well. It is evident, then, that he considered that the he-who-benefits-ought-to-pay argument outweighed the ideal-output argument. (Professor Lewis admittedly regarded inability to earn amortization quotas as, in itself, an argument in favour of covering these costs—but why is it an argument in the case of public utilities? No reason was given.) We can also gather that this argument, in conjunction with the ideal-output argument, outweighs a possible dislike of discrimination. Finally, he appears to imply that non-renewable assets need not be covered, unless they can be covered out of consumers' surplus (when they ought to be covered). The two arguments in favour of covering the permanent assets are, first, that he who benefits from the specialization of resources ought to pay, and, secondly, that investors (and taxpayers presumably) ought only to lose as a result of mistaken foresight.[2] But suppose discrimination is impossible. Then it appears to be implied that the permanent assets need not be covered, in which case the above two arguments are overruled. By what? Apparently only by the ideal-output argument. There thus seems to be an unexplained shift in the weighting of the arguments as we pass from escapable indivisible to inescapable costs.

[1] Loc. cit., p. 246. [2] Loc. cit., p. 246.

I, and many others, will find some of Professor Lewis's value judgements acceptable. To the extent that they are acceptable, it follows that the economic welfare calculus, with its limited value premises, is inadequate to decide the kind of question which we are trying to decide. It is notable that A. M. Henderson, in his summing-up of the controversy,[1] ignored these extra-economic value considerations, confining himself to economic welfare as we have defined it. We say this in order to emphasize our view that the economic welfare calculus, even given all the value judgements required in order to apply it, is an inadequate instrument. It should also be noticed that many people would want to say that the considerations raised by Professor Lewis are *economic* considerations.

We must now consider some further objections which have been raised against marginal-cost pricing. As we suggested in the previous chapter, the output and pricing policy adopted cannot, in practice, be treated as independent of investment criteria. This was pointed out by Mr. T. Wilson in the following passage:

. . . In theory one must then fall back upon consumers' and producers' surpluses and engage in the pleasant diversion of measuring areas under a series of curves. Unhappily such a procedure . . . could yield a large variety of answers from which anyone with an axe to grind could take his choice. Probably the only way to get at any sort of approximate answer would be to consider whether it would be possible to cover the total costs of the undertaking if it were run monopolistically. This is the sort of forecast which the monopolist himself has to make, so presumably a rough answer could be obtained. There is, however, this difference. Since the monopolist will try to exploit to at least this extent, he will have some check on the accuracy of his forecasting. A socialist undertaking run according to the Rule[2] will have no check at all, and will, therefore, be unable to build up the experience which the monopolist will possess.[3]

It may be argued that the question of new investment would not arise, because a larger output can always be obtained from the same plant, if output is adjusted until price equals marginal cost, and if marginal cost is, at that output, less than average cost. This, however, only applies when the investment is for the purpose of providing more of the same good in the same market. For instance, one cannot say that it is wrong to build another ship, or run

[1] *M.S.*
[2] See A. Lerner, *Economics of Control*, p. 64 (my note).
[3] Loc. cit., p. 458.

another train, because there are empty berths or seats on those one already has. The above objection may apply to the gas or electricity supply of a single town or district. But, even then, if one is considering the extension of such services to a new, but similar, market, it would be very helpful to know whether those services in the old areas could have paid their way. If we were wondering whether to build an underground railway in Glasgow, it would certainly help to know whether one in Birmingham could run at a profit. Thus, if we are considering the best output criterion for nationalized undertakings in general, we must not confine our attention to the case of public utilities which have a homogeneous product, and are already fairly fully developed, without much fresh territory to conquer.

Mr. Wilson's argument, especially when taken in conjunction with the well-known 'empire-building' argument, undoubtedly provides a strong reason for making the managers of a socialized undertaking cover total costs somehow. It is a strong argument, because there is no practical alternative criterion to profitability; and because the results of misinvestment can be much more harmful than a failure to achieve from moment to moment an 'ideal' output from a given plant, even supposing that there is such a thing in the real world as an 'ideal' output, and even supposing that, if there were, it could be discovered in practice.

The question of efficiency has also been raised.[1] By 'efficiency' we mean efficiency in attaining the lowest possible cost for a given output, given the plant and the prices of co-operating factors. A. M. Henderson excluded operating efficiency as a consideration because 'all systems of pricing of public utilities abandon the automatic incentive to efficiency which is supplied by the profit motive'.[2] This does not, in itself, seem an adequate reason. Dismissal for inefficiency might well be an incentive. In which case different systems could theoretically be evaluated according to the extent to which they make the discovery of inefficiency, in the above sense, possible. Nevertheless, Henderson may be right. Whatever the system, operating efficiency shows up only on the cost side. High costs can, in this field, often be prevented from showing themselves in the profit and loss account. On the other hand it may be argued, possibly with some justification, that subsidization, even when the subsidy is fixed, tends to make

---

[1] Meade and Fleming, pp. 323–4 and 335–7.   [2] *M.S.*, p. 234.

managers think that costs do not matter very much, and tends to make them careless about efficiency. Again, it is quite possible that an instruction to maximize profits would be more of an incentive to efficiency than, for instance, the instruction to cover average costs (especially if it was all too easy to cover them), although the profits earned would not directly benefit the managers.

Mr. Norris raised the problem of common costs (which may; however, be exceptional in public utilities); marginal costs are then indeterminate; and, even when there is only one product, they cannot be very precisely determined.[1] Professor Lewis has also made the important point that marginal cost may include some user cost.[2] A. M. Henderson remarked on this, and emphasized that user cost involves a guess at the unknowable, and that marginal cost ceases to be an objective magnitude and becomes, in part, a guess about the future. He added:

> I feel that there can be no doubt that the marginal cost principle is disqualified from being the sole or even the main principle of pricing on the score of administrative difficulty. It fails to supply a principle which is clear and unambiguous, and it is not possible for inspection to enforce compliance.[3]

The general case against marginal-cost pricing is clearly overwhelming. All the arguments, even the rather dubious purely theoretical ideal-output argument, are against it. In general, there is nothing to be said for it, but, in particular cases, some of the arguments could tell in its favour. First, it is conceivable that the distribution-of-real-income argument might be held to be favourable. This is only likely to be the case when the consumers of the product of some public utility are more or less coincident with some social, or income, class or group. But this may happen. For instance, it might be desired to redistribute real income in favour of the inhabitants of undeveloped areas. Charging for electricity at marginal cost would tend to have this effect. Secondly, in certain cases the ideal-output argument may be in favour. This is the case when marginal cost is zero. A zero marginal cost means that the good in question could not be transformed into anything else. Therefore the complication engendered by the fact that price is not equal to marginal cost elsewhere does not arise. Moreover, when marginal cost is zero, all the other 'optimum' conditions of

[1] Loc. cit., p. 58.   [2] Loc. cit., p. 232.
[3] R.E.S., p. 17.

production and exchange do not require to be satisfied. If marginal cost is zero, one can be fairly sure that some people could be made better off without making anyone worse off, simply by lowering the price. Admittedly there will be some small production changes elsewhere, both on account of substitution and income effects. But, at least, the deduction is very much less shaky than when marginal cost is not very small.

It should be noted that zero or near-zero short-run marginal cost is very common. We may instance museums, parks, bridges, passenger-trains and buses, broadcasting, water-supply, and sometimes even roads (certainly in the case of light traffic). It at once springs to mind that usage of most of these facilities is already free at the margin. Museums, parks, bridges, and water normally cost one nothing to consume. The charge for one's wireless licence does not vary with the amount one listens. Roads are free except to motorists, who pay a small charge for immediate usage in the shape of the petrol tax. They are entirely free to pedestrians and bicyclists. This is, presumably, because marginal-cost pricing is supported by the common-sense value judgement, 'Surely people should be allowed to use something as much as they like if it costs nothing'. We may ask why an exception is always made in the case of transport. There is nothing more obvious than that, if a bus or train or ship is running half-empty, it would cost next to nothing to carry an extra passenger. Part of the answer lies in the equation of supply and demand. Museums, parks, and bridges are not often full. Broadcasting has an infinite capacity, and can never be fully used. The theoretical pricing rule, when marginal cost is zero, is 'Lower price until the service is fully used—if necessary to zero'. This could hardly be done in the case of buses or trains. Everyone would wait until the last moment for the price to come down, when there would be a horrid scramble. It would obviously be impracticable to hold an auction at every station at which the train stopped. Equally, if transport were free, there would be no criterion for when it was desirable or not to make an indivisible change, i.e. run another bus, or another train. Also the 'ideal' would not be attained. People who wanted to travel very badly would be crowded out by joy-riders, who would not have travelled if they had had to pay anything.

Administrative impossibility, fluctuating prices, and the leaving of an enormous number of small but indivisible changes to the whim of the manager, combine to make marginal-cost pricing impossible in the case of transport. It should be noticed that those who believe that the road–rail question can be settled on marginal-cost principles do not consider true marginal cost. They average costs to some extent, thereby ignoring some consumers' surplus. It is obviously right to do so. But it means that the best resolution of such problems is a matter of judgement, and not of scientific principle. When, for instance, A. M. Henderson wrote, '. . . The inefficiency arises from attempts to force traffic to go by rail when the marginal cost is lower than for road transport, although the pricing system is such that the road charge is the lower',[1] he means that, say, an extra 100,000 passengers per annum could be carried by rail at an average extra cost per head which would be small compared to the average extra cost if they went by road. If we really followed short-run marginal-cost principles, the road–rail problem would certainly not be solved. In such cases as this, one can only take 'marginal cost' in a very broad, and theoretically illegitimate, sense.

This leaves us with such things as water, museums, parks, broadcasting, roads, and bridges. They are free at the margin, except for motor-traffic on the roads. The arguments against them being free, are (a) that there is no criterion for when to build more museums, roads, &c., and (b) that their costs may contribute to marginal taxation. Where such things are provided for out of local finance, the danger of over-development is not very serious. The ratepayers would have something to say, and in the end the district would lose population. Also marginal taxation is not thereby increased. With broadcasting the danger is also slight, and, again, the costs are (more than) recovered from consumers. Moreover in many of these cases broader considerations of welfare and culture would, in many people's minds, justify a development which could not be justified by any purely economic argument. The case of roads is more difficult. The lack of any good criterion could lead either to underdevelopment or overdevelopment. In practice, in England, where something is financed through the central budget, underdevelopment is more likely in cases where political emotions are not strongly aroused. Overdevelopment is more probable where the investment is self-financing, and the undertaking is better placed than others to draw upon the public's

[1] *M.S.*, p. 241.

consumers' surplus. But if some check on investment in roads were required, it could be provided by limiting the investment to such as can be financed out of consumers' surplus, by vehicle taxation and local rates. This is, of course, no answer to the question 'Should a particular new road be built from A to B?' The theoretical answer would require at least an estimation of consumers' surplus on this particular road, and of loss of producers' surplus on the railways. No tolerable system of pricing could possibly yield an automatic investment criterion here. It appears, then, that the investment-criterion argument cannot be used against a free road system: though, paradoxically, there may be a case for tolls if desirable development is being retarded by the exigencies of central finance.

Let us now sum up the argument as far as we have progressed. First, we may say that when marginal cost is zero there is a good prima facie case for making the service free. When there is also some investment check, and the losses can be covered other than by marginal taxation, and in an equitable manner, then the case for making the services free, or almost free, is well established. Second, when marginal cost is not small, but average costs are considerably higher than marginal costs, there may be a weak prima facie case for charging somewhat less than average cost for the service, but never for actually charging marginal cost. The prima facie case is stronger (i.e. we could have more confidence that the gainers could overcompensate the losers) the lower marginal cost is in relation to average cost. It only becomes very strong when marginal cost is zero, and the overheads could be covered without upsetting the 'optimum' conditions.

The prima facie case may often have to be over-ruled by one or other of the arguments mentioned above. But, if marginal cost is zero and nothing is charged, or if the policy is to charge rather less than average cost when there is a large divergence between average and marginal cost, then the objections (a) that marginal cost is indeterminate, and (b) that the instruction 'produce until price equals marginal cost' is administratively impossible, or would result in inconveniently fluctuating prices, do not apply. These are really only strong objections against trying to operate the Lerner 'rule'. The objections to the prima facie case which have so far been raised and which remain are:

(a) a possible unfavourable redistribution of income;

(b) the he-who-benefits-should-pay kind of argument;

(c) the lack-of-a-criterion-for-indivisible-changes argument;

(d) the fact that it may be impossible to cover overheads without increasing marginal taxation;

(e) the fact that subsidization may tend to cause inefficiency by encouraging the idea that, since there is no harm in making a loss, costs do not matter much.

Some of the above objections will apply in some cases and not in others. The extent to which they will apply depends very much on the method chosen for meeting the loss which will arise from reducing charges below average costs. A. M. Henderson has reviewed the different methods in this light.[1] There are, broadly speaking, three possibilities—national taxation, local taxation, and price discrimination by means of multi-part tariffs.[2]

The first possibility, national taxation, is clearly the worst. It implies an increase in taxation at the margin of effort, and will also normally result in an increase of indirect taxation. It also implies subsidization with, possibly, a consequent decrease in managerial efficiency. These effects may offset what would otherwise be the theoretical advantages, even in cases where marginal cost is zero. To some extent one's common-sense judgement is warped in such a matter, because the benefits of making a service free are, in some cases, obvious. The offsetting effect of increased taxation is very widely spread, and any ill effects will scarcely be noticeable if only a single case is considered. When, however, taxation has already reached a high proportion of the national income, it may be worth while to guard against this form of myopia. Furthermore, all the other three arguments (a), (b), and (c) may weigh against it. There is likely to be some income redistribution, which might be unfavourable. Some people will pay for benefits they do not receive, and there is no check on 'empire-building' investment. It would clearly be very difficult to find a case in which one could, given any plausible set of value judgements, say with some reasonable degree of confidence that it would be right to reduce price below average cost, and finance the cost by an increase in general taxation (i.e. adopt the Hotelling–Lerner solution).

---

[1] M.S.

[2] Where there is a multi-part tariff, when I refer to the charge or price, I mean the charge which varies directly with the amount of the good or service consumed by the individual, e.g. the charge per kilowatt-hour for electricity, or per therm for gas.

The second method is local taxation in the form of rates. Where the benefits of the public service are local, this means of payment is superior on all counts to national taxation. Marginal taxation is not increased; subsidization is not required; redistributional effects are likely to be small; and, broadly speaking, those who benefit pay.[1] Furthermore, there is much more likely to be a check on investment. Where the benefits of the service are widespread, however, this method of payment can be ruled out by the redistribution and the he-who-benefits-should-pay argument. For instance, if a large and expensive bridge was built to carry national roads and railway lines, no one would argue that it ought to be a charge on local rates.

The third method is the multi-part tariff. This method may not enable the 'ideal' output to be produced. The overhead charge will normally have to be greater than the expense which can be directly attributed to each consumer (e.g. installation charges for electricity, &c.), and certain people who would just be willing to pay consumer cost may be excluded. Motor-car taxation will, for instance, exclude a fringe of would-be motorists. Alternatively, the variable charge will have to be greater than marginal cost. The multi-part tariff is, in fact, only an approximation to the theoretical 'ideal' of perfect discrimination. This we would not hold as a serious argument against it. As we have seen, *the* ideal output only exists in theory. Except when marginal cost is zero, and overheads can, in fact, be met out of surplus of some kind, it is indeterminate. And, in any case, we have seen that the theory, which lies behind the concept of an 'ideal output', has at best only a very rough and ready application to the real world. It is a mistake to suppose that anything except a very rough approximation to the 'ideal', even when it is theoretically determinate, can be confidently held to be beneficial. On all other counts the multi-part tariff is superior, even to a charge on rates, where it is applicable. If the charge is on rates, some will pay who get no benefit. Similarly, a multi-part tariff prevents any significant redistribution of income, which is, on the whole, likely to be an advantage. It also provides a check on investment. The finance of the undertaking is autonomous.[2] This may be an advantage, because those who are experienced in the running of the business can take all or most of the decisions. Furthermore, the

[1] This would be more true if full rating of industrial and agricultural property were restored.　　　　　　　　　　[2] See Henderson, *M.S.*, p. 234.

managers have a reasonably definite pricing system, and they can gain the experience necessary to decide whether some new undertaking would pay for itself with that pricing system. But the danger of any generalization must be noted at this point. If of two strongly competing industries one can exploit a multi-part tariff, and the other cannot, the first may be overdeveloped relative to the second. This is very probably the case with gas and electricity in England.[1]

There is one special disadvantage of the multi-part tariff; it normally involves discrimination, which may be thought to be unfair. The larger the difference between marginal and average cost, and the nearer to marginal cost one tries to get, the greater the discrimination would have to be. Whether discrimination can be worked in this way depends mainly on whether suitable impersonal categories (e.g. size of motor-car, or house) can be found as a basis for discrimination. In my judgement, and for the usual reasons, it would be folly to strain after the 'ideal' by attempting to discriminate in a manner which would be regarded as unfair. Here my emphasis is rather different to that of Professor Lewis, simply because I do not believe one can attach much weight to the 'optimum' output argument.

We can safely conclude that where it is possible to finance losses, due to charging less than average cost, either by means of the rates, or better still by a multi-part or two-part tariff, then the case for reducing price below average cost (assuming that marginal cost is substantially less than average cost) is very much stronger than if part or all of the loss has to be borne by national taxation. Where these methods are not available, and therefore the whole loss would have to be borne by general marginal taxation, and where the service is one that is consumed by individuals,[2] then I

[1] See I. M. D. Little, *The Price of Fuel*, O.U.P., 1953, chs. v–vii.

[2] Henderson (*M.S.*, p. 237) treats defence as a public utility paid for out of general taxation. But things such as battleships are not consumed by individuals —and they play no part in the 'welfare' scheme we examine. It is absurd to say that defence ought to be financed through general taxation arranged so that the taxpayer pays no more than the consumer's surplus he derives from it. Ought those, who would not be willing to contribute anything to defence, to have their income-tax reduced? Individual preferences play no part where there is no mechanism by which they can be expressed. When people vote, they do not vote on particular issues; and, in any case, the price mechanism is not a 'Yes'-'No' affair. There are no wasted votes, and no minorities. This is remarked on, because there is a tendency to pretend that consumers' preferences are expressed in the same sort of way through the ballot-box as they are through the price mechanism.

think we would, at least, require to have the following conditions satisfied:

(*a*) either that almost all individuals benefit to some extent, or that the income redistribution would be favourable;

(*b*) that marginal cost is very small in relation to average cost;

(*c*) that a multiplicity of indivisible decisions is not, as a result, left without any criterion.

Can we pause at this stage of the argument and draw any general conclusions? The only conclusion that seems to emerge is that nationalized industries should *at least* aim to cover total costs, and even here one might occasionally want to make exceptions. But the fact that one cannot draw up general rules as to tariffs and output policy must not be taken to imply that the economist has no contribution to make to the problem in particular cases. We have earlier dismissed the idea that the ratio of price:marginal cost should be made equal to some average (unknown) value for that ratio in the economy. We have also seen that there is nothing ideal about the 'proportionality' thesis.[1] But that is different from saying that relative prices and relative marginal products do not matter. We saw that the idea lying behind a rise or fall in a price:marginal-cost ratio is the shift of factors to industries where the value of their marginal product will be greater.[2] Now where a good has one or a few strong substitutes, and where the demand for these goods taken together is inelastic, one may be able to predict the direction that these factor movements would take and hence be able to predict, with fair confidence, that an increase in the national income would result from a change in pricing policy.[3] One may also of course take into account the possibility of changes in factor supply, in income distribution, and external economies. But the point is that detailed study may well enable one to make recommendations with some confidence; in particular cases many of the general objections to the application of 'welfare' analysis may be seen to have little weight. In my opinion this detailed approach is the proper one to make: and generalities about price:marginal-cost ratios, or the use of particular kinds of tariffs, are rather useless,

[1] See pp. 162–5 above.

[2] See pp. 162–3 above.

[3] It has been emphasized in earlier chapters that this is not sufficient evidence, even combined with a favourable redistribution, that such a change is desirable: but, while insufficient, it is still evidence.

and may easily be worse than useless. This, however, is not the place to descend into such detail.[1]

Let us return to generalities concerning the price and output policy of nationalized industry. There is one problem we have not yet mentioned, the solution to which has some bearing on the output of nationalized industries. This is the problem of deciding what total costs should be deemed to be. It may, at first, seem surprising that there should be such a problem, which certainly does not exist under private ownership. It is the case, however, when an industry is nationalized, that its overhead costs are determined by the compensation paid to the dispossessed owners. There can certainly be no particular reason why its overheads should be fixed in this way, because the amount of compensation is itself determined by varying methods, and may be quite arbitrary. If overheads are not necessarily to be related to the compensation paid, then how are they to be fixed? This apparently opens up the possibility that they can be adjusted until 'covering total costs' would amount to the same thing as 'producing until marginal cost equals price'. Average cost could be forced into equality with marginal cost.

This is, of course, a silly suggestion. It inevitably does away with the whole object of covering total costs, and is open to all the grave objections which have been made to the policy of producing until price equals marginal cost, covering the overheads by national taxation. Moreover, if we require that covering overheads should provide experience which helps to decide whether new investment in a new but similar, or imperfect, market is desirable, then it is important that the nationalized industry should start off with overheads which bear some reasonably close relation to the value (in some sense) of the equipment and goodwill which it takes over.

The last consideration mentioned above would appear to give us at least one reason for valuing the overheads of a nationalized industry in a particular manner. It is a commonplace that the historical cost of equipment is irrelevant, and that it is the replacement cost that matters. But the reason for this, and the reason why *all* overheads are not irrelevant, is not always made clear. The reasons are, first, that depreciation should be based on replacement

---

[1] My *Price of Fuel* is an example of the method I suggest. The matter is further discussed in the preface to that book.

costs and should be covered by price, if the often more or less routine investment of depreciation funds is to be under the direct control of the undertaking itself, and, secondly, that only if capital is valued at replacement cost is the experience gained in covering total costs of greatest value as a guide to making new investment decisions. Is it, however, adequate to say that the overheads should be determined by replacement costs? A. M. Henderson has discussed this question. The problem, as he set it, is to determine how much the industry should pay to the Exchequer after covering its current expenses. This becomes the problem of determining the valuation that is to be set on its capital equipment, since the annual payment will then be determined as the normal yield expected on an investment of this class. To quote:

What is relevant is the replacement cost of the equipment, and this should be the basis of valuation. In this way, there is an automatic increase in the amount of the annual payment in periods of high prices and a fall in periods of depression.[1]

He went on to say that this basic replacement-cost figure needs to be modified, because some of the equipment would not be replaced if the decision had to be taken anew. He wrote: 'In this case, we require the highest price we would be willing to pay to replace this equipment.'[1] Only in this case? Suppose that we would be willing to pay more than replacement cost? If windfall losses are to be subtracted, presumably windfall gains should be added. He continued:

The sum we are seeking is the current value of the equipment such that, if a normal return is paid, then the taxpayers will not be subsidizing consumers of the product of the industry, though they will bear the capital losses from investment which has turned out to be unjustified.[2]

This appears to be the sum we are seeking, because, he suggests, we really want to ask ourselves what we would be willing to pay to replace the equipment. It does not seem clear why this is the question we should ask ourselves unless, either for reasons of income distribution or for reasons such as Professor Lewis's, we think that taxpayers ought to bear the losses of mistaken investment, and ought not to have to subsidize consumers. In any case capital valuation on the basis of a normal return does not seem to

[1] Henderson, *R.E.S.*, p. 21.   [2] Ibid.

be a modification of the replacement-cost principle. It seems to be a quite different and alternative basis of valuation.

Suppose that, in accordance with this scheme, the capital value is, on takeover, determined by multiplying the current profits by the number of years purchase corresponding to the yield expected by investors on an investment of the same class. The annual payment is thus apparently equal to the profits before nationalization, and the pricing policy remains broadly unchanged so long as operating costs remain the same. Alternatively, if no account is taken of risk, and the interest charge is determined by gilt-edged rates, then the annual payment would be somewhat less than the pre-nationalization profits, and price could be slightly reduced.

A new investment after nationalization will then be made if the industry convinces the Exchequer that it will thereby be able to increase its annual payment in proportion (assuming that the normal yield does not change), given that it continues to charge the same price.[1] If the investment is made, and the expected yield does not result, then a higher price must not be charged. The implication is that the new capital must be revalued in accordance with the actual yield of the new investment; otherwise, the taxpayers would not be bearing the loss.[2] The annual payment of the industry would thus be adjusted up or down according as new investment was successful or the reverse. This would mean that a mistaken investment would appear to be immediately condoned. As far as the industry and the public was concerned, its mistakes would be covered up as soon as made—and likewise its successes. This might not be a good thing.

Admittedly it does not follow from the mistake of, say, erecting an unnecessary factory that one should make the further mistake of not using the factory in what might be, in theory, in the short run, the best manner. On the other hand, if overheads are always adjusted so that the average cost of this factory is covered, then there remains no obvious indication that the industry is now too

[1] Cf. Henderson, *R.E.S.*, p. 23.

[2] Apart from this revaluation, the annual payment scheme seems to come to the same as that advocated by E. F. M. Durbin, 'Economic Calculus in a Planned Economy', *E.J.*, Dec. 1936, where he says: 'Make the largest output you can consistent with earning normal profit on the cost of replacing your plant. When through a change in market conditions you cannot earn normal profit at all, then earn the biggest profit you can.' This instruction is subject to the same objections as we make to the annual payments scheme.

large. If the annual payment was not adjusted then the industry might use its monopoly power in order to meet its obligations. The taxpayer would not then pay the penalty of the mistake, but at least the consequent increase of excess capacity would indicate that the industry ought to contract. Equally if the new investment was particularly successful, a resultant increase in overhead charges might tend to hide the fact that further expansion was desirable. Again, if demand increased or decreased, there would be similar reasons against immediately adjusting the annual payment upwards or downwards. There are thus arguments against adjusting overhead charges, more often than very occasionally, to what the industry can, in fact, pay when operating at or near full capacity.

Suppose, however, that a new investment failed to give the expected yield, not so much because costs or demand were miscalculated, but because there was a general fall in prices. There is then a strong case for reducing the annual payment. This would automatically occur if the equipment was revalued at replacement cost. Similarly, if there was a general rise in prices, not only the depreciation but also the interest component of the annual payment should rise. The failure or success of an investment which is the result of a change in the general level of prices should not be attributed to the foolishness or wisdom of the managers, and there is no reason why such gains or losses should not be hidden. Furthermore, if the annual payment was not thus revised, output would be expanded or contracted as a result of a purely historical accident—the accident of whether the equipment was purchased when prices were relatively high or low—and this, at least, cannot be a good reason for a change in output policy.

This somewhat clumsy idea of a fluctuating annual payment only results from the fact that we have presumed that the managers would be instructed to adopt a price which would enable them to pay the annual payment. In fact, if interest on the capital value was charged at private industrial rates, we would simply have been discussing how we should vary the annual payment so that the managers, in taking it as their guiding star, would in fact maximize profits, or minimize losses, in the same way as they did under private enterprise.

We do not want to imply that, when an industry is nationalized, the equipment should be valued at replacement cost. On the contrary, when the new management takes over, there is no point in burdening them, even on paper, with the results of the past mistakes of others, nor indeed in valuing the equipment in such a way that they can pay an exceptional return from scratch. The initial valuation should certainly be made on a normal yield basis, and, unless there are special reasons (as there may often be) for supposing that the public has seriously underestimated or overestimated the prospective yield, or the risk involved, the Stock Exchange valuation may be taken. (Although it is, of course, inconsistent to take the Stock Exchange valuation, and then require the industry to pay only gilt-edged rates on the value of the capital thus determined.)

The trend of the discussion will probably have disappointed some readers, since the proposal so far is simply that there should be a capital reorganization at the time of take-over, and that thereafter the public monopoly should, as far as short-term output is concerned, continue to behave in the same way as the private monopoly would have done (although within the framework of covering total costs it may of course try to produce the 'best' output). The only difference is that the interest charge would be reduced if gilt-edged rates of interest were now charged.

A. M. Henderson suggested, however, that the amount of the annual payment might be modified for various reasons; thus it might have its annual payment lowered to make price more nearly equal to marginal cost, if the excess of average over marginal cost was unduly high; or, if it justified general encouragement because of defence requirements, indirect social benefits, or external economies. Alternatively, it might have its annual payment raised for the opposite kind of reason. He added:

It may seem pointless to start with a more or less precise figure and then to submit it to a host of adjustments of so vague a nature. The justification is simply that in many, if not most, industries there will be no very convincing case for making any of them.[1]

We certainly agree with this. But, supposing that it was felt that some interference with monopolistic pricing *was* justified, we doubt whether this interference would best be made by means of an adjustment of the annual payment which the industry would be expected to make.

Let us suppose that the annual payment is reduced, so that the

[1] *R.E.S.*, p. 22.

industry is not, in effect, expected to cover its total costs, as we have tried to define them earlier. New investment would then be undertaken if it was expected that charging the same price for the product would permit the annual payment to be increased by sufficient to cover interest and amortization on the full cost of the new equipment, although the corresponding full interest charge would not necessarily be exacted.[1] It is clear that this involves a more exacting criterion for new investment than does profitability. The criterion is now profitability given a certain price less than monopoly price. So long as the reduction of the annual payment is small, we cannot claim this as a disadvantage, since, as we saw earlier, profitability might err on either side of the 'ideal'. If the reduction in the annual payment was, however, fairly large, an undue restriction of investment might result.

Further, if the annual payment was not increased by the full interest and amortization charge on the new equipment—which, if the investment were successful, could have been paid—then the price charged must be lowered. In that case the ratio of price to average cost would be changed. Evidently, if it is only 'correct' to make new investments which, at the same price as before, can cover their total costs, then, if the same average-cost: price ratio is to be retained, the industry must be required to pay the full interest charge. On the other hand, if the annual payment was, in the first instance, modified for general social reasons (for instance, if it was increased for distilleries), then we should presumably require that more, or less, than a normal return must be made on the new capital. If the annual payment is to be modified for many different reasons, it is surely wrong to suggest a single investment criterion, to wit, 'make an investment if, on the basis of the old price, full costs can be covered'. If, for general social reasons, we wished to encourage or discourage an industry, we should correspondingly not want it to be able to cover total costs, or be more than able to cover them.

We thus see that there would be a number of disadvantages if the annual payment was adjusted for some of the reasons specified. First, it would make it more difficult to find a general investment criterion, and to judge the investment performance of the industry, and this, in turn, makes the problem of deciding on the right investments more difficult. Secondly, it would be clumsy. Too

[1] Ibid., p. 23.

many reasons have been advanced for altering it; a change in the price level; a particularly successful or unsuccessful new investment; external economies and diseconomies; general social reasons, and so on. Thirdly, if it was correct to alter it for such reasons as A. M. Henderson put forward, there would be a temptation to alter it for more arbitrary non-economic reasons. Whether or not to alter it for reasons of general social advantage is a matter of judgement about which there could be considerable difference of opinion (indirect social benefits, external economies, &c., cannot be objectively determined). Decisions on such matters might, in a democratic community, well be aired in public, and therefore should not be lost to view as they would tend to be if incorporated in a change in the annual payment, which would also have to fluctuate with changes in the general level of prices, and with the success or failure of new investments.

A. M. Henderson also suggested that, in addition to being able to vary the annual payment, the government may also give specific subsidies or levy special taxes.[1] Yet interferences on the ground of the price: marginal-cost ratio, defence requirements, and indirect social benefits, are apparently all to be dealt with by a variation of the annual payment. Indirect taxation is also included. Thus it is said: '. . . the need for a contribution from indirect taxation is a reason for raising the annual payment in all nationalized industries'.[1] Even unintentional subsidization, owing to the failure of an investment plan, is dealt with by varying the annual payment. What, then, is there left to be dealt with by means of specific taxes or subsidies? The important point about subsidies and taxes is that they are abnormal payments; they conflict with the established norm of covering total costs (however defined). Being abnormal, they attract attention. Therefore I would wish to rank as subsidies or taxes payments which should be subject to public discussion. Among these I would include payments (or modifications of payments) to or from industries for reasons of general social advantage, external economies, defence, &c.—and would even prefer to include among them any payment for the purpose of approximating to the 'optimum' conditions, because I believe that common sense, backed by public opinion, may often be a better guide than pure welfare theory in deciding whether a change would satisfy our criterion of desirability.

[1] *R.E.S.*, p. 23.

But, even supposing that any special encouragement or discouragement of an industry is dealt with by means of taxation or subsidization, there are still disadvantages in a system under which output is determined by the obligation to balance after a certain annual payment is met. Suppose that there is an increase in the demand for the product, and that output cannot be quickly expanded. The same price must be charged if the industry is not to make too much profit. This would involve queueing or rationing or an increase in imports, which is certainly not, as a general rule, ideal. It would be wrong to suggest that the taxpayer ought never to benefit by the increase in demand. Certainly theory suggests that the price should be raised, and the exceptional profit made. Only then is the product 'ideally' distributed (we have seen in Chapter IX that the 'optimum' exchange conditions are the least shaky of all the 'optimum' conditions, and that their fulfilment is presupposed by the 'optimum' production conditions). This argument admittedly may not apply in some cases, where income-distribution effects are important and cannot be compensated, but it surely applies in others. Another disadvantage of the annual payment method is that it 'permits' losses (if the industry cannot avoid making a loss), but never permits exceptional profits, since these can always be avoided. There may thus be a tendency for general taxation to increase. Again, it is likely to be more difficult to aim at making a definite amount of profit from year to year than it is to aim at maximizing profit in the long run. This remains just as true if the instruction is to break even, taking the good years with the bad. All business experience is built up on the profit-maximizing basis. Also, if too much profit is to be avoided, and there happens to be a tendency to make too much, then there may be little incentive to avoid waste. The balance might be struck by inefficiency, rather than by increasing output.

Some of the above disadvantages might be overcome if the instruction to break even was overridden by the instruction that the industry should always make as much profit as it could, consistent with operating at full practical capacity. The abnormal profits, if any, should be reduced only by increased output as and when new investment made that possible. This raises the question of what should happen to any exceptional profits made. First, of course, they would be subject to profits and income-tax. The residue could be retained if required to finance an agreed investment programme:

anything left should probably be paid to the Treasury. It may be argued that, for political reasons, exceptional profits should not be made in a nationalized industry. They might, for instance, incite demands for wage increases. This difficulty might be met by instituting a suitable purchase-tax if and when an industry began to earn a quasi-rent on its equipment. The purchase-tax would be removed when output could be expanded sufficiently to meet the excess demand.[1]

Thus it is suggested that the annual payment be altered only for two reasons: either (a) because the general price-level, and therefore replacement costs, had changed considerably, or (b) for the purpose of writing off mistaken investment. These capital re-organizations would be made only occasionally, when the need for them had become obvious. Secondly, it is suggested that the instruction to break even be overridden by the instruction that as much profit as is consistent with full capacity should always be made. If the average cost of marginal firms is more than covered, then output should be expanded through new investment. Thirdly, if it is thought that interference is definitely required in order to make price more nearly equal to marginal cost, or for general social or military reasons, then this should be effected by means of taxation or subsidization.

New investment should, in general, be undertaken if it is expected that its full costs can be covered, assuming that the same rate of taxation or subsidization (if any) remains. This gives us the usual profitability criterion for investment, subject to the general encouragement or discouragement implicit in the taxation or subsidization of the industry. Only if the taxation or subsidization is for the purpose of making price nearer to marginal cost do we tend to lose sight of the normal profitability criterion of investment. We anticipate, however, that interference on the grounds of reducing price to make it nearer to marginal cost would seldom, if ever, be obviously necessary, except possibly in the case of fairly fully developed industries where investment was unimportant, and probably not often even in this latter case, since the greater output would usually be obtained by discriminatory pricing, or by local

---

[1] In some cases a permanent rent might be earned on intra-marginal units, in which case the Treasury should receive the abnormal profit corresponding to this rent. In some cases, however, such rents will have been capitalized when the industry was taken over, and would therefore be included in the normal annual payment.

taxation; and where it could not be so obtained, it would seldom, if ever, appear to be desirable.

Finally, we would add that control by price-fixing cannot be eliminated as a possibility. In abnormal times, as when a particularly severe shortage develops, or when there is considerable inflationary pressure, then rationing and price-fixing may be required to ensure equitable distribution, or to prevent a wage inflation by holding down the cost of living.

Some disadvantages still remain. Nothing in the above instructions serves to prevent an industry, which is faced with a chronic decline of demand, from exerting its monopoly power[1] to meet the annual payment in spite of the decline in demand. Whereas, by the suggested overriding instruction, we have introduced some element of price flexibility when demand increases, no corresponding flexibility in a downward direction is in evidence. Also there is nothing to prevent the industry from using one of its products to subsidize another. There is also the already mentioned possibility that the instruction to break even may result in inefficiency, if and when it is very easy to break even.

The above kind of consideration raises the question of whether it is not possible to introduce into public enterprise some element of competition. In other words, cannot profit-maximization sometimes serve in its traditional capacity as an output regulator? Thus it has been suggested that, for some industries, it would be better to have several boards which would compete against each other, rather than one central board. There would, however, be disadvantages in not having a central board for an industry. In any industry there are probably certain economies of 'co-ordination', such as central research and the dissemination of information. Perhaps more important in some people's view is the fact that the industry would become more difficult to control if there was no single central organization responsible to the Minister. In normal times this would not matter very much, and might be an advan-

---

[1] A public monopoly might have much more monopoly power than a private monopoly. Whereas the ratio of price to marginal cost in the latter is seldom likely to be significantly different from the average 'degree of monopoly', this might not be true of a public monopoly. Private enterprise, however monopolistic, is always limited by the threat of potential competition, or public control. There is little evidence that the text-book short-run 'exploitation' behaviour is a real phenomenon. On the other hand, the lack of the above threats might, in public enterprise, be offset by the increased influence of parliamentary, or public, opinion.

tage, but if we have to cater for the possibility of 'abnormality' then it might certainly be a disadvantage.

But, in any case, the same presumed advantages, which would result from having an industry split up into a number of competing boards, could be rather better obtained with a central board, if that board adopted a suitable policy. Thus, in a multi-plant industry, the individual plants, or mines, could be instructed each individually to maximize its profits. If the product were homogeneous, or if there were a small number of homogeneous products, then each plant would behave as if in perfect competition. Oligopolistic competition or restraints could be discouraged by the central board. In such a case the board would not be maximizing its profits. It would not control the price, and the individual managers would, in fact, be making price equal to marginal cost. But in an industry with rising costs, if the above policy was applied, losses would not result; indeed, considerable profits might sometimes be made. In that case most of the objections to marginal-cost pricing vanish; we would have the competitive industry of pure theory. In some cases this would seem to be the best solution.

We believe that much the same solution could be applied to many imperfectly competitive industries (we beg the question of the definition of such an industry). There is no longer, of course, a single price, but many prices and many products. The board would not itself be instructed to maximize profits, because that would, in the end, mean fewer and fewer commodities, and larger and larger plants. Standardization may be a good thing in some cases, and the central board would have to decide when it should be imposed, but the decision to standardize as much as possible should not be forced on it by the instruction to maximize profits. The individual plants, or firms, would act without day to day interference as under private enterprise. As we shall argue in a later chapter, welfare theory cannot tell us that resources are wrongly distributed within an industry of this kind, and there would be nothing to be gained, and possibly much to lose, by attempting to make each plant produce some abstractly defined 'ideal' output. Such a solution does not imply that there are no possible advantages to be gained from nationalization in such a case. Entry would be 'free', that is, abnormal profits would be taken as a sign that more plants and more products, or possibly more plants and the same number of products, are needed. Thus demand might become more elastic for each plant. Purists could then take some comfort from the fact that price would be nearer to short-run marginal cost than it is likely to be under private enterprise, if entry is in any way restricted. The central board could also institute research, spread useful information on productive methods rapidly, and discourage any tendency to oligopolistic agreement.

In both the above cases the central board would be responsible for investment policy, although subject to ministerial control. In general it would seek to expand the industry when marginal plants were more than covering their average costs, and to contract it in the opposite case. It would, in fact, have the guidance of the normal profitability criterion as to when investment or disinvestment was required; and in the imperfect competition case it would also have the guidance of profitability in deciding which lines of production should be developed, and which restricted.

The above kind of scheme, whereby the central board of the industry exists in order to ensure that competition acts in the way in which it is supposed to act, has many advantages. As far as managers are concerned their instructions are simple and stimulating, and what they are used to. The board has the best practical guide for its investment policy.[1] Queueing is avoided when demand is in excess of supply, and, on the other hand, price reductions are semi-automatic when demand falls off. There is thus more flexibility than when an annual payment regulates output (the annual payment would remain as a datum-line of normal profitability for the industry, but it would not determine output).

But the above competitive solution,[2] which does away with the necessity of keeping a close watch on the annual payment, since that no longer determines output, is certainly not a universal panacea, although it might be widely applicable. If, for instance, the industry consisted mainly of a few large firms with falling costs, then the instruction to maximize profits would not be determinate (some element of indeterminacy would no doubt always be present

[1] We showed in Ch. X not only that profitability is the only practical and generally applicable guide, but also that it cannot, in the case of the imperfectly competitive industry without significant indivisibilities, be shown to be, even in theory, wrong.

[2] A very similar solution has been proposed by Mr. C. A. R. Crosland in his article, 'Prices and Costs in Nationalized Undertakings', *O.E.P.*, N.S., no. 3, Jan. 1950. I am indebted to the author for several of the suggestions embodied in this chapter.

in any imperfectly competitive industry—but, in many cases, it would not be great enough to matter). Each firm would require to know what assumptions it should make about the behaviour of other firms. If each acted independently, treating price as a parameter, heavy losses might be made. The competitive solution would then be open to all the objections urged against marginal-cost pricing, and more. The central board or the government would have to control the price. Even if this were done the individual firms could not be allowed to maximize profits on the basis of the given price, because they would then make marginal cost equal to price,[1] and the board would find that the price, at which the resultant output could be sold, would involve it in heavy losses. Again we have all the disadvantages of the marginalist solution. Therefore unless total costs can be covered by discrimination, resort must be had to average cost pricing. In which case the board must, in some way, control the output of the individual plants, so that overheads are covered. We are then back at the annual payment method of output determination.

In the above paragraphs some emphasis has been placed on nationalized industries making profits. The larger the nationalized sector the more important it becomes that this sector taken as a whole should make profits (and/or that some of its products should be taxed). The present nationalized sector is already large enough for it to be probable that the only general convention we have— that each industry should try to break even—is causing serious damage to the economy. A very large part of the savings of the community comes nowadays from corporations. Indeed private corporations save more than they invest, in addition to which they make profits and pay tax on them, which is also a contribution to

---

[1] To let managers maximize profits on the basis of a fixed price, adjusted by the central board until supply equals demand, would be the only practical method of getting marginal-cost pricing. That price is equal to marginal cost is, after all, a deduction from profit-maximization *with* a constant price—and whenever these postulates are realized, price is *by definition* equal to marginal cost. This deduction, as is usual in economics, cannot be verified, because marginal cost is not precisely identifiable (including, as it must, user cost). It was a mistake of the advocates of the extreme decentralized marginalist solution to take the condition, 'let price equal marginal cost', which is the fundamental 'welfare' theorem implicit in the theory of pure competition, and attempt to apply it directly. This cannot be done for the reason that marginal cost is not a perfectly objective magnitude. The only possible way of getting marginal-cost pricing *is* by aping the postulates of pure competition theory, on the assumption that managers, when told to do so, do in fact maximize profits.

governmental savings. The nationalized industries do not save at all; in fact they probably dissave although not supposed to do so. At the same time they are very heavy investors.

Moreover, most goods produced in the private sector are indirectly taxed. They thus make a contribution towards financing investment and government expenditure via indirect taxation, via contributing to the profit and income-tax of corporations, and via corporation saving. In contrast the products of the nationalized industries probably make a negative contribution.

This may seem a far cry from welfare economics: but there is in fact an intimate connexion. The large volume of taxation required to be raised cannot be raised in any very ideal way. But it will almost certainly be raised in a worse way than it need be if a range of products is automatically made exempt from taxation, however good prima facie candidates they might be. Moreover the total volume of taxation required will be pound for pound higher the smaller the contribution of these same goods to non-governmental savings. This is not to say that all nationalized industries should be expected to make some contribution to the finance of investment, or government expenditure. But where it can be seen that a particular industry could make good profits without any apparent 'distortion' of output, then it seems manifestly wrong that it should throw the whole burden of finding the savings required for its own investment on to the government or the rest of the economy. Where, finally, an approach to the best pricing policy would automatically result in large profits (as in the case of the National Coal Board) which would make possible the reduction of harmful taxation on other goods, the view that nationalized industries should *at least* cover costs becomes very much of an understatement.

The discussion we have had in this chapter of some of the possible methods of running public concerns is only, of course, a sketch drawn mainly, though not entirely, from the economic point of view. However, it suffices, I think, to show that there is not any one best method. From the economic angle we have to conclude that the best method depends on the nature of the product or products and on the nature of the industry. Just as the latter part of this chapter showed that there is no one best method of arriving at a certain output, so the first part showed that there is no one way of determining what the best output is. The best output, and the best method of arriving at it, are not indeed separable problems.

We can only decide what is the best thing to do in each particular case taking everything into consideration. The answer will be different in each case. And it will also depend on who decides; the problem is not a scientific one, about which we can expect to obtain universal, or almost universal, agreement. The decision is influenced by many different considerations of different kinds which cannot be weighed in any very objective way.

This whole chapter, and especially the latter part of it, has been somewhat of a digression from our main theme. But it may have been useful to stray away from pure theory, and see what the theory looks like when one tries to apply it. One cannot very well appreciate its usefulness, or lack of it, unless one watches it performing.

CHAPTER XII

THE VALUATION OF THE NATIONAL INCOME

In Chapter II we used the condition $\sum p_2 q_2 \geqslant \sum p_2 q_1$ (the q's referring to quantities bought by some individual) as a sufficient criterion for saying that the individual chose situation II rather than situation I. Similarly, if $\sum p_1 q_1 \geqslant \sum p_1 q_2$ we said that he chose situation I rather than II. If these two conditions both held, a contradiction arose.

We are now going to examine the same conditions when the q's refer not to quantities purchased by a single individual, but to the total quantities bought by a group of individuals. Where the group is relevant we will use capitals (P's and Q's) and where the individual is relevant small letters (p's and q's). By a group of individuals we do not mean a collective. A collective can be said to choose, and can therefore be treated as an economic individual, although it may be composed of many actual individuals. By definition, then, a group of individuals cannot be said to choose. The recipients of the national income are assumed to form a group but not a collective, and we shall, in general, assume that the Q's of the formula refer to the total quantities of different kinds of goods comprising the (real) national income, and that the P's refer to the market-prices of these goods.[1] When speaking of welfare, we use the same criterion for changes in an individual's welfare as we have used throughout ('on a higher behaviour line', or, if this cannot be known, the index-number criteria $\sum p_2 q_2 \geqslant \sum p_2 q_1$, and $\sum p_1 q_1 < \sum p_1 q_2$), and the same value judgements as before are presupposed.

From the above paragraph it follows that no obvious meaning in terms of choice attaches to $\sum P_2 Q_2 \geqslant \sum P_2 Q_1$ or $\sum P_1 Q_1 < \sum P_1 Q_2$. The first condition is shorthand for 'the money value of the real national income in period II is not less than the real income of period I valued at period II prices'. The second condition is shorthand for 'the money value of the real national income in period I is less than the real income of period II valued at period I prices'. When we are concerned with an 'economic man', $\sum p_2 q_2 \geqslant \sum p_2 q_1$

---

[1] Let us, for the moment, assume that all goods comprising the national income are consumed by individuals and have a market-price.

implied $\sum p_1 q_1 < \sum p_1 q_2$; this followed from the definition of consistency. But now that we are dealing with groups, $\sum P_2 Q_2 \geqslant \sum P_2 Q_1$ does not imply $\sum P_1 Q_1 < \sum P_1 Q_2$. It can easily be seen that the two sentences above, for which $\sum P_2 Q_2 \geqslant \sum P_2 Q_1$ and $\sum P_1 Q_1 < \sum P_1 Q_2$ are shorthand, are not contradictory. Even if every individual comprising the group was perfectly consistent, so that for every individual $\sum p_2 q_2 \geqslant \sum p_2 q_1$ implied $\sum p_1 q_1 < \sum p_1 q_2$, it would still not follow that we could not have both $\sum P_2 Q_2 \geqslant \sum P_2 Q_1$ and $\sum P_1 Q_1 \geqslant \sum P_1 Q_2$, when we summed the budgets of all the individuals.

Now it is usually thought that $\sum P_2 Q_2 \geqslant \sum P_2 Q_1$ contradicts $\sum P_1 Q_1 \geqslant \sum P_1 Q_2$, but this is only because these index numbers have been given meanings or definitions (apart from the obvious meanings given above) which make them contradictory. It is our purpose to examine the suggested definitions. Professor Hicks proposed such a definition in the following passage:

Thus, what the condition $\sum P_2 Q_2 > \sum P_2 Q_1$ tells us is that there is some redistribution of the Q_1s which would make every member of the group less well off than he actually is in the II situation. For, if the corresponding inequality were to hold for every individual separately, it would hold for the group as a whole.

As compared with this particular distribution, every other distribution of the Q_1s would make some people better off and some worse off. Consequently, if there is one distribution of the Q_1s in which every member of the group is worse off than he actually is in the II situation there can be no distribution in which everyone is better off, or even as well off. Thus, if we start from any actual distribution of wealth in the I situation, what the condition $\sum P_2 Q_2 > \sum P_2 Q_1$ tells us is that it is impossible to reach, by redistribution, a position in which everyone is as well off as he is in the II situation.

This would seem to be quite acceptable as a definition of increase in real social income.[1]

[1] J. R. Hicks, 'The Valuation of the Social Income', *Economica*, May 1940. I have substituted capitals for the sake of uniformity. It should also be noted that, although the definiendum is here 'real social income', Professor Hicks seems to assume in the same article that this is equivalent to 'welfare'. Finally it should be noted that it must be the case that the condition shows that there is a distribution of the Q_1s, *in which the optimum exchange conditions are satisfied*, which makes every member of the group worse off than he is in the II situation. But the condition does in fact show this. See P. A. Samuelson, 'Evaluation of Real National Income', *O.E.P.*, Jan. 1950, p. 8, n. 1: also C. M. Kennedy, 'An Alternative Proof of a Theorem in Welfare Economics', *O.E.P.*, Feb. 1954.

Now, for some reason, it is supposed that a good definition of 'real social income' must pass the base-reversal test. In other words, if $\sum P_2 Q_2 \geqslant \sum P_2 Q_1$ entails 'real social income is higher in II than I', then $\sum P_1 Q_1 < \sum P_1 Q_2$ must entail 'real social income is lower in I than II. It should be noted that this 'must' is a matter of elegance and convenience. There is no logical or philosophical reason why such a definition should pass the base-reversal test, because, as we have seen, the meaning of $\sum P_2 Q_2 \geqslant \sum P_2 Q_1$, which is implied by the conventional usage of the symbols, does not contradict the similar meaning of $\sum P_1 Q_1 \geqslant \sum P_1 Q_2$. When dealing with groups, there is no logical reason why we should not accept $\sum P_2 Q_2 \geqslant \sum P_2 Q_1$ as a definition of increased social income, and disregard the fact that $\sum P_1 Q_1$ may be greater than $\sum P_1 Q_2$.

Professor Kuznets has, however, criticized this Hicksian definition, saying that it must pass the base-reversal test.[1] Now it is evident that, given the formula $\sum P_2 Q_2 \geqslant \sum P_2 Q_1$, it does not matter how the goods were distributed in the first period. One can imagine the Q_1s were distributed in any way one likes in the first period. With each such different distribution there would be a different set of prices (P_1s), but these do not enter into the formula. Further, no distribution in the first period is logically inconsistent with our having arrived at the actual distribution and prices of the second period. This enabled Professor Hicks to say that $\sum P_2 Q_2 \geqslant \sum P_2 Q_1$ proves that there could have been some distribution in the first period such that, if we had still arrived at the actual position of period II, the formula $\sum p_2 q_2 \geqslant \sum p_2 q_1$ would have held for every individual. Thus $\sum P_2 Q_2 \geqslant \sum P_2 Q_1$ shows that, given the total quantities of the first period, the progress of history could conceivably have been such that every individual would now be better off. This is the meaning of Professor Hicks's definition of an increase in real social income.

What then, is the correct base-reversal of this Hicksian definition? Using a formula based on the prices of the first year, we must see that the analogous argument holds. Thus we must see that it is possible to redistribute the Q_2s in the formula $\sum P_1 Q_1 < \sum P_1 Q_2$ so that the inequality will hold for every individual. Since the P_2s do not appear in the formula, it is obvious that this is the case. In other words, it is possible to distribute the goods of the second

[1] S. Kuznets, 'On the Valuation of Social Income—Reflections on Professor Hicks's article', p. 4, *Economica*, Feb. and May 1948.

period in such a way that each individual's first period income would have been insufficient to buy what he could thus have in the second period, if goods were suitably redistributed. Thus if $\sum P_1 Q_1 < \sum P_1 Q_2$ the base-reversal test is satisfied, and Professor Kuznets's criticism is met.

But Professor Kuznets wrote:

But suppose we reverse the requirement, and ask whether it is impossible to make *everyone* as well off as in situation I by any redistribution of the actual quantities acquired in situation II. If it is impossible, then real income in I is greater than in II.[1]

We now see that if $\sum P_1 Q_1 < \sum P_1 Q_2$, then it is always possible, by redistributing the quantities of the second period, to make $\sum p_1 q_1 < \sum p_1 q_2$ for every individual. But, unfortunately, this is insufficient to show that everyone could be better off in the second period. For that, $\sum p_2 q_2 \geqslant \sum p_2 q_1$ must hold for every individual ($\sum p_2 q_2 \geqslant \sum p_2 q_1$ implies $\sum p_1 q_1 < \sum p_1 q_2$, but the reverse does not hold true). What Professor Kuznets had in mind in suggesting that Professor Hicks's definition did not pass the base-reversal test was that $\sum P_2 Q_2 \geqslant \sum P_2 Q_1$ does not prove that $\sum p_2 q_2 \geqslant \sum p_2 q_1$ could be made to hold for every individual, by redistributing the quantities of the second period. Thus he produces an example of two classes, rich and poor, who consume respectively luxuries and necessities, and argues that even if $\sum P_2 Q_2 \geqslant \sum P_2 Q_1$, then we cannot necessarily make both rich and poor better off unless luxuries can be substituted for necessities.[1]

This is perfectly true, but irrelevant to Professor Hicks's original definition.[2] Professor Kuznets goes on to say:

If we are to determine unequivocally an increase in welfare in situation II over situation I, we must assume not only a constancy of wants in the sense of a constancy of each individual's appraisal of different goods but also that either (a) all goods can be substituted for one another in the full range, or (b) the structure of the goods aggregate in the two situations is such that no specific good, to the extent that it cannot be replaced by another, is reduced in output.[1]

Now if all goods are merely, in some degree, substitutes, the fulfilment of either (a) or (b) will only ensure that it cannot be proved

[1] Loc. cit., p. 4.
[2] Professor Hicks in a comment on Professor Kuznets's article implicitly abandons his former criterion, and agrees with Professor Kuznets's criticisms ('The Valuation of the Social Income—A Comment on Professor Kuznets's reflections', *Economica*, Aug. 1948).

to be impossible, in the second period, to make $\sum p_2 q_2 \geqslant \sum p_2 q_1$ for every individual. If it is to be proved possible to make every individual better off, condition (a) should read 'all goods are perfect substitutes'. But if all goods are perfect substitutes (a) is irrelevant, and condition (b) should read simply 'no good is reduced in output'. The larger the inequality $\sum P_2 Q_2 > \sum P_2 Q_1$ the less substitutable must goods be for it to be possible, in the second period, to make $\sum p_2 q_2 > \sum p_2 q_1$ for everyone. But the definition is not supposed to depend on the magnitude of the inequality. However small it is, indeed even if $\sum P_2 Q_2 = \sum P_2 Q_1$, 'real social income' or 'welfare' is said to have increased. It does not require any proof to see that $\sum P_2 Q_2 = \sum P_2 Q_1$ does not demonstrate the possibility of making $\sum p_2 q_2 \geqslant \sum p_2 q_1$ for every individual, unless it is true that the output of no good has decreased.

Therefore if we are required to prove that everyone could be made better off, before we can conclude that welfare or real social income has increased, we could never say that welfare or real social income had increased, because it would never happen that the output of no good was less than before. Remembering the value premises we require in order to speak of an increase in welfare, it would also be necessary to add that the distribution of real income must not have changed for the worse. It is evident that such a definition is useless.

Let us return to the original Hicksian definition. Professor Hicks proposed, in effect, that we can say welfare, or real social income, has increased over an earlier period if there could have been some distribution of the goods produced in that earlier period which would make every individual better off now as compared with then, in the sense of being now able to choose that earlier *pretended* position if he wanted. Thus, by this definition, we have to say the welfare of society has increased, when the poor are poorer, and even though it might be impossible to restore them to their former position without making the rich worse off in their turn. They have only the consolation that there might have been at the earlier period a distribution which would have made them, and everyone else, worse off than at present. I don't think many people would on this account want to say that welfare, or real social income, had increased.

Nevertheless, this Hicksian definition leads to the correct solution. Let us recall the sufficient criterion, which we laid down in

Chapter VI, for an increase in welfare: (a) the income distribution of the second position must be not less favourable than that of the initial position, and (b) it must not be possible to reach the second position merely by redistributing money. Now Professor Hicks showed, in the above quotation, that no redistribution of the quantities of the first position could have made $\sum p_2 q_2 < \sum p_2 q_1$ hold for every individual now, assuming that the actual second position is unaltered by the earlier redistribution. It shows, in fact, that, if the two positions could have been put to the vote, those who stood to lose by the move could not profitably have bribed those who stood to gain to vote against it. This follows because if $\sum p_2 q_2$ remained equal to, or greater than, $\sum p_2 q_1$ for *any* individual, then that individual would not have been successfully bribed. $\sum P_2 Q_2 \geqslant \sum P_2 Q_1$ shows, in short, that the Scitovsky criterion is satisfied. Professor Hicks had, in fact, abandoned, in his 1940 article, the Kaldor–Hicks criterion, and adopted the later-defined Scitovsky criterion. As soon as we introduce a value judgement about income distribution it thus ceases to matter whether the gainers could overcompensate the losers or not—it ceases to matter whether $\sum p_2 q_2 > \sum p_2 q_1$ could be made to hold for every individual in the second period. Therefore we can conclude that welfare in period II is greater than in period I if $\sum P_2 Q_2 \geqslant \sum P_2 Q_1$ and if the distribution of real income is no worse in the second period.[1]

This criterion is a welfare criterion, but not a criterion for a desirable change (see Chapter VI, p. 111). The reason why it is only the former is that we have shown only that the goods actually produced in the first situation could not have made everyone as well off as in the second position. We have not shown that some redistribution in the first situation could not have produced a still better position, account being taken of the fact that the pattern of output would have adjusted itself to the redistribution. In terms of the Utility Possibility Diagram (Fig. XII) the curve represents the utility possibilities of the set of goods corresponding to position (I), not the set of factors of production corresponding to position (I). By 'real income' being better distributed at II, we mean that I' is better than I, where the set of goods at I' is the same as at I. $\sum P_2 Q_2 > \sum P_2 Q_1$ proves that II is north-east of I'.

---

[1] This, however, assumes that the disutility of work has not increased. If a man is just induced to move to an unpleasant area where he produces twice as much, and earns twice as much, the national income increases, but not welfare.

This 'welfare' criterion has been criticized on the grounds of redundancy.[1] It is said that if anyone can say that I' is better than I, then he could equally well have said that II is better than I. Supposing that II is the present position, and I represents a past year, is this the case? Direct inspection of I is impossible, since there are no time machines. Of course, it may still be reasonable to make a judgement directly, eschewing the evidence of index-

FIG. XII

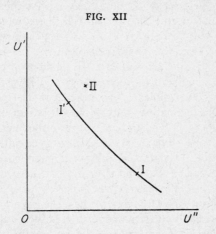

numbers, and evidence of the distribution of wealth, by reading novels, social surveys, &c. But perhaps most people would think that quantitative evidence in the form of index-numbers of output or consumption, and figures relating to the distribution of wealth, was of assistance in forming a judgement. Since the former tell one only that I' is south-west of II, it is difficult to believe that our analysis is entirely superfluous.

The above welfare criterion (it is, of course, only a sufficient criterion, and not a definition) must not be subjected to any base-reversal test. We said above that there was no logical reason why the condition $\sum P_1 Q_1 < \sum P_1 Q_2$ should also be required to hold. Just as we found that some changes could be recommended although the gainers could not compensate the losers, so we find that if real income is better distributed, and if $\sum P_2 Q_2 \geqslant \sum P_2 Q_1$, then the second position is better than the first, even although it is also

[1] C. M. Kennedy, 'The Economic Welfare Function and Dr. Little's Criterion', *R.E.S.* **xx** (2), no. 52, 1952-3. See also p. 106 above.

the case that $\sum P_1 Q_1 \geqslant \sum P_1 Q_2$. Similarly the first position is better than the second position if $\sum P_1 Q_1 \geqslant \sum P_1 Q_2$ and if there has been an unfavourable change in distribution between the two positions, even although $\sum P_2 Q_2 \geqslant \sum P_2 Q_1$.[1]

Now the index-number $\sum P_2 Q_2 / \sum P_2 Q_1$ is arrived at by dividing the uncorrected index-number $\sum P_2 Q_2 / \sum P_1 Q_1$ by the Laspeyre price index-number $\sum P_2 Q_1 / \sum P_1 Q_1$. Thus our analysis indicates the superiority of the Laspeyre price index when it is considered that income distribution has changed in a favourable manner. In fact, only by the use of the Laspeyre index can we say that welfare has increased. Similarly, the index-number $\sum P_1 Q_2 / \sum P_1 Q_1$ may be arrived at by dividing the uncorrected index by the Paasche price index-number $\sum P_2 Q_2 / \sum P_1 Q_2$. Only by using the Paasche index can we say that welfare has decreased. In a democratic community, with universal suffrage, income distribution will normally tend to move in a favourable direction in the eyes of most people. The use of the Laspeyre index is then indicated. Those who believe that, in a capitalist community, income distribution must always be changing unfavourably, however it changes, should always use the Paasche price index.

The above discussion is very formal. We have been assuming that we have exactly the same population of identical men in both periods. In fact, of course, people die, and are born. The longer the interval over which we are making the comparison the worse this difficulty becomes. Also we have been assuming that all individuals are choosers, which is far from being true. Hardly any individual chooses all the goods he consumes, and some choose none of them. But we have seen that people think, to some extent, in terms of averages, or in terms of social groups, and such concepts fulfil rather better than actual individuals the requirement of continuity of choice. In thinking about the welfare of the country, one may be prepared to ignore distribution within social groups which have only a small range of real income distribution.

We have also been assuming that we have had an unchanging 'population' of goods. But if a new good is introduced the formal analysis is upset. If some good, which is available in the second

---

[1] But it should be noted that a contradiction could still arise if the change in distribution were neutral. In this case one would require both $\sum P_2 Q_2 > \sum P_2 Q_1$ and $\sum P_1 Q_1 < \sum P_1 Q_2$ for position II to be better than position I, and analogously for I to be better than II.

situation, is not available in the first, then we do not require an index-number to tell us that a redistribution of goods could not have put everyone on the same or a higher behaviour line as in the second situation, because the behaviour lines of all those who consume some of the new good are formally incomparable with those of the earlier period. Thus the introduction of a new good formally prevents us from saying that welfare has increased, and, similarly, if a good ceases to be produced, it would prevent us from saying that welfare had decreased. Quality changes also can obviously invalidate the analysis.

Then, of course, we have the fact that no index-number can be perfect. The price index must always be arrived at by sampling. Also, of course, the national-income totals themselves are not perfect. But, even if the index-numbers were perfect, our analysis would not fit the real world very well. We thus reach what is by now a very familiar conclusion. Not only must any change in the distribution of income be judged favourable, but also $\sum P_2 Q_2$ must exceed $\sum P_2 Q_1$ by a good large margin before one can have any confidence in one's conclusion. How large this margin must be is a matter of judgement.

We have said in an earlier chapter that, in practice, welfare conclusions cannot be tested. But the comparison of national-income totals does provide a certain very rough test of the applicability of the welfare analysis. Let us suppose that two people agree to accept the two fundamental value judgements of welfare economics. Let us also suppose that they both agree that income distribution did not change unfavourably between the two periods in question. We may also limit ourselves to the question whether *consumption* rose (we have so far assumed, in discussing national income comparisons, that all goods are consumed by individuals). We will suppose that an index-number of consumption seems to indicate that consumption rose. We ask, need these two people agree that consumption rose? Obviously not, for both can recognize the fact that the real world is not very like the world presupposed by the formal analysis. If one wishes to maintain that consumption has risen, and the other that consumption has fallen, neither can possibly *prove* his case. Nor could he prove it, however perfect the statistical techniques might be. Of course, if the index-number showed a terrific rise, the person who maintained that consumption had fallen would look silly. One might cease to trust his judgement, but he could never be proved wrong. If, however, the index-number showed only a small rise, it really becomes quite meaningless to say that consumption has either risen or fallen. The extent of the rise which the index-number would have to show before everyone, who agreed on the theoretical value premises required, would also agree on the practical conclusion, is a rough index of the applicability of welfare analysis. This is the case, because the only way of testing welfare analysis is by inviting agreement or disagreement with the conclusions from those who accept the premises.

The reader may be surprised to find that I have treated judgements about consumption in the same way as I treated welfare judgements. In the above paragraph it was implied that the former kind of judgement requires value premises, just as the latter does. We have already seen that the word 'welfare' is an ethical word. But words like 'real income' and 'consumption' are not, of course, ethical words. Nevertheless such a statement as 'the real income of the community decreased between 1939 and 1949' strongly suggests that there was a change for the bad; and similarly if it was said to have increased. I have therefore proposed that the phrases 'increase (decrease) of welfare' and 'increase (decrease) of real income' should both be logically subsequent to a judgement about the desirability or otherwise of any change in the distribution of welfare (or real income). To say 'the real income of the community is greater' is not much different from saying 'the income of the community is really greater', which is again not much different from 'the community is better off'. We have therefore treated 'increase of real income' and 'increase of welfare' as synonymous. Now in the above paragraph changes in consumption, not real income, were discussed. But to say 'Consumption has increased, &c.' suggests almost as strongly as 'Real income has increased, &c.' that something good has happened. If no change in the output of any good occurs, 'real income' has a fairly precise descriptive meaning (although of course any discussion of what should be included in 'real income' is a discussion of values). It simply refers, in a closed community, to the total collection of goods and services sold. Similarly, consumption refers to the aggregate collection of goods and services consumed. But the question whether this collection becomes larger or smaller, when its composition changes, does not admit of any precise, objective, purely descriptive answer. The answer given depends inevitably on the relative importance attached to the different kinds of goods consumed. For this reason, before it is said that consumption is greater, we require that our criterion for a desirable economic change be satisfied, i.e. the distribution of consumption must not be worse, and it must not be possible that a redistribution of the goods, consumed in the initial situation, should have put every individual in a position with respect to consumption which would be chosen rather than the position actually reached in the second period. If this criterion is satisfied it is concluded that consumption is greater.

Unfortunately, for people to agree on such questions as whether welfare has increased or decreased, it is insufficient that they should agree on the initial value premises required. They know that within wide limits it is still possible to disagree because the theoretical anlysis is not perfectly applicable. It is all a matter of judgement where the limits lie, but within these limits, consciously or unconsciously, honestly or dishonestly, one can be led to reach one conclusion, or the other, from ulterior motives. The surface argument may be about how well the welfare analysis fits the real world. The real argument may be about whether a socialist government is a good thing, or not. There is thus the ever-present danger that welfare economics may degenerate into a kind of scholastic tub-thumping.

After this digression, let us return to rather more technical matters, and tie up some loose ends. We have shown that there can be no welfare significance in national-income comparisons unless a value judgement about changes in distribution is presupposed. But statisticians, when they present us with national-income totals, whether valued at current prices or at those of some base year, do not, of course, wish to make any such presupposition. They wish to present such data as will be useful as a basis from which other people can draw inferences about welfare, or changes in consumption or real income, if they wish to do so. They can, however, preserve this neutrality without any difficulty. They can, for instance, say that the total market-value of consumption goods in 1947 was ten per cent. greater than the value of the consumption goods of 1939 measured at 1947 prices. What they should not do is to conclude that consumption increased. There is, after all, no such *thing* as consumption, the size of which can be measured. The first of the above two statements is objective and neutral. The second is neither one nor the other. We may at once add that the general practice of statisticians, and that in particular of the compilers of the national-income figures, leaves little or nothing to be desired in this respect.

But we have said that statisticians may wish to provide data from which others can draw inferences about real income, real wages, and so on. This raises two questions: first, what prices should be used? and, second, what things should be included in an index which people can use as a guide to welfare? As regards the first question, we have so far assumed that market-prices are used. The formal reason for using market-prices is clear. They are the prices which individuals have to pay, and our theory regards welfare, real income, &c., as a function of, or logical construction from, the welfares or real incomes of 'individuals'. We have, however, pointed out that this theoretical concept can at best only be very roughly applied to a changing population of changing tastes, not all members of which are choosers. Since this is the case, does there remain any good reason for using market-prices, rather than costs, as weights?

At the formal level a precise reason could be given for using market-prices. At the applied level—which is the level we are interested in—only imprecise reasons can be given. It is probably better to use the weights which pure theory suggests, if there is no particular reason for choosing others, since this procedure brings the logic of the comparison more into the open. This is really only a pedagogic reason. Secondly, it is conceivable, though unlikely, that prices and costs would diverge enough to make the market-price comparison more reliable (the sense in which one comparison can be said to be more reliable than another was made clear in our discussion of the problem of testing the applicability of the analysis). Lastly, although the comparison cannot possibly be given a precise meaning in terms of actual individuals, the individual is usually held to be of importance, and the use of market-prices as weights is more consistent with this kind of social philosophy than the use of an index based on factor costs would be. I think that there is thus some slight reason for concluding that, on the whole, an index, which is to serve as a guide to making welfare, or real income, judgements, would be better based on market-prices—although in almost all cases an index based on factor costs would be just as useful.

The second question—What should be included in the 'guide-to-welfare' index?—we have by-passed by assuming an economy in which all goods are consumed by individuals, that is by assuming an economy with no saving, and no collective or government consumption. Let us thus continue to by-pass this question until we have discussed the significance of comparisons of national-income totals in which the goods are weighted by factor costs (including, of course, profits), and not by market-prices.

The factor-cost index is supposed to measure production in some sense. Now the production of an economy consists of a heterogeneous collection of goods of various kinds (each kind of good being itself regarded as homogeneous). There is only one clear and obvious sense in which a heterogeneous collection can be said to be larger, and that is when there is more of one kind of good and no less of any kind. Accepting this, it follows that production can never be said to have increased if the output of any one good has declined. This is exactly analogous to the view that welfare cannot be said to be greater if any individual is harmed, a view which results from the mistaken idea that the welfare of the community is a heterogeneous collection of the welfares of the individuals comprising the community.

Analogous to the Kaldor–Hicks definition of an increase in welfare, we have the view that production can be said to be greater if resources could be rearranged in such a way that the production of every good would be greater. Just as the fulfilment of the Kaldor–Hicks criterion indicated, at best, a potential increase in welfare, so, of course, the change by which the output of every good could be increased can only be correctly and accurately described as a potential increase in production.[1] This may seem unduly pedantic. I hope, however, that I have said enough about the suggestiveness of economic language to show that pedantic accuracy of description is highly desirable, if one wishes to preserve any neutrality towards the facts one tries to describe.

Now if average full costs were equal to marginal costs, the ratios of the weights used in a factor-cost index would be equal to the transformation rates of the goods.[2] In that case the condition

[1] If all goods are valued at factor cost the same total must be reached as is reached when each factor used is weighted by the amount it is paid. Thus an index which measures potential changes in production must also be a measure of the amount of resources used, assuming that all factors, including entrepreneurship, are included. In other words, potential production is the same thing as production potential.

[2] Cf. J. Hicks, 'The Valuation of the Social Income', *Economica*, May 1940, pp. 119–20.

$\sum P_2 Q_2 > \sum P_2 Q_1$ would show, for very small changes in production, that, in the second period, more than the goods of the first period could have been produced. In other words, it would show that production potential had increased. Thus, ideally, the factor-cost national-income measure can be said to be a measure of production potential. It should be noted that, given this interpretation, we do have a contradiction if both $\sum P_2 Q_2 > \sum P_2 Q_1$ and $\sum P_1 Q_1 > \sum P_1 Q_2$. It would then be the case that the goods of the second period could have been produced in the first period, but the goods of the first period could also have been produced in the second period. If this is true, we clearly cannot speak of an increase in production potential. Thus, unlike an increase in welfare, an increase in production requires both $\sum P_2 Q_2 > \sum P_2 Q_1$ and $\sum P_1 Q_1 < \sum P_1 Q_2$.

But the above theory of changes in production potential is 'extremely shaky'. To quote Professor Hicks:

... It is on this sort of structure that actual index numbers of production are based; but it has to be recognized that it is extremely shaky from a theoretical point of view. Returns are not always constant; prices (ex tax) are not always equal to marginal cost; once these assumptions are dropped the whole argument loses its validity. . . . Some people may be tempted to rush in with the suggestion that a constant degree of market imperfection and constant marginal costs would mend the situation, and is not too bad a hypothesis; but there seem to be crushing objections against this. While there may be some sense in which it is normal for marginal costs to be constant under imperfect competition, that sense can hardly be relevant here, where we are thinking about a whole economy, not a single firm, so that the specificity of factors is of first-rate importance to us. Further, unless we have some way of measuring marginal costs directly, we need to assume not only a constant degree of market imperfection, but the same degree of market imperfection in all industries—and that assumption is hardly tolerable.[1]

It should be noticed that, in the previous paragraph, it was stated that this analysis was valid only for small changes in production. But of course index-numbers are applied where more than marginal changes in the output of individual goods must be allowed for. In this event the analysis is valid only if transformation curves are straight lines. This is a far stronger assumption than constant returns to scale, and implies that there is only one factor of production, or that factors are employed in the same proportions for

[1] J. Hicks, 'The Valuation of the Social Income', ibid., p. 121.

all outputs. The normal assumption of economic theory is, of course, a diminishing rate of transformation as the output of one good is increased and that of another reduced: and therefore we should see what the index-numbers can tell us about production on this assumption.

Now, since the transformation curve is concave, $\sum P_2 Q_2 > \sum P_2 Q_1$ does *not* tell us that the goods represented by the point Q_1 could have been produced with the factors and techniques of the second situation. Similarly $\sum P_1 Q_1 > \sum P_1 Q_2$ tells us nothing about the production possibilities of the two situations. Just as the *convexity* of behaviour lines prevents one from inferring anything about utility possibilities from $\sum P_1 Q_2 > \sum P_1 Q_1$ or from $\sum P_2 Q_1 > \sum P_2 Q_2$, so the concavity of transformation curves prevents one inferring anything about production potential from the reverse inequalities. But equally $\sum P_1 Q_2 > \sum P_1 Q_1$ and $\sum P_2 Q_1 > \sum P_2 Q_2$ enable one to infer something about production potential. The former tells us that the goods of the second position could not have been produced with the factors and techniques of the first situation even if the production possibility function were linear, and *a fortiori* if it is concave: and the latter that the goods of the first position could not have been produced with the factors and techniques of the second situation.

In order to infer that the production potential of the second situation is higher than that of the first one would require at least that $\sum P_1 Q_2 > \sum P_1 Q_1$, and that $\sum P_2 Q_2 > \sum P_2 Q_1$ (the latter in order to avoid a contradiction). But in fact, it is doubtful whether this is enough—for the phrase 'an increase in production potential' would seem to imply that the factors and techniques of the second situation could more than produce *any* set of goods which could have been produced with the factors of the first situation: and this no mere index-number can tell us. If then the phrase is used when these index-number criteria are satisfied, it is important to remember that they merely mean that the second situation could more than produce the *actual* goods produced in the first, and the first could not have produced the actual goods of the second.[1]

It may occur to the reader that the approach via, as it were, the goods potential of a situation, and the approach via the utility potential of a set of goods should be combined, and the utility

[1] The above analysis of 'production potential' is based on P. A. Samuelson, 'Evaluation of Real National Income', *O.E.P.*, Jan. 1950.

potential of the two situations be compared, free play being allowed to the sets of goods to accommodate themselves to the different distributions of wealth. If this is done, the result is the conclusion that index-numbers can tell us nothing about the utility or welfare potential of different situations with different transformation curves (see Samuelson, loc. cit., above, p. 17).[1] From the point of view of using predicted changes in the national income as a guide to policy this is unfortunate. The fact that the actual goods of the first situation (which may be thought of as the *status quo*) could not make everyone as well off as they would be in the second situation is not a sufficient reason to move to the second situation, in that it might still be the case that *some* set of goods, which would have been produced in the first situation if money had been suitably redistributed, could have made everyone better off than they would have been in the second situation.

Struck perhaps by the shakiness of the transformation rate approach to production indices, Professor Kuznets has tried to introduce, or reintroduce, a different concept of production. Thus he writes:

> The widespread tendency to identify social income as a measure of welfare, with social income as a measure of productivity . . . is grounded upon the sound notion that the 'product', taken as the yield of resources, cannot differ from the welfare equivalent, for the simple reason that the latter represents the positive result of the use of resources, and that resources have no weight independent of the positive result of their employment.[2]

This passage seems to be a recommendation to use the word 'product' in the same sense as the word 'welfare'. Thus, to say 'the "product" . . . cannot differ from the welfare equivalent' is only another way of saying ' "product" is equivalent to "welfare" '. If 'production' thus always meant 'welfare production', and it is accepted that the best index for a guide to welfare is the market-price index, then, of course, the best production index is, *ipso facto*, the market-price index. Professor Kuznets's claim that the production measure and the 'welfare' measure should be identical would be established. But, in fact, 'production' does not mean 'welfare production', although the statement 'production is greater' may tend to suggest that something good has occurred. It is, however,

---

[1] The reader can also easily satisfy himself of the truth of this with the aid of a diagram containing transformation curves and community-indifference curves, as defined in Ch. XIII. [2] S. Kuznets, loc. cit., p. 124.

obviously not contradictory to say that production has increased, but welfare has diminished. Welfare is not necessarily the positive result of the use of resources. To suppose that 'welfare production' and 'production' really mean the same is again to confuse the two ideas which Professor Hicks separated out in the article cited.

In addition to arguing that a 'welfare' measure and a 'production' measure must really be the same, Professor Kuznets also argues that the market-price index, as a matter of fact, is a better measure of production potential. This is rather confusing, because, if it were true that a 'welfare' measure and a 'production' measure *must* be the same, then there is no need to show that, as a matter of fact, they are the same. But to take the last argument on its own merits, the claim is that marginal costs are better represented if indirect taxes (*less*, presumably, subsidies) are added on. The assumption on which this claim is based is that the cost of free government services to firms can be equated to the amount of net indirect tax paid. Thus factors would be weighted by the payments to them, *less* direct tax, *plus* transfers, *plus* final free public services. (That is, national income is equal to rent, interest, profits, wages and salaries, *less* direct tax *plus* transfers *plus* final free public services.)

If we agree, for the sake of argument only, that disposable income *plus* final free government services (equal to the usual 'welfare' measure *less* free intermediate services) is what ought to go into a 'welfare' index, then the two indices would coincide. It is possible that Professor Kuznets's resultant production index would be better than the ordinary one, which takes no account of changes in intermediate governmental services. For instance, if there was an increase in essential intermediate services, *without* an increase in indirect tax, his index would show a fall in productive potential, which would be correct, since the previous collection of final goods could no longer be reproduced. On the other hand, if there was simply a change in indirect taxation, without any change in production or intermediate services, Professor Kuznets's index would normally show a change in productive potential, which would be incorrect. There would seem to be no particular reason to suppose that this index would be better than the ordinary one, although, in view of the shakiness of any index, it could hardly matter very much which we used, especially since they would be most unlikely to give very different results.

It was necessary to discuss an index based on factor costs, because this is the only possible index for those goods and services which are not bought by individuals, and which, therefore, have no market valuation. Thus the market-price index can refer only to goods chosen directly by individuals. Now goods which are chosen collectively may be divided into two classes—'welfare goods' and 'non-welfare goods'. Some people might want to declare the latter a null-class, and claim that battleships and tanks contributed to people's welfare. I think, however, that most people who so thought would not want to say that battleships contributed to current welfare; they would rather regard such things as a kind of insurance, rather than actually as constituents of a good life. Although it is a matter of opinion what kinds of things should be classed as 'non-welfare goods', the statistician who wants to produce an index which will be most useful as a guide to welfare must make a guess as to what most people would want to see included. Roughly speaking, I think most people would want to fit into this category, or regard as costs rather than utilities, those goods and services which are not individually chosen, and would not be regretted by many people if a diminution of them did not tend to a reduction in the amount of any other kind of good—such things as justice, police, and defence. The admittance of a category of non-welfare collective goods implies, of course, that we do not ourselves believe that disposable income *plus* government free final services of all sorts comprises the contents of the best index for welfare purposes.

Thus we have three sectors of the economy: (*a*) a collective non-welfare sector, (*b*) a collective welfare sector, and (*c*) a sector the goods of which are individually chosen (this is, by definition, a welfare sector). We will still assume, for the moment, that there is no saving.

The first sector (*a*) is, by definition, excluded. But clearly both (*b*) and (*c*) must be included. In sector (*b*) the only possible index seeks to answer the question 'Could last year's collection of goods have been produced this year?' Now, as far as sector (*c*) is concerned, we have argued that the market-price index should be used, and that it is a guide to welfare in that it tells us whether any redistribution of income, given last year's goods, could have made every individual as well off as he is this year (given a constant population of choosers, &c.). The question arises as to what justification there can be for lumping together two such conceptually different indices. The resultant would be a hybrid to which no definite meaning could be attached. Some writers have satisfied their consciences by making the very dubious *ad hoc* assumption that publicly provided goods would just fetch their cost price on the market. We have, however, contended that the sector (*c*) index cannot possibly have any precise meaning in terms of actual individuals anyway. And Professor Hicks has shown that the factor-cost index also can have no precise meaning. We can therefore cheerfully lump the two indices together, since what we are looking for is the index which will be of most assistance to most people for drawing welfare conclusions; we are not looking for an index with a precise meaning. That would, in any case, be a wild-goose chase. On the other hand, it would be an advantage to have a separate index for both sectors. This is because many people are interested in their comparative growth, their respective magnitudes being of considerable social significance.

We must now consider the question of how best to treat savings. Savings can hardly be left out of a welfare measure. No one would want to say that people are worse off because they freely decide to save more. They might say that their standard of living had fallen, but not their welfare. Therefore, savings should, in my opinion, be considered to contribute to current welfare. But all saving, except saving by public bodies, arises in the individualist sector. (Admittedly, there are private collective savings, but perfectly clear-cut lines of division are impossible. The two collectivist sectors together may be taken to apply to what is usually called the public sector of the economy. This division is less distorted by the adoption of the convention that undistributed profits are individual savings than it would be by including them in the public collective sector.) Therefore it would appear that all such savings are, for welfare purposes, to be included in the individualist sector, whatever the class of investment to which they correspond. This is not, however, altogether paradoxical, for current investment has no direct relevance to the present happiness of individuals. But current savings do contribute to people's happiness so long as they believe that their savings will retain their value.

Professor Kuznets adopts a different view of savings. He believes that the decision to save should be regarded as a decision to make some real investment. He then suggests that the investment total and the consumption total may be added, because the value of capital goods is, in theory, the discounted value of their future yields. He considers that this treatment approximates better to the true meaning of savings decisions. It is difficult to agree with this, when a decision to save is independent of, and by no means always accompanied by, a decision to invest.

Professor Kuznets writes:

We must value in terms of current welfare also such parts (of total output) as represent a net addition to (or a net draft upon) the country's capital, whether under private or public auspices.[1]

But surely, if an appeal has to be made to future yields, this has not been done. The expected future 'yield' of an individual's savings is based on the rate of interest, and the price level of consumption goods now, and in the recent past. It seems to me that we approach more closely to the meaning of individual decisions to save if we adopt the alternative view that a decision to save is a decision to accumulate purchasing power over future goods of the kind available in the saving situation. This view is consistent with adding in private savings to the welfare sector, without requiring any elaborate assumption about the relation of the discounted value of the yield to the present value of resources. The only practical differences between these views are, (1) that, on the present view, public saving should be excluded from the welfare index, and (2) that the income totals should be deflated by a price index comprising consumption goods only.

Both views have, however, a common disadvantage. In a time of rising prices, caused perhaps by the devotion of much investment to the non-welfare sector, the value of people's savings falls. Some people would then probably want to say that saving was only an illusory contribution to welfare. They would want to make a distinction between their being really better off, and their only thinking they were better off. This, however, raises all the difficulties associated with assuming that $\sum p_2 q_2 > \sum p_2 q_1$ is an adequate criterion of individual welfare. The most that one can say is that, so long as one lays emphasis on individual choices, it seems more consistent to accept the view that savings contribute to current welfare, whether they are being used to finance battleships or consumption-goods factories; and our discussion of the welfare mea-

[1] Loc. cit., p. 13.

sure for the predominantly individualist sector of the economy *is* based on the assumption that great emphasis is laid on individual choices.

It must, however, be admitted that the above discussion is very academic, for it is most unlikely that a budget surplus or deficit would, in normal times, make sufficient difference for it to be reasonable to suppose that one treatment would result in a better guide to welfare than the other. Under abnormal conditions, such as a very severe inflation, no measure based on a quantity index would be of any value. The condition $\sum p_2 q_2 > \sum p_2 q_1$ would have little relevance, even in relation to an individual's welfare, if prices were changing very rapidly, and no relevance to the welfare of the community, unless it was at least given that the resultant large changes in income distribution were approved of.

We conclude that the most useful guide for the purpose of making welfare judgements would be to have two indices, one comprising private savings *plus* private consumption, using a market-price index as deflator, and the other comprising the output of final collective 'welfare goods', using an index of costs as deflator. But such indices cannot be treated as *measures* of welfare. They would be better regarded as providing some evidence, which people may use to assist them to make welfare judgements, if they want to.

CHAPTER XIII

WELFARE THEORY AND INTERNATIONAL TRADE

WE do not propose to analyse the welfare implications of all the manifold different trade policies which a country might adopt. We shall content ourselves with three of the most important topics: first, the 'gains' from international trade; secondly, the 'gains' which can accrue to a country as a result of raising a tariff barrier; and, lastly, the question of the desirability of free trade.

A correct statement of the 'gains' which may accrue to a hitherto isolated country as a result of entering upon international trade can be most simply made in terms of the analysis of the national income which we made in the last chapter.

Let us first postulate that all the 'optimum' conditions of production and exchange are satisfied in a certain country. Let the money value of the national income be $\sum P_1 Q_1$. The fact that all the 'optimum' conditions are satisfied implies that no other set of goods (such as Q_0) which could be produced would suffice to make everyone as well off as they, in fact, are. In other words, the gainers by a movement away from the production aggregate, described by $\sum P_1 Q_1$, would not be able to compensate the losers. This implies that $\sum P_1 Q_1 \geqslant \sum P_1 Q_0$, because, as we saw in the last chapter, this condition describes a situation such that the Q_0's could not be distributed in such a way as to make everyone as well off as in situation I.

Next, let us suppose that the trade barriers are removed, and that relative world prices are not identical with the price-relatives in the hitherto isolated country. Trade therefore takes place, and we will suppose that a new equilibrium results, such that the national income of the country in question is now $\sum P_2 Q_2$. We assume that all the 'optimum' conditions are again satisfied. It once more follows that no other set of goods which could be obtained by production or exchange would suffice to make everyone as well off as in the post-trade equilibrium position.

Now among these other sets of goods which could be obtained is the set produced in the pre-trade equilibrium position. It therefore follows that $\sum P_2 Q_2 \geqslant \sum P_2 Q_1$. The interpretation of this inequality is the same as in the last chapter. If the distribution of real income is no worse in the second situation, then welfare can be said to have increased. We would not require to assume 'optimum' conditions of production and exchange within the country if it could be assumed that production would be in no way altered by the opening of trade. In that case, the above argument also shows that the post-trade position is better than the pre-trade position, in that the set of goods produced within the country, after trade has commenced, would be incapable of making every individual as well off as he is with the goods he actually consumes.

Thus we see that the correct statement of the 'gains' from trade is not that the 'gainers' could overcompensate the 'losers'. That is not, as we saw in the last chapter, implied by the condition $\sum P_2 Q_2 \geqslant \sum P_2 Q_1$. In his article 'The Gains from International Trade'[1] to which the above argument owes much, Professor Samuelson states that 'more of every commodity can be secured with less of every productive service. This ensures us that by Utopian co-operation everyone can be made better off as a result of trade.'[2] This conclusion, that everyone could be made better off, presupposes the possibility of a production pattern different to that of the actual post-trade equilibrium position. Thus Professor Samuelson argues that trade could make everyone better off, and not that a redistribution of the goods actually obtained by trade could make everyone better off. Our statement is rather different. We say that the post-trade position is actually better than the pre-trade position, if the distribution of real income has not deteriorated.

We have said nothing about productive services. At the formal level they can be dealt with by the inclusion of leisure among the 'products'. It may also be noticed that the above argument makes no mention of comparative costs in the foreign country. When we are considering the gains which may accrue to a single country, this is not necessary. All that is required is that comparative world *prices* should be out of line with comparative real costs in the home country.

The gains-from-trade argument has usually been stated in a form which shows that both countries will gain from embarking on some

---

[1] *C.J.E.P.S.*, vol. v, May 1939, reprinted in *Readings in the Theory of International Trade* (Blakiston, 1949).   [2] Loc. cit. (Blakiston, 1949), p. 238.

trade. For this argument to be valid, it is further required that all the 'optimum' conditions of production and exchange should be satisfied in both countries, or, if all countries are involved, in every country, so that transformation rates are equal to comparative real costs; or else it must be assumed that production is unaltered in every country, so that the problem becomes merely one of exchange. Then so long as trade does not shift the distribution of real income in an unfavourable manner, either between individuals in one country or between countries, it follows that trade increases welfare. The argument in favour of universal free trade simply results from pushing the gains-from-trade argument to its logical limits. If to the above assumptions we add universal full-employment, and the absence of external economies, &c., then we arrive at the theory that free trade 'maximizes world welfare', because it results in the fulfilment of all the 'optimum' conditions of production and exchange throughout the world. But it is only 'world welfare' that is supposed to be maximized. An individual country may gain by a restrictive policy, just as an individual monopolist may so gain. This brings us to the question of tariffs.

In considering tariffs, we will first deal with the simple two-country two-good case. This, and other international trade problems, can be dealt with graphically with the assistance of the device known as the 'community-indifference' curve.

The 'community-indifference' curve has been defined by Professor Scitovsky in a manner which does not involve us in the absurdity of treating a community as a person, when it is actual individuals, or small social groups within the community, in terms of which community welfare (or indifference) is defined. To quote:

In a Cartesian plane whose axes measure physical quantities of two commodities, say bread and wine, designate by p_0 the amounts of these goods possessed by the community and assume that they are distributed among its members in a given way. Assume next that the community is induced by a rise in the price of bread to give up a certain quantity of it, say $b_0 b_1$. Then it is possible exactly to compensate everybody for his loss of satisfaction by distributing a certain quantity, say $w_0 w_1$, of wine. p_1 therefore is a point of indifference to p_0, in the sense that it represents for each member of the community the same welfare that he enjoyed at p_0. In a similar way, we can draw all points of the community-indifference curve going through p_0.

It will be noticed that there is not one but an infinite number of community-indifference curves going through p_0 corresponding to different distribution of welfare (i.e. of bread and wine) among members of the community.[1]

Fig. XIII illustrates the above quotation. It must be noticed that the compensating quantity of wine, $w_0 w_1$, must be that quantity which will suffice to make everyone exactly as well off as

FIG. XIII

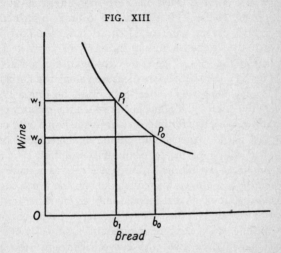

before, given that the quantities of the new situation, Ob_1 bread and Ow_1 wine, are distributed in such a way that the 'optimum' conditions of exchange are satisfied. This must be so, because otherwise the point p_1 would not be uniquely determined. We must also assume that bread and wine were 'optimally' distributed in the first place. Secondly, it should be noticed that it is only true that the quantities represented by p_1 *could* make everyone as well off as before.

Thus a 'community-indifference' curve through a point B may be briefly defined as the locus of all points representing the various quantities of two goods which, if 'optimally' distributed, would just suffice to put every individual on to the same behaviour line

[1] T. de Scitovszky, 'A Reconsideration of the Theory of Tariffs', *R.E.S.*, vol. ix, 1942. Reprinted in *Readings in the Theory of International Trade* (Blakiston, 1949). The reference is to pp. 364–5 of the latter text. On the construction of 'community-indifference' curves from individual ones, see W. J. Bammol, 'The Community Indifference Map: A Construction', *R.E.S.*, vol. xvii, 1949–50.

as he was on in the situation B. In other words, all points lying above, or to the right of, this curve represent collections of goods such that the Kaldor–Hicks criterion is satisfied with reference to the position B; and similarly the Kaldor–Hicks criterion fails to be satisfied for all points lying to the left of, or below, the 'community-indifference' curve. As Professor Scitovsky says, there may be any number of 'community-indifference' curves going through any point B, each one corresponding to a different distribution of 'welfare'. It follows, of course, that 'community-indifference' curves can cut. Let us now see how Professor Scitovsky used the 'community-indifference' curve technique to demonstrate the 'gains' which may result from imposing a tariff.

In Fig. XIV home goods are measured along the horizontal axis, and imports along the vertical axis from the origin O. OR represents the quantity of home goods which the country can retain, or export in exchange for imports. RF is the home offer curve, and is defined as the locus of the points of tangency of price lines through R with appropriate 'community-indifference' curves. We say *appropriate* 'community-indifference' curves because the curve to which the price line is tangential must be one which corresponds to the distribution of real income implied by some initial distribution of money, and the set of prices represented by the slope of the price line. RG is the foreign offer curve, similarly defined. The intersection of these two offer curves determines the free-trade equilibrium point A, where the home country retains OS home goods, and exports RS in return for OT imports. Thus OS home goods and OT foreign goods are available for consumption at home.[1]

Now suppose that the home country places a tariff on imports. The result is to create a divergence between the rate at which the country exchanges home goods for imports, and the equilibrium home market-rate of exchange between them. The latter must always be equal to the slope of some home 'community-indifference' curve, because at an equilibrium point all individual behaviour lines have the same slope. Thus, at that point, the rate at which every individual would require to be compensated by home

[1] Fig. XIV only presents the case where each country produces one good. But it can be adapted without loss to deal with the more general case. See J. E. Meade, 'A Geometry of International Trade', George Allen and Unwin, 1952, Ch. II.

goods, or vice versa, is the same. It follows that the 'community-indifference' curve has the same slope, which must be equal to the market rate of exchange. This was why we could legitimately trace out a community offer curve by the condition of tangency of price lines with 'community-indifference' curves in just the same way as an individual's offer curve can be traced out.

FIG. XIV

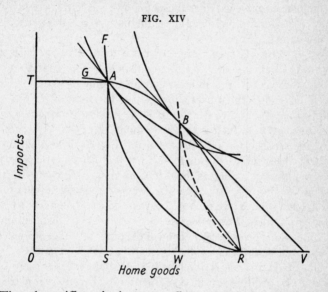

Thus the tariff results in a new offer curve which is the locus of all points such that the ratio of the difference between the market valuation and the ex-tariff valuation, to the ex-tariff valuation of imports, is equal to the tariff rate. In Fig. XIV the broken curve RB represents a tariff-distorted offer curve of this kind. It is drawn to pass through the point B, which is a point of tangency of the foreign offer curve and a home 'community-indifference' curve.

Since B is the highest point of the 'community-indifference field' through which the foreign offer curve passes, a tariff which will distort the original offer curve to pass through B is said to be an 'optimum' tariff. The sense in which such a tariff is optimum will be discussed, but, first, let us see what tariff does enable us to reach the point B. At B, BW is imported. The home market valuation of these imports, in terms of exports, is WV, but only

WR is actually exported to pay for them. Hence, the total duty paid is RV, and, since the ex-tariff value of imports is WR, the tariff rate expressed as a percentage is $VR/WR \times 100$. It can be seen that this ratio VR/WR is determined solely by the slope of the foreigner's offer curve at the point of tangency B, and by the position of B. In other words, it is determined solely by the elasticity of the foreign offer curve at the point B. Thus if this elasticity is known, the tariff which would enable us to reach the position B is also known.

We must now discuss the question of whether B can be correctly said to be better than A, or better than any other point on the foreign offer curve. It is evident that the 'community-indifference' curve through B must pass above and to the right of A. This indicates that for a move from B to A the Kaldor–Hicks criterion is not satisfied, or, which is the same thing, the Scitovsky criterion must be satisfied for a movement from A to B. According to our criterion, this suffices for us to say that it is better to impose the 'optimum' tariff so long as the distribution of real income is better in the B position. In a similar way, a movement along the foreigner's offer curve to B is always to be recommended, so long as the movement does not cause an unfavourable redistribution of real income. This is because none of the other sets of goods obtainable would be sufficient to make everyone as well off as at B.

The above analysis is different from that of Professor Scitovsky, because he neglects real income distribution (unless it results in a contradiction) and holds that welfare can be said to have increased if, and only if, both the Kaldor–Hicks and the Scitovsky criteria are satisfied for the movement from A to B. To quote:

If the indifference curve tangential to the foreigner's offer curve intersects another indifference curve between its point of tangency and the latter's point of intersection with the foreigner's offer curve, we must, according to our convention [the requirement that both the Kaldor–Hicks and the Scitovsky criterion must be satisfied] regard the corresponding trade policies as equally favourable to national welfare.[1]

'Equally favourable' must here mean 'indeterminate'. It is maintained that a movement from A to B is indeterminate if their respective 'community-indifference' curves cut between A and B, because, in that case, B would lie below A's curve, and the Kaldor–Hicks criterion would not be satisfied. We have shown that the

[1] Loc. cit. (Blakiston, 1949), p. 371.

Kaldor–Hicks criterion is irrelevant if the other criteria are satisfied, and therefore it would not matter if the curves did intersect in the manner described.[1]

So far, we have considered only the exchange of goods, it being assumed that one country produces only 'home goods' and the other only 'imports', so that the only production 'optimum' conditions which are relevant are those concerned with the 'optimum' employment of factors. These conditions must either be assumed to be satisfied, or else the deviations from the 'optimum' conditions must be unaltered by the tariff, because otherwise nothing formal can be said about the advantages or disadvantages of a tariff. Now foreign exchange can be considered in the same light as production, since it is a way of 'transforming' one good into another. In the 'optimum' position B the exchange conditions are, by the definition of 'community-indifference' curves, satisfied. Also the rate of 'community-indifference' (i.e. the rate at which every individual who consumes both is willing to exchange imports for home goods) is equal to the transformation rate, i.e. to the rate at which it is possible to induce the foreigner to give up imports for exports (the slope of his offer curve). Therefore all the transformation or production conditions are also satisfied at B (we also assume the factor employment conditions to be satisfied).

In these circumstances, if B is regarded as symbolizing a position in which all 'optimum' conditions are satisfied so far as the importing country is concerned, and remain satisfied through any process of compensation, then the Kaldor–Hicks criterion must be satisfied for a move to B.[2] This, however, does not mean that the community-indifference curves cannot intersect, since they are defined to show whether or not particular sets of goods are adequate to make everyone as well off. Thus whereas the gainers can always compensate those who lose by a change to a *policy* of having 'optimum' tariffs, it may not be true that the particular set of goods designated by the point B would suffice. What this really shows is that 'community-indifference' curves are irrelevant to the analysis of a policy of putting all the optimum conditions of production and exchange into operation.[3]

[1] Although a contradiction may still arise if the welfare distributions, while different, are ethically neutral.

[2] See pp. 109–10 above.

[3] On all this see J. de V. Graaf, 'On Optimum Tariff Structures', *R.E.S.*, xvii (1), 1949–50.

It is not, of course, necessary to assume that the foreigner only produces 'imports', and the home country only 'home goods'. The only difference is that if some of each are produced in both countries, then the home rate of transformation will also be equal to the relative home market prices, and hence to the slope of the foreigner's offer curve.[1] Thus all the 'optimum' conditions of production and exchange are satisfied from the point of view of the home country.

It is also clear from Fig. XIV that if we call B the second position, thus concerning ourselves with a movement to B, then the condition $\sum P_2 Q_2 \geqslant \sum P_2 Q_1$ is satisfied, wherever the first position lies on the foreign offer curve. Thus, in the diagram, if we value imports in terms of home goods, $\sum P_2 Q_2 = OV$. If we take any other point on the foreign offer curve, and construct a line parallel to BV, its point of intersection with OV will represent $\sum P_2 Q_1$. Inspection then shows that $\sum P_2 Q_2$ must be greater than $\sum P_2 Q_1$ so long as the foreign offer curve is concave to the origin. If the foreign offer curve is a straight line (infinite terms-of-trade elasticity of foreign reciprocal demand), then $\sum P_2 Q_2$ is equal to $\sum P_2 Q_1$, and the 'optimum' tariff is zero, the free trade position being, in that case, already one in which the foreign offer curve is tangential to a 'community-indifference' curve. Thus the analysis of the 'optimum' tariff in terms of the national income also yields the conclusion that the 'optimum' tariff is (in theory) best, but only if it causes a not-unfavourable redistribution of real income.

We must now concern ourselves with the formula which has been evolved for determining the 'optimum' tariff. We have seen, in effect, that it can be worked out as that tariff which will maximize the level of the national income. The real value of the national income is a maximum if every conceivable movement which fulfils the two conditions $(a) \sum P_2 Q_2 \geqslant \sum P_2 Q_1$ and (b) a not-unfavourable redistribution of real income, has been carried out.

Now
$$\sum P_2 Q_2 = \sum (P_1 + \Delta P)(Q_1 + \Delta Q)$$
$$= \sum P_1 Q_1 + \sum Q_1 \Delta P + \sum P_1 \Delta Q \text{ (neglecting second orders of smallness),}$$

[1] Cf. W. W. Leontief, 'The use of Indifference Curves in the Analysis of Foreign Trade', *Q.J.E.* (1933), reprinted in *Readings in the Theory of International Trade* (Blakiston, 1949); or J. E. Meade, *The Geometry of International Trade*, George Allen and Unwin, 1952.

and
$$\sum P_2 Q_1 = \sum (P_1 + \Delta P) Q_1$$
$$= \sum P_1 Q_1 + \sum Q_1 \Delta P,$$
$$\therefore \sum P_2 Q_2 - \sum P_2 Q_1 = \sum P_1 \Delta Q.$$

Therefore, we have $\sum P_2 Q_2 \geqslant \sum P_2 Q_1$, if $\sum P_1 \Delta Q$ is positive or zero. $\sum P_1 \Delta Q$ is the value of the changes in quantities, measured at the old prices. It follows that real national income is maximized if $\sum P_1 \Delta Q = 0$, or, when we are concerned with small changes, if $\sum P_1 \delta Q$ is zero.

Now suppose that we have a tariff T_I, expressed as a fraction of the price received by the foreigner P_I, and wish to determine whether it is 'optimum'. It is 'optimum' if for a small change in the tariff (δT_I), $\sum P_1 \delta Q = 0$. When we thus alter the tariff, the value of the change in exports, measured at the old prices, will be $P_E \delta E$, and the home value of the change in imports is similarly $P_I (1 + T_I) \delta I$. Therefore when T is 'optimum' we have the equation:

$$P_E \delta E - P_I (1 + T_I) \delta I = 0. \qquad (1)$$

The expression on the left-hand side also measures the value of the changes in the quantities of goods to the foreigner, where P_E and P_I represent the prices in terms of the foreigner's currency before the small change in the tariff is made. Now, since the value of the change in imports must equal the value of the change in exports, we also have the condition

$$\delta(P_I I) = \delta(P_E E),$$
$$\therefore \qquad P_I \delta I + I \delta P_I = P_E \delta E + E \delta P_E,$$
$$\therefore \ P_I \delta I (1 + 1/\eta_s) = P_E \delta E (1 - 1/\eta_d) \text{ where } \eta_s \text{ is the elasticity of}$$

foreign supply, and η_d the elasticity of foreign demand, and the P's are measured in terms of the foreign currency.

$$\therefore \qquad \frac{P_I \delta I}{P_E \delta E} = \frac{1 - 1/\eta_d}{1 + 1/\eta_s}. \qquad (2)$$

But since $P_I \delta I / P_E \delta E$ is the same whether P_I / P_E is expressed in terms of the home or the foreign currency, it follows from (1) that

$$\frac{P_I \delta I}{P_E \delta E} = \frac{1}{1 + T_I}.$$

Whence
$$T_I = \frac{1 + 1/\eta_s}{1 - 1/\eta_d} - 1,$$

$$\therefore \qquad T_I = \frac{1/\eta_s + 1/\eta_d}{1 - 1/\eta_d}.$$

The elasticities in the above formula refer, of course, to those which rule after the tariff is imposed. The guesswork which is consequently involved could, in theory, be reduced or eliminated by a trial and error process of approximation to the 'optimum' tariff.[1]

It may be noticed that the 'optimum' tariff could equally well take the form of a tax on exports. Thus equation (1) could be written:

$$P_I \delta I - P_E(1 - T_E)\,\delta E = 0, \qquad (3)$$

where T_E is the 'optimum' export tax expressed as a fraction of the full foreign value of exports. Whence the 'optimum' export tax equals $(1/\eta_d + 1/\eta_s)/(1 + 1/\eta_s)$. (If the export tax was expressed as a fraction of the *home* value of exports, we would have

$$P_1 \delta I - P_E\{1/(1 + T_E)\}\,\delta E = 0,$$

and expressed in this form the 'optimum' export tax would equal the 'optimum' import tax.) The 'optimum' tariff(s) could also be levied partly on exports and partly on imports. Let us write equation (1):

$$P_E(1 - T_E)\,\delta E - P_1(1 + T_1)\,\delta I = 0. \qquad (4)$$

Whence from (2)

$$\frac{1 - T_E}{1 + T_1} = \frac{1 - 1/\eta_d}{1 + 1/\eta_s}.$$

A possible solution is that $T_E = 1/\eta_d$, and $T_1 = 1/\eta_s$. This is the result arrived at, in a different manner, by Professor Lerner.[2]

The analysis has thus far been limited to the two-good case.[3] Where, in fact, the general elasticities of foreign supply and demand are weighted averages of specific ones, the imposition of a general import tariff, based on such overall averages, could fail to satisfy the Scitovsky criterion, because the tariff might be much too high for some goods and too low for others. The multi-good case

[1] The above derivation of the 'optimum' tariff substantially follows that of Professor R. F. Kahn in 'Tariffs and the Terms of Trade', *R.E.S.*, vol. xv (1), no. 37. The formula was, however, first deduced by Bickerdike and Edgeworth. See Bickerdike's review of Professor Pigou's *Protective and Preferential Import Duties*, *E.J.* (1907), pp. 98–102, and Edgeworth, *Collected Papers*, vol. ii, p. 361.

[2] *Economics of Control*, pp. 382–3.

[3] Strictly speaking, three goods are involved, since a third good (which is neither exported nor imported) is required as a *numéraire* in terms of which to express the prices of exports and imports.

has been analysed by J. de V. Graaf.[1] Each import would need to be taxed at a rate depending not only on its own elasticity of supply, but also on all the cross-elasticities of supply of other imports with respect to its price: and similarly each export would need to be taxed at a rate depending not only on its own foreign elasticity of demand, but also on the cross-elasticity of demand for all other exports with respect to price.

Recognizing, then, that a tariff, arrived at by treating exports and imports each as one good, would hardly be 'optimal' let us revert to a discussion of the realism of this concept of an 'optimum' tariff, and also of the realism of the idea that there are, or may be, gains from foreign trade.

That there may be gains from foreign trade is indeed obvious. The rates of transformation through foreign trade may be very different from those rates which prevail in the home industries. In the extreme case, it may be impossible to obtain a certain good at home, however large the quantity of other goods sacrificed. Inequalities may occur which are of a different order to such inequalities as one might expect to prevail, between market rates of exchange and transformation rates at home, as a result of monopoly or market imperfection. To say that there may be gains from trade is analogous to saying that it is conceivable that a monopoly might restrict output in such a way that it would be obvious that welfare could be increased by increasing its output.

On the other hand, to push the gains-from-trade argument to the point of claiming that universal free trade is ideal, is going much too far. Here we have the argument that whenever there is any difference, however small, between home and foreign rates of transformation, then welfare could be increased. But we have already emphasized often enough that the theoretical argument is too unrealistic for us to have any confidence that any improvement could be made unless the divergences from 'optimum' conditions are large. In fact, the pure economic-theory case for universal free trade, aimed at the satisfaction of all the 'optimum' conditions of production and exchange throughout the world, is analogous to the general case against monopoly (of any degree) and imperfect competition of all kinds. Both cases are very shaky, presupposing, as they do, that many 'optimum' conditions are exactly satisfied, which never could be so satisfied.

[1] Loc. cit., above.

The idea that free trade maximizes world welfare not only presupposes 'optimum' conditions of production and exchange within all countries and full employment, but also ignores the distribution of real income between countries. A free-trader can make some defence to the first charge. Production and exchange conditions within countries may be taken as data; and trade take place on the basis of comparative prices, and not comparative costs. He may further plausibly argue that free trade would, if anything, tend to decrease degrees of monopoly within countries, and conclude that it may, at least, effect an improvement, even if it cannot be held to 'maximize world welfare'.

Against the second charge, to the effect that the free-trader ignores the distribution of real income between countries, there is no good defence. Even in cases where we should have some confidence that the gainers could compensate the losers, there are no grounds for saying that the result would be an increase in welfare, or good. There is therefore no good sense in which free trade is ideal or optimal. Analogous to our previous analysis, it appears that we must maintain that it can only legitimately be said that a change in international trading relations is economically desirable if it does not shift the distribution of real income between countries in an unfavourable manner, and if the losers could not bribe the gainers to oppose the change. But we must remember that the justification for the second test is that, if it is not satisfied, then it would have been better simply to shift purchasing power. Where there exists no political possibility of supplying free goods or purchasing power to countries which, it is held, ought to benefit (for any reason whether moral or political), then it is hypocrisy to maintain that any measure taken by such a country to improve its terms of trade is economically wrong.

The above discussion might conceivably be objected to on the ground that comparisons of real income between different countries are meaningless. Such comparisons are not necessarily implied, because one can, of course, maintain that it would be desirable if America gave some dollars to Tahiti, without saying that it would be desirable because the Americans are really wealthier than South Sea Islanders. Nevertheless, the grounds for thinking it desirable would often be a comparison of real income. Whether international real-income comparisons mean anything or not depends on the particular comparison made. There is no possible doubt that one is making a true descriptive statement if one says: 'Real income in America is higher than in India.' On the other hand, one can very well doubt whether the question 'Is real income higher in England or in Switzerland?' is a question of ascertainable fact. I should say that it was not, and that this question could be correctly described as descriptively meaningless. International index-numbers of 'real income' per head certainly give next to no information to someone who knows both countries very well. But if someone does not know Switzerland, and some index-number says that real income per head is, say, 10 per cent. higher in Switzerland than in his own country, then it at least tells him that he is not very likely to decide that either is much better off than the other. But, of course, all this may be quite irrelevant to the question presupposed by our analysis, i.e. the question 'Would it be a good thing to benefit country A at the expense of country B?'

If we take the over-pessimistic view that everyone will always consider that a shift in the distribution of the real income of the world in favour of his own country is a good thing, then everyone can always maintain that a shift, which would cause this, would increase not merely the welfare of his own country, but indeed that of the world, even although his country could, for instance, be profitably bribed not to impose the tariff. Thus it is sometimes said that a tariff will benefit a country only by harming other countries to a greater extent than it gains itself. In welfare terms there is no good *a priori* ground for saying this.

The view that every government will always consider that any change which increases the welfare of its own country is a good thing, and that the erection of a tariff wall has this effect, has given rise to a theory which seeks to rationalize the fact that tariffs constitute a norm of international economic behaviour. If one government imposes a tariff for the sake of increasing welfare in its own country, other countries will be harmed. They can partly restore their previous position by themselves imposing tariffs in retaliation. The result may be to increase the height of the 'optimum' tariff in the original country, and so on. The competitive tariff warfare might conceivably go on until trade between the two countries is at vanishing point, but will stop short of that if a point is found such that the tariff-distorted offer curve of each country is tangential to a 'community-indifference' curve of the other country.[1] The

[1] For a diagrammatic treatment of tariff warfare, see T. de Scitovszky, 'A

country originally raising the tariff may or may not gain if retaliation results.

Thus, if we start from a position of free trade, tariff warfare will develop if each country fails to take account of the fact that retaliation will be made by other countries, and may do so even if account is taken of the possibility of retaliation. Each country may expect that the effects of its tariff will be small on any other single country, and that therefore retaliation would not result. This is the theory of monopolistic competition applied to the international sphere. It has been said that 'to call the raising of tariffs on these assumptions irrational would be similar to calling competitive behaviour irrational'.[1] To which, of course, one may reply that competitive behaviour is indeed irrational if one has a case in which it is stupid to imagine that one's own actions would not influence those of others; hence the prevalence of oligopolistic practices. Nevertheless, if the gains from a tariff are obvious, assuming that retaliation does not result, a state of universal free trade might be unstable. At any moment some country might find too strong the temptation to take the immediate gains and let the future go. But then, it does not follow that others must follow suit. The fact that one country has broken the free trade rule does not alter the position as far as the others are concerned. As before, each may believe that it will gain by retaliation if his action does not cause others to retaliate too. If they do retaliate, the last case may well be worse than the first. On the other hand, a country may believe that others will take the long-sighted view, and see that retaliation will not pay them in the end; and that would be an excellent reason for imposing a tariff. The best chance of preventing a country from imposing a tariff is to convince it that others would retaliate. If we take the reasonable view that countries are oligopolists, then, to prevent anyone breaking the oligopolistic free trade game, it becomes necessary that each should be prepared to indulge in that retaliation which it knows is probably not in its own best interests (unless the preventive effects of the preparedness to retaliate are taken into account). The case is one of bluff and counterbluff. The outcome is quite indeterminate. It might even be free trade.

The above theory of international economic relations rests

Reconsideration of the Theory of Tariffs' (Blakiston, 1949), pp. 372-5. But see also H. G. Johnson, 'Optimum Tariff and Retaliation', *R.E.S.* xxi (2), 1953-4.
[1] T. de Scitovszky, loc. cit., p. 375.

partly on the belief that tariffs *obviously* increase the welfare of individual countries, if retaliation does not take place. We must, therefore, discuss the realism of the 'optimum' tariff idea. There is no need to elaborate all the assumptions which the theory of an 'optimum' tariff requires. Most of them have been discussed earlier in this book. In brief, all the 'optimum' conditions of production and exchange must be satisfied, both before and after the imposition of the tariff; or else there must be no change in production; or, at least, it must be true that the tariff will not make worse any divergences from 'optimum' conditions. It is clear that if there are only small divergences from 'optimum' conditions (if foreign supply and demand is fairly elastic) one could have little faith in the conclusion that the gainers could overcompensate the losers. If, on the other hand, foreign supply and demand were very inelastic, one might have some confidence that there would be potential gains as a result of a suitable tariff policy. But it should be noticed that the 'optimum' tariff formula requires a guess at the foreign elasticities of supply and demand (not to speak of the cross-elasticities!), which are likely to alter as a result of the tariff, especially if they were small in the first instance (the foreign elasticities may alter either apart from, or as a result of, retaliation).

Therefore governments who were really trying to increase welfare (on our individualistic assumptions[1]) might not impose tariffs of the magnitude which the optimum tariff formula would suggest, even if they all acted monopolistically, and not oligopolistically. Indeed, if this was their only object, they might not impose any tariffs at all, because the benefits of the tariff might not be obvious. And where any increase in economic welfare is not obvious, one is quite entitled to distrust the theory which predicts such an effect. That the benefits, if they exist, are not obvious is proved, I think, by the fact that so many people, economists and politicians, have been able to deny that they exist, without looking silly.

Furthermore, if one is to have any confidence in the theoretical benefits being real, the foreign elasticities must be low. They are

---

[1] A state whose 'welfare' theory was based on collectivist central valuations might be more likely to try to exploit its position. As we have said, 'welfare' theory is much more applicable in such a state. The theoretical 'benefits' would be much more likely to be real—and they would certainly be more obvious, since their reality does not depend on judgements about the well-being of individuals.

not likely to be low if the country in question is trading with many others in a state of free multilateral trade. But it is only under such conditions that it is plausible to suggest that a country might ignore the possibility of retaliation. A tacit oligopolistic agreement not to indulge in economic warfare would be quite likely to obtain.

Also governments do not, unlike many theoretical welfare economists, ignore income distribution. Many tariffs, which might otherwise have been imposed, would not be imposed because they would shift income distribution in an unfavourable manner.

Finally, it should be noted that, on our assumptions, an export tax is just as good as an import tax. That export taxes are not imposed, except for quite different reasons by some primary producing countries, seems to be evidence that the motive for raising tariff walls is not primarily a desire to increase welfare at home by exploitation of the foreigner. It seems fair to conclude that, if there were no other reason than the 'static welfare' reason for building tariff walls, it is quite possible that the tariff problem would not be a very serious one.

But, as Professor Scitovsky says, there are other motives for raising tariffs. The principal one is that tariffs are good for employment. It is obvious that tariff barriers will tend to give the country concerned a favourable balance of foreign trade, which will tend to increase employment. It is also obvious that a specific tariff will sometimes prevent frictional unemployment. It is certain that countries are much more likely to impose tariffs when there is an employment, or balance of trade, crisis than on account of the rather sophisticated argument that they will (apart from the improvement in employment) increase welfare. Then there is the infant industry argument. Tariffs may be raised as protection for a new industry, which will justify itself in the long run. Yet, in the short run, it may be unable to establish itself without protection, because of the lack of the external economies which exist in a more fully industrialized country. It may also be justified (as far as the country itself is concerned) by dynamic arguments—industrialization proceeds by geometric progression, and inventions breed inventions. Thus protection can also be classed as an obvious reason for raising tariffs.

Finally, of course, tariffs are used for the purpose of insulating a country from the foreign trade which it would expect to become impossible in the event of war. This may be done by all countries, those who plan to attack and those who expect to be attacked. But it may also be advisable for countries who expect to remain neutral, since their trade may, nevertheless, be seriously upset by the outbreak of war.

The picture which seems to emerge is one of oligopolistic, rather than monopolistic, competition with a variety of motives taking the place of the profit motive. The most important of these would seem to be the frictional- or cyclical-unemployment motive or the balance-of-payments motive, while the motive which is most closely analogous to the profit motive, i.e. the 'welfare' motive, may well be one of the least significant.

We may now turn to the most important conclusion which Professor Scitovsky has drawn from his application of the theory of monopolistic competition to international economic relations. He writes:

> But it is not enough to declare the desirability of free trade and trust that enlightenment will bring it about; nor is it enough to create initial conditions favourable to it; it must be imposed and enforced. . . . We [economists] can only tell that some form of compulsion is necessary to ensure free trade.[1]

We agree that a tacit oligopolistic understanding between countries is insufficient to ensure free trade. The next stage, if it is desired to enforce it, is to reduce the tacit understanding to a written agreement. But written agreements without the possibility of sanctions are not very potent. It is hardly likely that complete free trade could be obtained by treaty. If, then, the written agreement fails, what next? Should economic sanctions be applied? Would the threat to wage economic warfare prevent economic warfare? Such a threat might prevent a country imposing a tariff, in the belief that other countries would refrain from retaliation on the ground that it was not in their own best long-run interest. But some countries, as we shall see, might still be better off even if tariff warfare resulted. No doubt, if the threatened economic sanctions were fierce enough, and went beyond the assurance of retaliation, taking, for instance, the form of a complete embargo on trade, the errant country could easily be brought to heel, if it was a small country. But if the said country were large, the sacrifice involved

---

[1] Loc. cit. (Blakiston, 1949), p. 389. The same passage is partially quoted with approval as the conclusion of Professor R. F. Kahn's article, 'Tariffs and the Terms of Trade', loc. cit.

in waging economic war on it would be great, in which case the attempt would probably fail, or the bluff be called. If large countries are agreed on free trade, they can impose it; but small countries cannot impose it on large ones. If some of the small countries would gain by having tariffs, how can the large ones claim that it is in the interests of all that they should be forcibly prevented from imposing them?[1]

We have already argued that, on the usual 'welfare' premises, there is no reason to say that free trade is desirable, unless one believes that the free-trade distribution of real income between countries is best. We therefore cannot accept, as a deduction from welfare theory, the major premise that free trade is desirable. But, it will be said, surely every country will end up worse off as a result of tariff warfare. This is not necessarily the case, even on the usual static premises, and even ignoring external economies. But even if it were the case, it would hardly be a good argument for making sure that tariff warfare, or worse, would immediately result from any one country breaking the free-trade rule.

As things actually are, the argument that there is no country which would not be better off under a system of free multilateral world trade than it is under a tariff-permeated system is certainly open to doubt. Again, it may be objected that it would be better to make a country gifts rather than permit it to help itself by means of tariffs. If we bring in wider considerations, such as the consequent possibility of economic domination, or at least the suspicion that loans and gifts may be a form of unwanted cultural and economic infiltration, then it is by no means certain that it would be better to assist a country directly, even if such assistance (to be given solely on the grounds that the country to be assisted was poor) did become a political possibility.

The implicit assumption that free trade is a good thing, or that it 'maximizes world welfare', ignoring, as it does, the distribution of real income, is very likely to give rise to accusations of cant and hypocrisy against those economists, or politicians, who make this assumption. Let us hasten to add that it is not only the free-trader economists who tend to make certain hidden assumptions about the desirability of a certain international distribution of income. Our

---

[1] This is not to say that small countries are better off than they would be under free trade, given the present tariff structure. It may, for example, be the U.S.A. which benefits.

appeal is that those economists who put their economics before
their politics should endeavour to make explicit all the premises
required for the deduction of their conclusions.

Thus we reject the syllogism 'Free trade is desirable. Free trade
cannot exist unless it is imposed by force. Therefore free trade must
be imposed by force.' The idea that there exists some *a priori*
ground for saying that free trade is desirable is the direct result
of having a welfare theory which ignores the distribution of
real income. It has also led to the aggressive conclusion that free
trade must be enforced. There is no good sense in which free trade
is the best possible state of affairs for the world. The fact that the
opposite conclusion is traditional in economics may have arisen as
a result of the identification of the interests of all countries with
those of the most highly developed countries, where economic
theory thrives. But it may also have arisen as a result of the suggestive influence of economic terminology.

This is not to say that a lowering of tariffs—but not necessarily
by all countries—would not be a good thing. I think it would be.
But it seems to me that a reduction of trade barriers is more likely
to result if the free-trade dogma is abandoned, and if it is recognized that any lowering of tariffs, which cannot be freely negotiated
without pressure, and which is therefore likely to benefit all parties,
cannot claim support from any generally acceptable economic
theory.

CHAPTER XIV

WELFARE THEORY AND POLITICS

IT might seem that a chapter on politics is out of place in a theoretical work. This would be the case if welfare theory were pure theory, but this it never is. We have argued that it is a calculus with an ethical interpretation. The putting into practice of its recommendations inevitably requires political changes. Whether one attacks or defends the theory, the reader can draw political inferences from one's arguments. The author must know this, and also know that the reader realizes that he knows. Consequently, the author must realize that he is always open to the suspicion that his political inclinations have coloured his comment on the theory. Since the validity of welfare theory is so much a matter of judgement, and so little a matter of precise measurement, it is difficult to guard against such bias, and difficult to defend oneself against charges of bias. In such circumstances, it seems best for the author to be open about what he believes to be the political implications.

Furthermore, it has not been my intention merely to present the theory, but also to discuss the logical status of its propositions, and to give their correct interpretation; to discuss the reality of its assumptions, and to assess its importance. Now much of the importance of the theory lies in the fact that it has been used to give an apparently respectable scientific basis to political arguments. Indeed, one might easily come to the cynical conclusion that that has been its only importance. But it is, in any case, clear that one cannot have a general appreciation of the theory without looking at its political aspect. Without further defence, we will therefore launch into a political discussion.

It will be assumed that the protagonists on both sides, or all sides, accept the two fundamental value judgements of welfare theory, that is, roughly speaking, they accept the view that it is a good thing that individuals should have what they want, and that they themselves know best what they want. Of course, everyone makes exceptions to this rule. Some people may think that health services should be an exception, and that these should be free, in terms of money, to the individual, and be charged to the community. Others will believe that they should be brought within the sphere in which the theory of economic welfare is supposed to operate—and that welfare would be increased if they were. In the limit, some people might believe that everything, or almost everything, including, of course, labour, should be freely given—relying on some entirely different source of motivation to that of individual gain. It is ironical that what is coming to be called the Welfare State is a state in which much is provided free, and in which the personal gain motive is weakened, but not apparently replaced—with the result that the sphere within which the theory of welfare can be applied is smaller. We assume, however, that there is at least a considerable portion of the economy within which it is agreed that the theory of welfare should be applied, if it can be applied. These assumptions have, it seems, been accepted by all the political economists whose views we shall discuss.

Historically, the economic calculus, in a crude form, was used to support the doctrine of *laissez-faire*. At first the rationale of the economic system was but dimly grasped; there was no distinction of logic and fact. The world was a logical place, and economists picked out sufficient of this logic for many of them to be awed by its rational nature. It seemed a miraculous fact that the profit motive, operating through a price mechanism, could—indeed must—lead to the best of all possible worlds. Here was a perfect harmony of self-interest and social morality. That the economic system, which had been designed by no man, should exhibit a kind of perfection was surely evidence of the benevolence of nature, or of divine purpose. Thus *laissez-faire* could become a creed, and intervention immoral. Philosophers had often tried to prove the coincidence of duty and self-interest, and to demonstrate that it must always be profitable to do one's duty. But the creed of *laissez-faire* demonstrated the same coincidence in a more comfortable way. It showed that it was one's duty to make profits.

As the economic calculus was more clearly developed, this metaphysical awe vanished, and it became possible to compare the actual system with a logical idea. In particular, it came to be believed by most economists that the *laissez-faire* distribution of wealth did not accord with the utilitarian ideal which provided the ethical basis of economics. Nevertheless, fancy was still, to some extent, mistaken for fact, and although monopoly and market imperfections were emphasized and discussed, it was still widely believed that, for the most part, the economic system tended towards a stable competitive equilibrium, which exhibited the ideal properties of the logical theory of pure competition; these properties being identical with the 'optimum' conditions of production and exchange. Wealth might be redistributed, and monopolies controlled, but only against the background of a predominantly *laissez-faire* system.

Then came the development of Keynesian economics, and of the theory of imperfect competition in the hands of Professor Chamberlin and Mrs. Robinson. The first provided the death-blow to the classical assumption of a full-employment equilibrium. We, however, are concerned only with the static theory of welfare, which rests on the assumption of full employment of productive resources, and full use of what is produced. With the political implications of the failure of a *laissez-faire* economy to achieve these presupposed conditions we do not concern ourselves. I shall only remark that it is widely agreed on all sides that control of some kind should be made whenever and wherever large disequilibria occur, and whenever employment is not 'full' (meaning formally by 'full' employment that level of employment which will maximize welfare in a changing and dynamic world). The theory of imperfect competition is more our concern. The chief importance of this theory lies in the fact that it has convinced most economists that 'imperfections' are the rule, and not the exception, and therefore that the 'optimum' conditions of production and exchange are seldom, if ever, fulfilled in the real world.

At the same time, Professor von Mises[1] challenged socialism on the ground that it necessarily destroyed a rational economic system—that is one in which the 'optimum' conditions can be (more or less) fulfilled. At a logical level this challenge was completely answered by socialist economists, principally Professors Lange[2] and Lerner,[3] who laid bare the welfare skeleton of the theory of pure competition, and showed that this skeleton was not logically incompatible with socialist institutions, and the collective ownership of property. But this was not all. Pure competition was ideal, but then the capitalistic world never was, and never could be, purely competitive, and the degree of monopoly was clearly

[1] See *Collectionist Economic Planning*, ed. F. A. Hayek.
[2] 'On the Economic Theory of Socialism', *R.E.S.*, Oct. 1936.
[3] 'Economic Theory and Socialist Economy', *R.E.S.*, 1934; 'A note on Socialist Economics', *R.E.S.*, 1936; 'Statics and Dynamics in Socialist Economics', *E.J.*, June 1937.

increasing. The theory of imperfect competition seemed to show that, even where competition was fiercest, it was not 'pure', and the 'optimum' conditions were not fulfilled. The distinction between monopoly and competition was blurred. Practically speaking, all competition was monopolistic or oligopolistic; and therefore price was not equal to marginal cost. The scope of the traditional pure economic argument against monopoly was greatly widened. It became, in fact, almost universal. The world was a world of monopolies; a world in which resources were chronically maldistributed.

Thus Professor von Mises's challenge gave rise to the' blueprint' of a socialist economy in which the managers of decentralized industrial boards automatically pursue a policy by which resources are ideally distributed by obeying the simple rule of employing factors until the value of their marginal products are equal to the price paid for them. Thus, not only could a socialist economy be 'rational', but it could be much more 'rational' than *laissez-faire*, the imperfections of which were admitted.[1] Thus, and with some irony, the static welfare-theory armament of the supporters of *laissez-faire* was seized by their opponents, and effectively used against them. Lange, perceiving the irony, has proposed to erect a statue to von Mises 'in the great hall of the Ministry of Socialization or of the Central Planning Board of the Socialist state'.[2] What we wish to do is to evaluate the claim that static welfare analysis provides an argument for socialism—to evaluate such a statement as '. . . the actual capitalist system is not one of perfect competition; it is one where oligopoly and monopolistic competition prevail. This adds a much more powerful argument to the economist's case for socialism',[3] or 'Price must be made equal to marginal cost. This is the contribution that pure economic theory has to make to the building up of a socialist economy.'[4]

First, let us remember that we have made income distribution an integral part of static welfare analysis. We must therefore take notice of such claims as 'Only a socialist economy can distribute

[1] This is, of course, an unfair comparison of an ideal with reality. The *laissez-faire* model, given enough assumptions, could bring about the 'optimum' distribution of resources as well as the socialist 'blueprint'. The socialist 'blueprint' model is 'superior' at the logical level in that it requires fewer postulates. It does not require the postulate of either a rising cost curve, or a perfectly elastic demand curve.   [2] Lange, loc. cit., p. 53.
[3] Ibid., p. 126.   [4] Lerner, *E.J.* (1937), p. 270.

incomes so as to attain the maximum social welfare'.[1] This claim
is merely emotive if the claimant does not say what income distribution he has in mind as ideal. No doubt there would be certain
distributions which would be incompatible with private enterprise. This incompatibility would follow from dynamic arguments,
such as the incentive argument. Where the driving force of the
economy is personal gain, and risks have to be taken, undoubtedly
certain distributions would be impossible without a serious decrease in welfare—and they might be possible under socialism,
where the government takes most of the risks, without causing
collapse as a result of the weakening of the motive of personal
gain (personal gain is surely the only possible effective motive
force for a free economy, whatever some idealists may think). But,
under a utopian socialist system (the so-called competitive solution
of the socialist problem), it is certain that some distributions of
income would also be incompatible with a high standard of living.
There is nothing more that can be said on this subject. One can
only leave it to the reader to judge whether the income distribution
he believes to be ideal is incompatible with capitalism, and possible
under socialism.

The second part of the static welfare case for socialism is that
price must be made equal to marginal cost, and this can be done
only in a socialist economy. There are really two problems here
which require examination; first, would it be a good thing, given a
socialist economy, to make price equal to marginal cost? And, second,
could price be made equal to marginal cost in a socialist economy?

Let us take the first question first. In earlier chapters we came to
the conclusion not only that the rule 'produce until price equals
marginal cost' was invalid for socialized industry in England, but
also that one could not reasonably attach very much weight to the
conclusions of welfare theory anyway, because such conclusions
are not testable, and because the concepts and postulates of the
theory obviously do not apply very well. It must be remembered,
however, that we were dealing with a country in which there is
much non-socialized industry; in which price is not equal to
marginal cost, and in which there is a high level of taxation. It was
these facts which made us conclude that pure economic theory does
not suggest that price should be equal to marginal cost in a few
socialized industries. But let us, for the sake of argument, beg our

[1] Lange, loc. cit., p. 123.

second question, and assume that price could be made everywhere equal to marginal cost in a fully socialized system. In Chapters VIII and IX we have already outlined and discussed the conditions under which it can be shown that such a reform would attain an 'optimum' position. Reference may be made to these chapters, but we will briefly review the conditions here.

All individuals must be 'economic men' in respect of all economic choices, the objects of which must be perfectly divisible. We have already said enough about this condition to show its unreality. Secondly, all the other 'optimum' conditions of exchange and production must be satisfied. We suggested that there is no reason to suppose that a socialist system would not often find it best to introduce rationing or production controls, in which case these conditions would be violated. In any case, we found it very hard to interpret the 'optimum' production conditions in view of the fact that 'job preferences' is not a precise concept. Third, it was necessary that there should be only poll taxation. We believe that it would be impossible to administer an equitable system of poll taxation. Lastly, we found that income distribution is determined by marginal productivities; and such an income distribution may not be held to be ideal. This distribution cannot be interfered with by taxation, because such taxation must necessarily be linked to income, and therefore would not be poll taxation.[1]

A defence may be made against some of these attacks. First, let us take it that an income distribution determined by marginal productivities, and by the price set-up resulting from marginal cost pricing, would be ideal. Then it may be argued that no taxation would be needed. A social dividend might even be paid. In reply, it must be said that even negative taxation of this kind would have to be equitably distributed to be tolerable. Such a distribution could not be linked to earnings. The dividend would have to be assessed on a personal basis; which would almost certainly become intolerable or administratively impossible. In any case, it would alter the supposedly 'ideal' real income distribution, if it was not linked to earnings.

But talk of a social dividend is optimistic. We have already

---

[1] We ignore the condition that factors must be in perfectly elastic supply, although this is a necessary condition for the marginal cost rule, because it is not a necessary condition for the Lernerian rule—'employ factors until the value of the marginal product equals the price of the factor'.

argued that the cost of the living of all non-workers, including the unemployed (for surely doles and family allowances would be paid), of defence, police, and justice, must be covered somehow, even if free health services, education, and other such welfare institutions were abolished. Against this we have only pure rents to set. Moreover such evidence as we have about marginal costs suggests strongly that industrial profits would be negative. Heavy taxation would undoubtedly be the order of the day—or, what comes to the same thing, people would be paid less than the value of their marginal products.

If defenders of the marginal cost doctrine are prepared to give up their claim to establish Utopia, some defence may be made against some of the above attacks. It would be best, in seeking to establish the best defence position, to surrender the claim that it would ever be possible, in a modern state, to fulfil the optimum factor-supply condition (condition II (c), Chapter VIII). It could then be said that, if price were equal to marginal cost, at least prices would be proportional to marginal costs (condition II (b), Chapter VIII), and also the factor-supply situation would at least not be made worse. Let us also presume that ordinary taxation could near enough reproduce any distribution which might be thought to be ideal.

The position is still very weak. Individuals must still be economic men, and goods and jobs perfectly divisible. Goods must not give rise to external economies or diseconomies of consumption. External economies and diseconomies of production must also be absent. Situations must not occur which make the fulfilment both of equilibrium and the 'optimum' conditions impossible. Rationing and controls might still be required. In the real world it is not obvious that some excess capacity is not a good thing. Prices cannot be varied with great rapidity, and consequently under marginal-cost pricing there would be a tendency of supply and demand to get out of line. We also saw in the last chapter that such a pricing policy would be quite impracticable where it left a multitude of small indivisible changes without any satisfactory rule of thumb as a criterion of whether they should be made. When we come to the long run the position becomes very much worse, because, as we saw, investment decisions are left high and dry without any practical criterion. There is no need to repeat all the arguments of Chapter XI on this score.

Then there is the question of whether the policy could be applied. Here we have the problems of joint costs and user costs which make marginal costs indeterminate. But, neglecting this, and assuming that they are determinate, there remains the problem that they are not known. Probably the nearest most managers could get would be to take average direct costs as a guide. This would normally mean running the plant flat out (if, as seems the case, average direct costs are fairly constant). But, when a plant goes flat out, user cost may become very serious. And, as has been pointed out, user cost is a matter of guess-work. Since marginal costs cannot be clearly known, one could never tell whether managers were abiding by the rules.

A retreat has to be made. 'Marginal costs' must be interpreted. They must be taken with a pinch of salt, or common sense. But, as soon as a retreat is made, and the need of interpretation admitted, then one is left with no universal rule or output criterion. Managers are left without any clear guidance. To sum this up, we may say that all the arguments of earlier chapters apply, except the argument that prices are not equal to marginal costs elsewhere. The removal of this argument, on which we laid little stress in Chapter XI, certainly does not convince me that marginal theory makes much contribution to the problem of how best to run a fully socialized system. If this is true, then it cannot be much of an argument in favour of socialism.

We must now emphasize that we have only been attacking one kind of socialism, which we have called 'utopian socialism'. Probably the great majority of socialist economists are already convinced that the marginal-cost scheme is absurd. Most practical socialists dismissed it from the first. Mr. D. Jay, in his *Socialist Case*, showed scanty respect for economic theory—perhaps he went too far in that direction. E. F. M. Durbin also showed some contempt for 'marginalism' in his article 'Economic Calculus in a Planned Economy',[1] and suffered in consequence a vitriolic attack from Professor Lerner.[2] Thus Professor Bergson, attributing the marginal-cost rule to Marshall and Professor Pigou, has written:

In recent years, however, the rule has had to be defended and reaffirmed on a number of occasions in the face of recurrent confusion. In this connexion, mention should be made of the contributions of Lerner

[1] *E.J.* (1936).
[2] See 'Statics and Dynamics in Socialist Economics', *E.J.* (1937).

and Hotelling. Both writers, Lerner with especial vigour, have championed the Marshall–Pigou position against doctrinal deviations.[1]

Possibly the logic of some of the deviationists was confused. The orthodox, however, have persistently confused logic and reality. Surely Marshall and Professor Pigou would not believe that one can be quite so positive and emphatic about the subject of welfare as are some of those who are thus said to be their disciples? The use of such a phrase as 'doctrinal deviation' also suggests that there may be some justification for a judgement such as that of Professor Wright:

> The moderate view that, on balance, the myth of the invisible hand is more nearly correct than the radical myth of the tender and omniscient mother-state, does not satisfy the emotional yearnings of those who are determined to find in economic doctrines an *ersatz* religion.[2]

Whether or not the omniscient mother-state is a myth is not our immediate concern. The myth we are concerned with is the myth that the economic calculus is an exact description of some possible world. There are signs that economic doctrines have tended to harden into dogmas which are defended with religious fervour, and that *laissez-faire* is not the only economic creed which has evoked an almost metaphysical awe.

The dismissal of the static welfare case for socialism implies the dismissal of the supposed welfare implications of the theory of imperfect competition. What are these implications? Accepting the view that the greater part of manufacturing industry is correctly described as oligopolistically competitive, it follows that short-run marginal cost is less than price.[3] Therefore the output of every

---

[1] *A Survey of Contemporary Economics*, ed. Howard Ellis, p. 425.

[2] D. McC. Wright, 'The Prospects for Capitalism', in *A Survey of Contemporary Economics*.

[3] Here we meet the theory on its own ground. Some economists believe, on the other hand, that business men seldom attempt to maximize profits in the short run. They must be right in some sectors at least, as is proved by the fact that second-hand prices, in times of strong demand, often exceed new uncontrolled prices. If business men tend to look to the long run, they will sell all they can at a price which they expect will enable them to make what they regard as a reasonable profit, without the danger of having their business disappear as a result of having provoked too much competition. If they sell less than is possible in times of strong demand, they will lose goodwill, driving their customers to look elsewhere. Consequently, it is quite probable that, ignoring short-run profit maximization, they will sometimes produce *beyond* the point at which marginal cost equals price. Similarly, no one producer wishes to incur the odium

firm ought to be expanded. Some labour might be drawn from outside manufacturing industry, for instance from agriculture, but it is evident that the required equality would come about mainly as a result of a rise in direct costs and a fall in price. There would be very little readjustment of productive resources. The chief change would be an increase in the real wages of manual labour at the expense of those who live on overheads. Thus it would appear that the chief argument against imperfect competition is one of the redistribution of income. But this redistribution can also be effected by taxation up to the point where there is a decrease in the supply of entrepreneurs, managers, and supervisory labour, i.e. a decrease in the supply of the middle classes.[1] Beyond that, profits may be squeezed to the point where they cease to be an adequate driving force for a capitalist economy. It is curious that this income redistribution argument is not the one which has been stressed.[2] The theory has, on the other hand, built up a formidable barrage of emotive phrases to convince one of its social importance —phrases such as 'productive inefficiency', 'misallocation of resources', 'restrictionism', 'degree of monopoly', and so on—to say nothing of the titles themselves '*imperfect* competition', and '*monopolistic* competition'. But, in the short run, even at the purely theoretical level, the charge of misallocation of resources has to wait upon a detailed study of the 'degrees of monopoly' which prevail. Moreover, we have shown that the theoretical level is a very shaky one. One certainly has no real cause to speak of misallocation

of raising prices—and it is always possible that some will not follow suit, in which case much goodwill would be lost. These considerations lend support to the view that the 'degree of monopoly' will decrease when demand is strong, and bear little or no relation to any actual or imagined elasticities of demand. Thus, although, in the text, we meet 'imperfect competition' on its own ground, that does not mean that we necessarily think that its short-run analysis often bears much relation to the facts. (For a discussion of business behaviour, in which marginal analysis is rejected, see P. W. S. Andrews, *Manufacturing Business*, Macmillan & Co. 1949.)

[1] i.e. up to the point where the optimum factor-supply condition is seriously upset, as far as those who live on overheads are concerned. The socialist economy faces the same problem, however, except in so far as it can take the risks; its managers must still be paid their supply price.

[2] It has, of course, been made, cf. Meade and Fleming, loc. cit., pp. 327–8. Probably the reason why it has not been stressed is that many economists wrongly believe that they are being perfectly scientific and objective if they say 'If price is not equal to marginal cost, welfare could be increased' and unscientific if they say 'Welfare could be increased by redistributing wealth in such and such a way.'

of resources unless by a detailed study one has at least shown that the shift of resources which would result from a change in some 'degree of monopoly' would increase the national income. Unless the ratio of marginal costs in two competing firms was very badly out of line with relative market values, one could surely have no reasonable confidence that this would be the result. Ideal outputs exist only in books on economics. In the real world there are no such things.

In the long run, the theoretical welfare implications of the doctrine of imperfect competition are rather different. Here the charge is that firms are too small, because, with a falling demand curve, the equality of long-run marginal cost and marginal revenue determines a size of plant which is smaller than that which corresponds to the lowest point on a long-run average cost curve.[1] But, except in the unreal case of pure oligopolistic competition (that is, where there is no product differentiation), the reason why the demand curve is falling is that every firm is producing a somewhat different product. Since the products are different, the removal of a firm is a non-marginal change involving consumers' surplus. Professor Hicks has remarked on the inconsistent procedure of deducing a falling demand curve from product differentiation, and then assuming that the firm is producing a unique product in arriving at the conclusion that the firm is too small, and there ought to be fewer firms of a larger size. Thus he writes:

> To emphasize the differences between the products for the purpose of getting a downward sloping demand curve for the individual firm, and then to neglect the differences between the products (irrational preferences!) for the purpose of neglecting the consumers' surplus, is both inconsistent and practically dangerous.[2]

---

[1] This theory can obviously only apply in a limited section of the economy. Schumpeter wrote: 'Such cases do occur, and it is right and proper to work them out. But, as the practical instances usually given show, they are fringe-end cases to be found mainly in the sectors furthest removed from all that is most characteristic of capitalist activity' (*Capitalism, Socialism and Democracy*, 2nd ed., p. 85). He notes: 'This is also shown by a theorem which we frequently meet with in expositions of the theory of imperfect competition, viz. the theorem that, under conditions of imperfect competition, producing or trading businesses tend to be irrationally small. Since imperfect competition is, at the same time, held to be an outstanding characteristic of modern industry, we are set to wondering what world these theorists live in . . .' (ibid.).

[2] J. R. Hicks, 'The Rehabilitation of Consumers' Surplus', *R.E.S.* (1940–1), p. 116.

Professor Hicks has also expressed himself on the most general formulation of the (welfare) theory of imperfect competition as follows:

But when we start from a position where there is an excess of price over marginal cost in the related industries, the social cost of producing a particular article is no longer represented by its marginal cost curve. . . . The social surplus equals consumers' surplus *plus* producers' surplus *minus* loss of potential surplus on other commodities; this may well be negative, when producers' surplus is positive. This is the possibility which has been uncovered by the modern theories of imperfect competition; it is, in fact, the correct and general statement of the possibility of loss due to imperfect competition.[1]

But it is not, of course, necessarily the case that a new firm, setting up in an imperfect market, will 'decrease welfare' (even on the Kaldor–Hicks definition) because, although it will ignore the loss of producers' surplus elsewhere which it causes, it will also be unable to tap all the consumers' surplus. The necessity of the introduction of consumers' and producers' surplus means that there is no clear way of deciding whether there are too many firms producing too many different things, or not. The case for standardization on a smaller range of commodities lies outside the pure static theory of welfare. It must rest on an overriding of consumers' choices, on the ground that people are irrational: or the ground must be that consumers never have the choice between the small range of cheaper goods and the larger range of more expensive ones, and therefore cannot show that they would really prefer the former.

My conclusion is that any general charge of maldistribution of resources on the ground that competition is not perfect cannot be substantiated from the basis of welfare theory. If the authority of Marshall and Professor Pigou can be evoked for 'marginalism', at least I can claim the support of Keynes, who, with Olympian disdain, wrote: 'There is no reason to suppose that the existing system seriously misemploys the factors of production which are in use.'[2]

Schumpeter came to the same conclusion, although, for other

[1] J. R. Hicks, loc. cit., p. 116.
[2] *The General Theory of Employment, Interest and Money*, p. 379.

mainly dynamic reasons,[1] he believed in the economic superiority of a socialist system. He remarked:

> Socially irrational allocation of resources is not nearly as frequent or important as it is made out to be. In some cases, moreover, it is no less likely to occur in a socialist economy. Excess capacity, also partly inevitable in a socialist economy, will often bear an interpretation which rebuts criticism.[2]

We have already remarked that the theory of imperfect competition has tended to blur the distinction, as far as welfare is concerned, between monopoly and competition. This is because the case against both is held to be the same, in that price is not equal to marginal cost. Yet, where there does exist a monopoly or a non-competitive oligopoly, which can foresee no potential competition, it is at least more likely that the phrase 'restriction of output' can be significantly used. Even so, we doubt whether there is a valid static-theory argument against monopoly in general. If we define a monopoly as a business whose negatively inclined short-run demand curve will not be significantly affected by the output or price decisions of any other business, it may still be true that few monopolies can be so confident of their long-run security that they can ever afford to 'exploit' the short-run position in the manner portrayed in the text-books.[3] And, even if they did so, it still may not be the case that relative marginal cost would be very badly out of line with relative prices—and, as we have seen, this inequality would have to be large before one was justified in speaking of misallocation of resources. Nevertheless, it seems very important to

---

[1] The exceptional (static) reason which Schumpeter gave for preferring a socialist system is the great saving which he believed would result from all earnings being paid net of taxation. To quote: 'For as a matter of commonsense it would be clearly absurd for the central board to pay out incomes first and, having done so, to run after the recipients in order to recover part of them' (op. cit., p. 199). But, if incomes are to be linked to marginal productivities, or even to the amount or kind of work done, they must be paid by local managements. Surely no one believes that an ideal income distribution can be determined without taking into account, not merely the amount and kind of work, but also the family circumstances of the worker. It is often forgotten that income distribution is not merely an inter-class but also an intra-class matter. If this is so, then the amount each worker was to receive would not only have to be paid by local managements, but would also require some calculation. P.A.Y.E. experience in this respect might convince some people that the great savings, envisaged on this account, would be non-existent. Yet, Schumpeter concluded that 'here we have got hold of one of the most significant titles to superiority that can be advanced in favour of the socialist plan' (ibid.).

[2] Ibid., p. 194.   [3] See above p. 266, n. 3.

retain a clear distinction between monopoly and competition. There may be important dynamic differences between the two. And there are certainly important social and ethical differences.

We must now take leave of the subjects of socialism and imperfect competition, and take notice of the fact that *laissez-faire* is not dead, but modified. Static welfare theory is still being used to support *laissez-faire*. Ruling out, for other reasons, the socialist competitive solution, or regardless of the danger of playing into the hands of the scientific static marginalists, some writers still extol the beauties of *laissez-faire*, in order to demonstrate the 'irrationality' and stupidity of planning. No one would, of course, go so far as to claim that *laissez-faire* is ideal. But, given that more or less full employment is maintained, by fiscal and financial policy, and given a suitable measure of income redistribution, it is claimed that, for the rest, the unimpeded price-mechanism is pretty good at solving the economic problem, and that planning will distort the allocation of resources in an irrational or uneconomic manner.

Unless the extent of the planning and its nature is described, there is little that can be said. At the one extreme, if planning takes no notice of costs whatever, it is clear that welfare theorists could object. But then probably no economist would advocate such planning. At the other extreme, if interference is only made when welfare theory indicates control as a solution for some problem, or when serious disequilibria occur, or in spheres in which welfare theory does not apply (we have in mind the question of standardization), or where it is particularly unplausible (in matters of investment), then clearly little or no case can be made out against planning. No general case can be made either way. Economic welfare theory is not so realistic that it can claim that the onus of proof always lies with the planners, although, of course, one's political views may lead one to this conclusion. Also it must be noted that planning in general is not a political issue. It only becomes one if the extent of planning is in question.

In some people's minds the real controversy between planners and anti-planners is not one to which welfare theory has any relevance. It is rather the question what kind of welfare theory is acceptable. The important issue is believed to be the question whether planning, of a degree to which anti-planners object, is compatible with the retention of a liberal set of values. The fear of these anti-planners is that the planners will inevitably tend to substitute their own values for those of the market.[1] If planning is so complete that no free market exists (some market must always exist, for if there is no free market a black or grey market is inevitable) no other outcome is possible. But even if a consumers' market exists, it may merely be used for the purpose of distributing that stock of goods which, the planners have decided, is to be made available for consumption. Any physical planning, and even financial planning by taxation or subsidy, implies some degree of divorce between production and market valuations, unless it is used merely to correct obvious discrepancies which may tend to occur spontaneously when decentralized profit maximization is the driving force, or, in a decentralized democratic socialistic system, the chief regulator of the economy.

Almost everyone agrees that some divorce between production and the dictates of a free market is desirable, even if the interference is only such as to prevent the production of brothels, or the unregulated sale of dangerous drugs. But our analysis has led us to the view that it is usually very difficult to be at all sure when, on our individualistic assumptions, one would do good by interference and when not. We have suggested that certain obvious cases for interference occur. The most obvious and important cases are the control of aggregate demand, and some measure of welfare redistribution. In such cases, intervention with the processes of *laissez-faire* obviously do good. Then there are cases where planning is inevitable and cannot be held to conflict with individuals' preferences, because the market mechanism does not allow these to express themselves (the obvious case being goods which can only be collectively consumed). There are also 'neutral' cases where it is far from obvious that planning will do good, but where it cannot be held to conflict with individual preferences, because it is very unplausible to suppose that they are adequately reflected by the market mechanism (the obvious example being aggregate investment). What is certain is that planning yields high returns at first, but that these returns decrease rapidly to a margin beyond which it cannot be said whether it does good or not.

There are, in fact, two such planning margins—an intensive and an extensive margin. People of an individualistic and liberal turn

[1] The theory that this is inevitable is put forward in Walter Eucken's article 'On the Theory of the Centrally Administered Economy: An Analysis of the German Experiment', *Economica*, May and Aug. 1948.

of mind, even supposing that they hold similar views about income and property distribution, may, nevertheless, differ widely about where the margins lie. There may thus be a fairly broad area of disagreement, without any ideological conflict. Nevertheless, if Smith wishes to extend planning further than the point, or points, beyond which Jones believes that it is far from obvious that welfare would be increased, then the latter is liable to suspect, rightly or wrongly, that Smith is beginning to substitute some other values for those of the market. Because of the fact that individual preferences can direct the economic system only in a comparatively crude manner, it is sometimes difficult to know whether the premises of those who disagree are really the same; or whether the issue lies between someone who sees the price-mechanism as a good method of democratic decentralization, and someone who believes in planning for reasons other than that it may correct some of the divergences from an individualistically determined optimum (however vague), which are certain to occur in a *laissez-faire* economy. Questions of welfare, real income, efficiency, &c., cannot be debated at all, at the economic level, if people are at variance on this latter kind of issue.

We may now sum up our discussion of the political implications of pure static welfare theory. We do not believe that it can be reasonably and honestly used in defence of, or against, any particular political system. The marginalist socialist 'blue-print' is a formal system of deductions of highly dubious applicability, even in an absolutist state, and certainly incapable of application in a democratic state. In my opinion, static welfare theory could only convince someone who was blind to realities, and very susceptible to emotive language, of the benefits of socialization. Equally, it could only convince someone who was similarly blind, and open to suggestion, of the benefits of *laissez-faire*. The theory suggests that some planning is beneficial. But planners cannot reasonably claim its support for much—probably not for enough to make planning a very controversial issue. These conclusions are reached in the face of the fact that the theory has been persistently used, by all sides, as a political weapon.

CHAPTER XV

CONCLUSIONS

THIS book might, in part, be described as a study of the usage of influential and persuasive language in economics. Wherever it has been found that the terminology of economics is, in this sense, normative, we have suggested that the ethical issues involved should be brought right into the open. Unless this is done, it is often not at all clear whether a dispute is one of fact, or one of value. A discussion, which is superficially objective and factual (because frankly ethical expressions are not used), but which is really about values, though the contestants may not realize it, is usually unhelpful, and may tend to create ill feeling.

I am far from suggesting that economists must try to be neutral on ethical issues (the fact that, for instance, I have chosen to give an exposition of the traditional welfare economics implies an acceptance of certain liberal values). As I have said, the distinction between economist *qua* economist, and economist *qua* ordinary mortal, is one that cannot be very easily maintained. Bringing ethical questions into the limelight does not imply any kind of neutrality. There is, admittedly, a tendency to think that once it has been shown that people differ on questions of value, then nothing more remains to be said. But this is a mistake. One can often convince someone, by reasoning with him, that one's own ethical beliefs are better than his. This is, however, different from trying to get one's opinions accepted by means of a propaganda use of language—different, that is, from trying to put something over by means of implicit persuasive definitions.

Thus I am not crusading against the use of all influential language in economics—that would be to oppose the use of all ethical judgements in the subject. I only want it to be recognized that many of our economic phrases are emotive. If this is not recognized, then many real, though apparently sham (because terminological), battles will continue to be fought. If, however, it is recognized that such battles may be real ones—of values—then they could be better waged, with more enlightenment for the spectators, if the decks were cleared of any encumbering pseudo-objective terminology. I am, in fact, suggesting a better separation, in economics, of different levels of discourse. This cannot be achieved if it is not recognized that many economic statements, which appear at first sight to be merely descriptive, have value implications. Among the most important of such phrases are 'increase of welfare' and 'increase of real income'.

I have rejected the utilitarian view that the logical calculus of 'welfare' economics should be interpreted in terms of satisfaction or happiness, on the ground that it is misleading to describe welfare economics as the science which studies the economic causes of the happiness of communities. So to describe it suggests a degree of objectivity and precision which is lacking. It is, for instance, very much a matter of opinion whether some given redistribution of money would increase or decrease happiness. I also claimed that there is an element of prescription in judgements about the happiness of communities. But even if I am wrong about this, it is, in any case, certain that people will slip into using prescriptive terminology—will slip from statements about happiness to statements about welfare, and thence to the use of words such as 'improvement' and 'benefit'—without paying much attention to the change. I have taken the view that the essential purpose of welfare economics is to prescribe, and that therefore certain questions of value are begged unless it is explicitly based on value judgements.

Thus my rejection of the utilitarian scheme of things has not been based on the perhaps rather dogmatic objection that satisfactions cannot be added, and certainly not on a 'denial' of interpersonal comparisons. As a matter of fact, I think that many people, in deciding what ought to be done, often employ some sort of hedonistic calculation. But such calculation is not *logically* essential to prescriptive economics. What we require are judgements about the sort of thing that ought to be done; and it does not matter to us what imaginative processes people employ to help them arrive at such judgements.

Accordingly I have proposed that welfare economics be based on the following sufficient criterion for a desirable economic change: an economic change is desirable if (*a*) it would result in a good redistribution of wealth, and if (*b*) the potential losers could not profitably bribe the potential gainers to oppose the change.[1] Two value judgements are presupposed by this criterion. The first

[1] This is subject to certain qualifications as to the sense of the word 'desirable' which it would be tedious to repeat at this point. See Ch. VI.

is that an individual becomes better off if he is enabled to reach a position higher up on his order of choice. The second is that the community is better off if one individual becomes better off, and none worse off. It is thought that both of these judgements would be widely acceptable. It has further been shown that the above criterion is sufficient, given enough *factual* assumptions, to deduce that a realization of the 'optimum' conditions of exchange and production would be a good thing, so long as a worse distribution of wealth would not result, or could be avoided by compensation.[1]

I have claimed that the above foundations are firm. Anyone may accept welfare economics on such a basis, or reject it. But the important thing is that it is clear what has to be accepted or rejected. If the conclusions follow from the axioms, and the meaning of the axioms is clear, then a system can be said, I think, to have firm foundations.

The suggested criterion is not, of course, objective. Whether a given economic change would be good or bad remains a matter of personal opinion. For it is a matter of opinion whether or not the change would cause a good, bad, or neutral redistribution of wealth or welfare. It must be emphasized that this does not imply that welfare economics is useless. Most people would accept the two fundamental value judgements. The theory, *if the required factual assumptions are deemed realistic enough*, in any particular case, enables such people to agree on the goodness or otherwise of the change, given that they give the same answer to the question about distribution. And even when there is no agreement about income distribution, useful conclusions may be reached, of the form 'This redistribution would be attained better by change *A*, than change *B*.'

Thus I think that welfare economics may best be considered as the study of whether or not one configuration of the economic system is better or worse than another and whether a change from one to the other should be made. Whenever these questions arise, whether explicitly or by implication, then I suggest that the answer be based on the above criterion. This means that welfare economics is not solely concerned with the development of 'optimum' conditions. It is concerned not only with prospective changes, but also with the results of actual changes which have occurred. It is

[1] We also, of course, have to assume that any induced non-economic changes are neutral or good.

obvious that the question whether economic welfare increased over some past period is a question in welfare economics. It is not quite so obvious that the same question whether posed with reference to real income, wealth, production, real wages, consumption, or standards of living, is also a question in welfare economics. But all these words or phrases belong to the pseudo-objective terminology of economics. They are substantival words which look as though they refer to something, changes in the magnitude of which may be measured; but this appearance is misleading. The size of a collection of incommensurable kinds is a concept which requires the assignment of weights, which determine the relative importance, *for some given purpose*, of the different kinds. One cannot, strictly speaking, discuss the question of changes in the size of such collections at all. The size of a thing *is* something objective, which is independent of the purpose of the measurement. But the 'size' of, say, the national real income has no such independence. Nevertheless, there is a correct answer (or rather, the form of a correct answer) to such a question as 'has real income increased?'. This is because the purpose, which determines the weighting, is suggested by the value implications of the sentence 'the real income of society has increased'. In other words, the purpose is to discover whether or not there has been an improvement. Consequently our 'welfare' theory tells us that the weights must be market prices, and that the answer to the question must then be determined by reference to our fundamental criterion.

Welfare economics is, then, likely to be useful if its factual assumptions are realistic enough. We saw that the question whether they are realistic enough is very difficult to answer, because the conclusions of the theory cannot, in practice, be tested. Whether its conclusions, in any particular case, are to be accepted or rejected is thus, even given agreement on all questions of value, a matter of judgement and opinion. There is no question of proof.

The first difficulty is that our criterion often, in practice, rests on the assumption that money may be redistributed without offending against any of the theoretical 'optimum' conditions. Such redistribution would frequently be an administrative or political impossibility.[1] Therefore many changes may have to be admitted to be

---

[1] Or it may be impossible because the potential losers have no 'lump-sums' which can be used to bribe the potential gainers. However, if there were no property, then a good redistribution of earned income by direct taxation would

desirable although they do not satisfy the criterion. Thus a change may be held to be good, if it effects a good redistribution, although, in theory, this redistribution could have been better carried out by 'neutral' money transfers. Therefore our criterion must be regarded only as a sufficient criterion for a desirable economic change, and not as a definition of 'an increase in economic welfare'. Its applicability, in opposing a particular change which would result in a good redistribution of real income, is limited by the practical possibility of carrying out the required redistribution in some better way.

But, in every case, the exact application of the theory would require the existence of eternal and perfectly consistent individuals, who choose between infinitely divisible goods of unchanging quality. In my opinion this unreality does not in itself suffice to make the conclusions of the theory worthless, but does make it silly to treat them as anything but rough guides to practice. It was argued that any divergence from 'optimum' conditions must be large before one could have any reasonable degree of confidence that an improvement would result from trying to satisfy them.

The above assumptions suffice only for the derivation of the 'optimum' exchange conditions, and, given perfect statistics, for the use of index-numbers in judging whether real income, consumption, &c., has changed. The 'optimum' conditions of production require many further unrealistic factual assumptions, and are, accordingly, less trustworthy. In particular, we found that the theorem that output ought to be adjusted until price equals marginal cost is extremely shaky, and we did not feel justified in taking much notice of it except in a few special cases. This theorem is the most important and the most controversial conclusion of welfare theory. It lies behind many of the widely accepted practical implications of economic theory. It is highly controversial because it is the only one of the 'optimum' conditions which also has serious political implications. The fact that I cannot bring myself to believe that the distinction between average and marginal cost is, more

satisfy our criterion. The potential losers could not profitably bribe the potential gainers to oppose the change, because the bribes required would be the exact equivalent of the proposed taxation. This would only not be the case if the bribe could be capitalized, and property transferred. Thus the fact that there might be no 'lump-sums' to transfer does not necessarily render the criterion inapplicable, although it does imply that it might not be a good thing to put the optimum labour-supply condition into operation, or make marginal cost equal to price.

than very seldom, of the slightest importance to the welfare of society, has led me to the view that this branch of economics— pure static welfare theory—is, or rather should be, of little or no political import.

We can, on the other hand, scarcely doubt that welfare theory is sufficiently realistic to tell us that relative costs of production should not be allowed to get too far out of line with relative market-prices. As a *rough* guide to what ought to be done, it is undoubtedly useful. If one says that welfare economics is useless one means that its precise conclusions cannot be taken seriously. The common-sense argument that if the market value of one thing is twice that of another, then it is usually worth producing if it does not cost more than twice as much—ambiguous though it is—is probably just as valuable, and is certainly less misleading than such conclusions as 'price ought to equal marginal cost'.

Common sense is sometimes bad theory, and then it may mislead. But it is often good, but crude, theory. Economic welfare is a subject in which rigour and refinement are probably worse than useless. Rough theory, or good common sense, is, in practice, what we require. It is satisfying, and impressive, that a rigorous logical system, with some apparent reality, should have been set up in the field of the social sciences: but we must not let ourselves be so impressed that we forget that its reality is obviously limited; and that the degree of such reality is a matter of judgement and opinion.

APPENDIX I

The Logic of Strong Ordering

by C. B. WINSTEN

IN economic theory the assumption of mathematical continuity is very convenient. Most of the geometrical reasoning based on various types of curves, such as demand curves, uses such an assumption. However, continuity is a deep notion and opens up the possibility of many bizarre and unrealistic situations, so that it is necessary, as far as possible, to have strong enough postulates for these situations to be precluded.

In the text and in Appendix II an axiom of strong ordering is used. This supposes that, for any two different collections of goods P and Q, one is definitely chosen rather than the other. There is also a transitivity axiom, that if P, Q, and R are three different collections, and P is chosen rather than Q, and Q rather than R, then in a choice between P and R, P will be chosen. However, if these axioms are taken as they stand, they still leave the possibility that, in one of the situations commonly considered in economics, the consumer's choice will not be determinate, even though his preference field is completely defined in accord with the axioms.

One preference field which gives this paradoxical result is the following:

FIG. XV

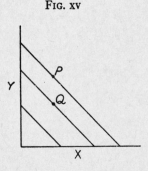

Suppose there are two goods X and Y, and suppose the points P and Q represent two collections of these goods. Draw lines at $45°$ to the axis through P and Q as shown in Fig. XV. Then suppose P is chosen rather than Q if it is on a higher line than Q. This defines the preference field unless P and Q lie on the same line.

On any particular line, order the collections of goods as follows:

FIG. XVI

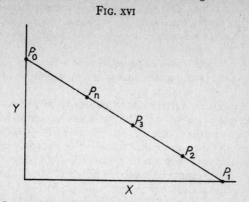

Let P_0, the extreme left-hand point of the line, be the least preferred on the line. Next above it, let P_1, the extreme right-hand point, be preferred. Now order the other points higher the farther to the left they are on the line, supposing that all the remaining points are preferred to P_1, and therefore, by the transitivity postulate, to P_0. Thus, in Fig. XVI, the points are ranked $P_3 > P_2 > P_1 > P_0$.

There is now no point on the line that is preferred to all the others. For since there is an assumption of mathematical continuity, however far to the left P_n is, provided it does not coincide with P_0, there is still another point P_{n+1} between P_0 and P_n, and this point will be preferred to P_n. In turn there will be another point between P_{n+1} and P_0 preferred to P_{n+1}. Thus we can continue to rise in the preference scale by getting closer to P_0, yet we never attain a maximum because P_0 itself is the least preferred point on the line.

Now suppose that the prices of X and Y are such that the line $P_0 P_1$ is a budget line. Then given this range of choices the consumer will prefer points on $P_0 P_1$ to others, but will not prefer any point on $P_0 P_1$ definitely above all others. This odd situation arises solely because of the assumption of continuity.

If we wish to avoid this paradox, while still retaining strong ordering, it seems adequate to replace the pair of postulates given above by the following pair:

1. In any closed and bounded set of the commodity space, one point is chosen.
2. If P and Q are two points both of which occur in two sets in the commodity space, and P is chosen in one of the sets, then Q will not be chosen in the other.

In the first of these postulates, we extend the range of possible choices from the start, and do not try to limit it to pairs at first. However, we limit it to bounded sets (which do not give the possibility of indefinitely large collections of goods) and also to closed sets (and these for present purposes we can say are sets which include their boundary lines).

The second postulate is one of consistency. It takes the place of the transitivity axiom, and implies that there is a definite ordering of P and Q.

The two postulates together imply transitivity, and therefore imply a strong ordering of the system. This result can be seen as follows:

Suppose in a pairwise choice, P is chosen rather than Q, and in another pairwise choice Q is chosen rather than R. Then in applying the consistency postulate to the two sets (P, Q) and (P, Q, R), since P is chosen in the set (P, Q), Q cannot be chosen in the set (P, Q, R). In the same way, applying the consistency postulate to (Q, R) and (P, Q, R), R cannot be chosen in (P, Q, R). Thus P is chosen in (P, Q, R), and so, applying the consistency postulate yet again to (P, Q, R) and (P, R), P is chosen from (P, R).

The two new postulates thus include the old postulates of strong ordering, but are strengthened to exclude the possibility given at the beginning of this note. In practice, of course, it would be entirely impossible to observe such subtleties of choice given above, but such postulates enable us to use rigorous mathematical reasoning without hedging the statements with exceptions.

APPENDIX II[1]

The Construction of a Behaviour-line System from Actual Choices[2]

DEFINITIONS:

1. A collection of goods is said to be *larger than* another collection if there is more of one kind, and no less of any kind. Similarly for *smaller than*.
2. A consumer is said to *choose* a certain collection A *rather than* B if, when he buys A, he could have bought B; i.e. in index-number form, if $\sum p_a q_a \geqslant \sum p_a q_b$.
3. A given *price-income situation* is a situation in which the consumer's income and all prices are given.

AXIOMS:[3]

I. A consumer chooses a larger collection of goods rather than a small collection.
II. If a consumer chooses A rather than B, and B rather than C, then he chooses A rather than C.
III. Every possible collection of goods is chosen in one and only one price-income situation.

Consider Fig. XVII.[4] X and Y are two goods, quantities of which are measured along the two axes. MN is a budget line (or price line). B represents the collection of goods chosen from the possibilities indicated by all the points on and below the line MN. It can therefore be said that B is chosen rather than any of these points (by definition 2).

Next, the budget line is rotated about the point B, continuously altering the price-income situation in such a way that the consumer could still just buy the collection B. In each of the resultant situations

[1] Except for the comment at the end, this appendix is the same as in the first edition. But since the subject has been treated in several further articles since it was written, a comment has been added at the end. I wrote in the first edition, 'this . . . construction is of no particular importance to welfare economics, or indeed any other kind of practical economics'. One might amend this judgement by deleting the words 'particular' and 'practical'.

[2] This construction is suggested by the work of Professor Samuelson in his *Foundations of Economic Analysis*, ch. vi, 'A Note on the Pure Theory of Consumers' Behaviour', *Economica*, 1938, and 'Consumption Theory in terms of Revealed Preference', ibid., Nov. 1948. Also my article 'A Reformation of the Theory of Consumers' Behaviour', *O.E.P.*, N.S., no. 1, Jan. 1949.

[3] These axioms are not quite sufficient. A further mathematical postulate is required. See p. 286.

[4] Borrowed from Samuelson, *Foundations of Economic Analysis*, p. 148.

a certain collection is chosen. The curve PBQ is the locus of the points representing these collections; it may be called an offer curve. Take any one of these points A; the line AB is then the budget line on which A is the chosen point. A is therefore chosen rather than B, and similarly for any other point on the curve PBQ, and *a fortiori* (by Axiom I) for any chosen point above the curve PBQ. This curve PBQ can only touch MN at B; elsewhere it must lie above it. If, as the budget line was rotated through B, a finite move to a point A was made only after

FIG. XVII

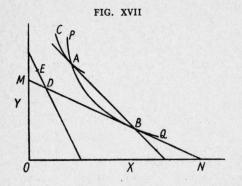

it had moved through some finite angle, then B would have been chosen in more than one price-income situation. This would occur whenever the consumer continued to consume exactly the same collection of goods in spite of a small change in their prices. It follows that the offer curve must be continuous, and tangential to MN at B.[1]

Now take the point A. In a similar manner, an offer curve can be drawn through A. Since it must, using the results obtained above, be tangential to AB at A, it must cut the curve $PABQ$, and therefore enlarge the area within which it can be said that all points are chosen rather than B. This follows because any point C on or above the new offer curve is chosen rather than A (that is, the relation $\sum p_c q_c \geqslant \sum p_c q_a$ holds) and A is chosen rather than B (the relation $\sum p_a q_a \geqslant \sum p_a q_b$ holds). The point A can slide along the curve PBQ and generate a family of similar new offer curves. Again, points can be taken on these latter curves, and new offer curves generated, and so on. Eventually a limit will be reached, and the boundary of the resultant area within which it can be said that all points are chosen rather than B can be shown to be a smooth convex curve. It will be called the *upper behaviour line* of B.

---

[1] If the offer curve approached MN at B' between M and B, then points between B and B' would not be chosen in any price-income situation, *contra* Axiom III.

Now let us take a point D on the budget line MN. We know already that B is chosen rather than D. Next rotate MN about D until D is itself the chosen point. We then know that D is chosen rather than any point E on the new budget line. Similarly D can, by moving along MN, generate a family of new budget lines, and so on, as for the previous construction. Again, we will reach a limit which will be called the *lower behaviour line* of B. This curve must also be continuous and convex to the origin.

It is now required to show that these two behaviour lines through B

FIG. XVIII

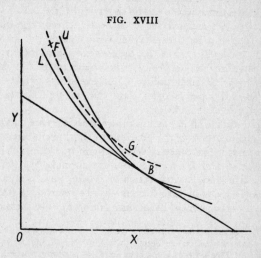

coincide. This will be proved by a *reductio ad absurdum*. Therefore in Fig. XVIII the two behaviour lines of B (BU and BL) are drawn separate. The area between the two may be called B's *region of ignorance*. Within this region let us take any point F, and construct a lower behaviour line of F (shown as a broken line in the diagram). The first possibility is that this lower behaviour line of F cuts the upper behaviour line of B, as in the figure. But then we would have some point, such as G, which would be chosen rather than B. But F would be chosen rather than G, and therefore, *a fortiori*, rather than B. Therefore, *contra hypothesi*, F would not lie in B's region of ignorance.

The next possibility is that the lower behaviour line of F passes through B itself. It might be thought that this would imply that F would be chosen rather than B. This is not, however, the case because the points on F's lower behaviour line (which is the boundary of the area containing points rather than which F is chosen) cannot themselves be held to be necessarily 'worse' than F. This possibility must therefore be excluded by a further postulate which will ensure that no point lies on more than one lower behaviour line. In mathematical terms the required postulate is to the effect that in the differential equation defining a set of lower behaviour lines—$dy/dx = f(x, y)$—f has continuous partial derivatives. This same postulate suffices also to exclude the remaining possibility that the lower behaviour line of F should cut that of B.

Therefore, given the above postulates, it follows that no region of ignorance can exist. The upper and lower behaviour lines of B must coincide in one curve which can be simply called the behaviour line of B. Thus the conventional set of smooth, convex, non-intersecting 'utility' curves can be derived from certain axioms about economic behaviour. It may be noticed that the convexity of utility curves is here deduced as a theorem. Convexity is the equivalent of Marshall's 'law' of diminishing marginal utility. Thus everything which could be deduced from this psychological 'law' can also be deduced from our axioms about economic choices.

These axioms are all implicit in the usual indifference curve analysis. They are not, of course, in the least realistic. But, given them, it becomes possible to arrange all conceivable collections[1] in order of choice, using as our criterion of choice the index-number formula $\sum p_a q_a \geqslant \sum p_a q_b$, which, by definition, is the criterion of A being chosen rather than B. Therefore the index-number formula may be regarded as fundamental to the theory of consumers' behaviour.[2] Here it must be mentioned that,

[1] Strictly speaking, those collections which lie on the same behaviour line as B cannot be determined to be 'better' or 'worse' than B, merely by observing market choices. This is because the behaviour line is a limit reached only as the result of an infinite process. Thus Professor Samuelson (*Economica*, Nov. 1948, p. 251) states 'the points lying literally on a frontier locus can never themselves be revealed to be better or worse than A. *If we wish, then, we may speak of them as being indifferent to A*' (my italics). If we supposed that observation of actual economic behaviour was the only conceivable method of construction of behaviour lines, then I think that Professor Samuelson would agree that the statement 'the points on A's behaviour line are indifferent to A' would be insignificant, or, in his terminology, operationally meaningless. But the behaviour-line system, given the assumption that utility is maximized, could conceivably be constructed by asking the consumer to name all collections 'better' and 'worse' than A. The points actually on the line could, then, be significantly said to be arranged in order of choice, because this order could in principle be discovered. Thus to call the points on a line indifferent to each other, is not merely misleading, but also rules out the (imaginary) methods of construction of behaviour-line systems by questions about hypothetical choices, or by confronting the consumer directly with choices between collections which he does not have to pay for.

[2] For certain purposes the construction of 'indifference curves', or behaviour lines, is unnecessary. Professor Samuelson (*Foundations of Economic Analysis*, pp. 111, 115) shows that all the theorems of demand theory can be derived from the proposition $\sum p \Delta x \leqslant 0$ implies $\sum (p+\Delta p) \Delta x < 0$. But this proposition can

if we are dealing with only two situations, then it is, of course, possible that an individual be on a higher behaviour line although it would not be possible for him to buy the goods of the former situation. What the above analysis tells us is that, if we could have as many other situations as we liked, then we could always bring the two initial situations into comparison by bringing in the other situations as stepping-stones. For instance, A may be on a higher indifference curve than Z, but it may not be true that $\sum p_a q_a \geqslant \sum p_a q_z$. Nevertheless, using this criterion, it must be possible to say that A is chosen rather than Z, by bringing in the fact that A is chosen rather than B, B rather than C, ... and Y rather than Z. Thus, it becomes possible to say that A is chosen rather than Z, although Z was not an immediate possibility. I do not think this is stretching the ordinary usage of the word 'choice' too far.

Finally, it may be said that this market-behaviour conception of behaviour lines is, in some ways, the most enlightening. It is well known that it is, in fact, impossible to draw up indifference curves by asking questions. For one thing the subject cannot rid his mind of the known exchange values of the collections he is asked to choose between. In practice the only way we can find out if a person is in a chosen position is by employing the index-number criterion $\sum p_2 q_2 \geqslant \sum p_2 q_1$, together with $\sum p_1 q_1 < \sum p_1 q_2$ as a test of consistency. If the employment of these tests gives no information (as when $\sum p_2 q_2 < \sum p_2 q_1$, and $\sum p_1 q_1 < \sum p_1 q_2$), then it might be possible to find a mediating point which would suffice for us to be able to say which was actually higher up on the order of choices. The behaviour line may be regarded as the ideal limit which would be attained if we could always bring every pair of situations into relation by means of the index-number criterion.

Further Comment

1. Professor Georgescu-Roegen has criticized Axiom II as being 'incorrect'.[1] By this he means that I could not stipulate that A should be chosen rather than C *in the sense of definition* 2. This is true, and I should have written 'A would be chosen rather than C if there was a free pairwise choice between the two'. Definition 2 then requires to be enlarged to ascribe a meaning to choice in a non-market situation. The critics of 'revealed preference' theory, or of my claim that the behaviour-

be deduced from the definition of consistency as follows. Given that an individual once bought the collection Q_1, rather than Q_0, that is, given that $\sum p_1 q_1 \geqslant \sum p_1 q_0$, then it follows that if he ever buys Q_0 it must not be the case that $\sum p_0 q_0 \geqslant \sum p_0 q_1$, because in that event he would have been able to buy Q_1, and he would then, by definition, have chosen Q_0 rather than Q_1, which would be inconsistent. Therefore $\sum p_1 q_1 \geqslant \sum p_1 q_0$ implies $\sum p_0 q_0 < \sum p_0 q_1$. Therefore $\sum p_1 (q_0 - q_1) \leqslant 0$ implies $\sum p_0 (q_0 - q_1) < 0$. Therefore $\sum p \, \Delta q \leqslant 0$ implies $\sum (p + \Delta p) \, \Delta q < 0$.

[1] 'Choice and Revealed Preference', *S.E.J.*, Oct. 1954.

line system was constructed from actual choices, would then say that
this was an illegitimate resort to choice in a non-market situation. If
revealed preference theorists had to limit themselves solely to observation, of course they could get nowhere. An observation that 'Smith
chose x' tells one only that Smith chose x, and did not choose any of
the other possibilities. The claim was (or should have been) that given
certain assumptions about people's choices (which need not all be
testable by observing only market behaviour) then the system of
curves can be built up by observing only behaviour. If, however, one
takes the view that the theory is pointless unless the assumptions are
testable in terms of market behaviour, Axiom II can be reformulated
to get over this difficulty.

Professor Georgescu-Roegen has shown[1] that this was the merit of
Professor Houthakker's so-called strong axiom.[2] Professor Houthakker's
axiom (which may be said to define 'semi-transitivity') is that if A is
chosen rather than B and B rather than C . . ., and Y rather than Z, then
Z must not be chosen rather than A. We may now extend the meaning
of 'chosen rather than' so as to be able to say that A is chosen rather than
Z in the above circumstances (I had already made this extension of the
meaning of choice, but in terms of full rather than semi-transitivity).
Now suppose that A is chosen rather than B, and C is chosen rather
than A, in the manner of Fig. XVII. These relations imply that A is
not chosen rather than C, and B not chosen rather than A.[3] But it is
obvious from the construction of Fig. XVII that C was not among the
possibilities when B was chosen—hence B was not chosen rather than
C, and never would be since, by Axiom III, B is not chosen in any other
price-income situation. Thus by the extended definition of 'chosen
rather than', and the relation of semi-transitivity, C chosen rather than
A, and A rather than B, implies C is chosen rather than B—which is
full transitivity.

But this restatement does not yet fully achieve the task of removing
altogether axioms which cannot be tested by market behaviour. Axiom I
clearly cannot be so tested. But in fact it would seem that Axiom I is
unnecessary, since definition 2 in fact does the required trick of en-
abling one to compare points on the budget line with those below it.
It seems to me difficult to object to this definition.

2. A flaw in the construction is the postulate that the differential
equation defining the set of lower behaviour lines should have continuous partial derivatives, since this cannot be given any testable
meaning in terms of economic choices. This postulate is not required

[1] Idem.   [2] 'Revealed Preference and Utility Function', *Economica*, 1950.
[3] An axiom to this effect (Samuelson's so-called 'weak axiom', see *Foundations*,
p. 151) should have been stated among the axioms, but is now contained in the
axiom of semi-transitivity.

to rule out the possibility that the lower behaviour line of F cuts that of B (see my cited *O.E.P.* article). But it is required to eliminate the possibility that it joins it at B. Thus if behaviour lines are branched as in Fig. V, p. 28, the construction appears impossible; supposing that in this diagram AC is the true behaviour line of C, then the present construction would trace the line AC as the upper behaviour line of C, but it would also trace the line BC as the lower behaviour line of C. So far as I can understand them, it appears that all other 'revealed preference' practitioners have made some similar analytic assumption. (See Georgescu-Roegen, loc. cit., p. 128.)

3. Another difficulty (also pointed to by Professor Georgescu-Roegen, loc. cit.,) is that Axiom III cannot be true unless some of both commodities are consumed—or in the general case some of everything. But in the general case this is obviously false. Scarcely anyone consumes something of everything. (But eliminating this axiom also upsets the usual conclusions of welfare economics (see pp. 25–26, and Appendix III, above) as well as revealed preference theory.) However, this does not seem to be an additional difficulty to that discussed in (2), since, given that we assume continuous partial derivatives, there is no need for the present axiom as well.

4. Professor Houthakker in the article cited has shown that the present kind of analysis can be extended to more than two goods. In so doing he shows that if transitivity holds good, then the behaviour lines can be integrated into surfaces. (This in fact had been already shown by Professor Georgescu-Roegen.[1]) He proves formally that the points on the surfaces are equivalent ($=$ symmetrical, reflexive, and transitive) to each other, so that they can be regarded as indifferent (since indifference is also an equivalence relation). This, however, does not mean that they could not be ordered by choice—for even if they were, they would still be equivalent in the sense of belonging to the same boundary line.

[1] 'The Pure Theory of Consumer's Behaviour', *Q.J.E.*, 1935–6.

APPENDIX III

Kinked Behaviour Lines and Boundary Optima

IT was stated in Chapter II that much of Welfare Economics remains valid even if it is not assumed that individual behaviour lines are smooth curves.

First consider the 'optimum' exchange condition. One can no longer speak in terms of the equality of different individual's marginal rates of substitution as a necessary condition for an optimum, because unique marginal rates of substitution are no longer assumed to exist. One can, however, still say that, with given totals of goods to be distributed, it is a *sufficient* condition of a Pareto optimum that all individuals should be free to trade as they please at a price which equates total supply and demand. This follows simply from the assumption that everyone's equilibrium point is where the budget line touches but does not intersect the highest behaviour line. It follows that no two individuals' behaviour lines (as in an Edgeworth box diagram) can intersect. It is, however, no longer necessary that there should be a single price, in that it would be possible to have a different price for those individuals with kinked curves, without shifting their equilibrium points at all.

Secondly, the condition that the marginal rate of transformation between two goods should equal the marginal rate of substitution no longer applies. Instead we have the condition that the marginal rate of transformation be equal to the relative equilibrium market prices of the two goods. If this condition is satisfied, then, for the reasons given in the above paragraph, the transformation curve cannot intersect any individual behaviour line. Taken in conjunction with the other 'optimum' conditions, this is a sufficient condition of a Pareto optimum. It is no longer a necessary condition in that it becomes possible for the transformation curve to intersect the price line without intersecting an individual behaviour line.

The theorem derived from these conditions, that if the production of all goods be carried to the point where marginal cost equals price, then (in the absence of external economies and diseconomies) a Pareto optimum is reached, remains valid. But it becomes a sufficient condition, rather than a sufficient and necessary one. The theorem that perfect competition fulfils this condition is unaffected.

That welfare economics is basically undisturbed by kinked behaviour lines is a point of more than purely technical interest. It may very well be true that in so far as people behave consistently at all, they behave in a manner which implies kinked lines. This is liable to be the case if people, to some extent at least, order their choices by reference to two or more guiding principles, arranged in order of priority but otherwise incommensurable. Let us take an example which illustrates the principle.[1] Suppose a man chooses between two goods on the basis of first a 'life' principle, and secondly a 'pleasure' principle, 'life' having top priority until it is fully satisfied. Until he has enough calories, vitamins, &c., for good health, the fact that he likes certain combinations more than others plays no part. Such a scheme of choice would produce a behaviour pattern of the type illustrated in Fig. XIX.

FIG. XIX

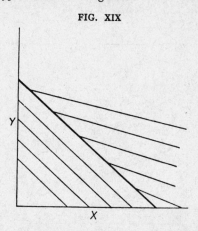

The heavy curve is the locus of points of satiation of the 'life' principle: only on and above this line does the 'pleasure' principle take over. The points on any given 'life' curve are all ordered by the pleasure principle; and they *cannot* therefore be described as indifference curves.

That kinks are likely to be very common can be seen by the following consideration. There are in most people's budgets some goods, with non-zero prices, of which no more would be consumed if there were an 'income-compensated' fall in their prices. (The fall in price must be 'income compensated' otherwise it might be claimed that the reason was that they are inferior goods.) This implies kinks. I personally would say that a great majority of the goods I consume are in this class. One reason for this is of course the indivisibility of many consumption goods. But another is the fact that (perhaps in order to simplify life a little, and not always be calculating) one pursues certain kinds of wants to satiation point before thinking of other ways of spending money.

The implications for welfare economics of kinked behaviour lines are

[1] The example is suggested by N. Georgescu-Roegen, 'Choice Expectations and Measurability', *Q.J.E.*, Nov. 1954.

the same as those of 'boundary optima'. The reader will have noticed in Chapter VIII that the illustrated optimum position was always within the 'box'. What happens if it is at the edge of the box as in Fig. XX?

Within the box there is no point at which the behaviour lines are tangential to each other. The 'optimal' points all lie along the left-hand and upper edges of the box, which thus form the contract curve. Consider one such point P. Through P are drawn two price lines (the dotted lines) one tangential to A's behaviour line, and the other to B's. Now either of these price lines, or any between them, would produce P

FIG. XX

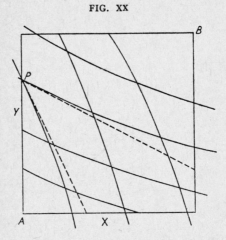

as an equilibrium point. From any point on either of them, it would pay both A and B to exchange until the limit was reached when A had no more X to give.

It follows from this that one cannot speak of equality of marginal rates of substitution. Nevertheless, it can easily be seen that, starting from any point on the diagram, a price must establish itself (if both trade freely, and the price falls or rises in response to excess supply or demand) which results in a position on the left or upper edge of the box. Consequently, as with kinked curves, it remains true that a single market price which equates supply and demand is a sufficient condition for the 'optimum' allocation of fixed collections of goods between individuals.[1] Modifications similar to those made above to allow for kinked behaviour lines apply to the other optimum conditions. Marginal cost pricing (together with the exchange conditions) remains a sufficient condition

[1] This case has been dealt with more generally by K. J. Arrow in 'An Extension of the Basic Theorems of Classical Welfare Economics', *Cowles Commission Papers*, N.S., no. 4.

of a Pareto optimum, while the theory that perfect competition leads (in the absence of external economies and costs) to a Pareto optimum also remains valid.[1]

At first glance 'boundary optima' may appear unrealistic: but this is only because our diagrams are limited to the two-good case. Second thoughts suggest that there is a large number of things one does not consume at all, and this is likely to apply to everyone. Indivisibility may be the most important reason for this: but not the only one, for most people will be able to think of many divisible things they do not consume. In general, when the commodity space is multi-dimensional one would therefore expect every consumer's equilibrium point to be on a boundary or corner of the space.

Finally, there is the question whether the mere statement of the 'optimum' conditions as being sufficient for achieving Pareto optima, rather than as necessary for any 'optimum', represents a significant weakening of welfare economics—whether, in fact, it makes it less applicable. At first sight it does weaken the theory. Thus the non-fulfilment of the 'optimum' conditions in the real world cannot any longer be taken as proof that one is not at a Pareto optimum. It could still be argued that putting the conditions into operation would ensure that one *was* at a Pareto optimum; and that it is better to be sure. This might not, however, seem very compelling. Therefore only disapproval of the pre-vailing distribution of wealth might be taken as a sufficient reason to make a change. In theory, therefore, this modification would seem to weaken welfare economics: but in practice it is very doubtful whether it does so. This is because the practical choice is never between keeping to the *status quo* or putting *all* the 'optimum' conditions into operation and so ensuring a Pareto optimum. In practice our choices are between 'sub-optimum' positions, and the case for a change is in terms of the probable satisfaction of Scitovsky or Kaldor–Hicks criteria.

All this is, however, of small importance. For the presence of only one consumer who has a unique rate of substitution equal to the relative prices of the two goods in question means that it remains a *necessary* condition for an 'optimum' that the rate of transformation should equal this rate of substitution. Unless it is so, this particular consumer could be made better off without harming anyone else if the relative outputs of the two goods were slightly changed—and this could not have been achieved by any new deal of the same output of goods. The upshot therefore seems to be to accept the 'optimum' conditions as necessary, and at the same time to recognize that boundary maxima and kinked behaviour lines are likely to be almost universal.

[1] Professor Arrow (loc. cit.) cites an exception: but it appears to be one which is ruled out by our assumption that behaviour lines do not slope north-eastwards.

APPENDIX IV

Direct versus Indirect Taxes[1]

THE usual analysis of direct versus indirect taxation (or subsidization) runs typically as follows:[2]

A single 'economic man' who spends his income on two goods (one of which may be 'money') is assumed. In Fig. XXI Q_0 is the equilibrium tax-free position. When an income-tax equal to AB of X is imposed, Q_1 is reached. The same sum could be raised by an indirect tax on Y, which would result in a position such as Q_2. From the usual convexity assumption it follows that Q_2 is worse than Q_1. Q.E.D.

FIG. XXI

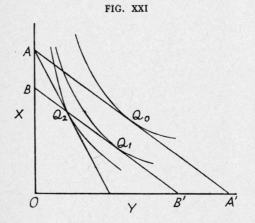

At first sight this result always looks like a conjuring trick. There is no overt reference to marginal costs. Yet it is well known that nothing can be proved without some such reference.[3] The covert reference is as follows: for the proof to be valid the government must be able to buy the same collection of goods whether the individual is at position Q_2 or at position Q_1. This it can do only if $Q_2 Q_1$ has the same slope as the

---

[1] This appendix is based on my article with the same title in *E.J.*, Sept. 1951.

[2] Cf. M. F. W. Joseph, 'The Excess Burden of Indirect Taxation', *R.E.S.*, June 1939; H. P. Wald, 'The Classical Indictment of Indirect Taxation', *Q.J.E.*, Aug. 1945; A. M. Henderson, 'The Case for Indirect Taxation', *E.J.*, Dec. 1948; A. T. Peacock and D. Berry, 'A Note on the Theory of Income Redistribution', *Economica*, Feb. 1951.

[3] Cf. the original Frisch–Hotelling controversy—*Econometrica*, 1939, pp. 145–60; in particular Professor Hotelling's final note, pp. 158–60.

transformation curve of X and Y (the curve showing the maximum amounts of X which could be produced given varying quantities of Y, and fixed amounts of all other goods). From this it follows that the slope of BB' must equal the relative marginal costs of the two goods. Thus, in Fig. XXI, relative marginal costs are assumed to be the same both at Q_2 and Q_1.

FIG. XXII

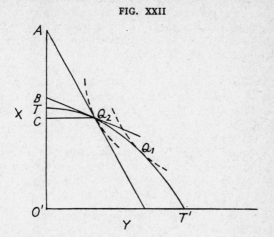

Although Fig. XXI is drawn with reference to a single individual, it may be presumed that it is designed to illustrate the relative effects, on each of many individuals, of two different tax systems of equal monetary incidence. Therefore, a considerable shift of production must be allowed for. This being the case, the assumption that relative marginal costs are the same at both Q_2 and Q_1 is in conflict with the normal assumption used in this connexion, that of a diminishing marginal rate of transformation. The analysis is excessively and un-necessarily partial in other ways. The prices of goods, other than those represented, may change when the indirect tax is substituted for the direct. When this is allowed for, it is even conceivable that any given individual would gain as a result of the change.

But none of this invalidates the usual conclusion (that the gainers could overcompensate the losers if direct taxes were substituted for indirect) *given that the supply of labour is not a variable.* In Fig. XXII the curve TQ_2Q_1T' is the transformation curve of X and Y, given the quantities of all other goods, and also given the quantities of X and Y demanded by the government.[1] At Q_1 relative price is assumed equal to

' [1] The assumption that the government's demands are absolute is made only

relative marginal cost (this is indicated by drawing in a 'community indifference' curve tangential to the transformation curve at Q_1). But at Q_2 this cannot hold, for Y has been made more expensive relative to X, while it has become relatively less costly to produce (at the margin). Thus the fact that the position Q_2 is not 'optimum' follows simply from the divergence of relative prices and relative marginal costs. No other proof is required or possible. But we shall show that the equalization of relative marginal costs and relative prices is not a sufficient condition for an improvement, even given that the distribution of wealth is not adversely affected, *unless* one makes the quite unwarranted and special assumption that the supply of labour is unaffected.

The contrary view has been put by A. M. Henderson, who argued that the fact that all marginal taxation is a tax on work (it can also be regarded as a subsidy on leisure, as far as substitution effects are concerned) does not destroy the case against indirect taxation.[1] The argument is that both indirect and direct taxes sin against the necessary 'optimum' condition that the rate of substitution of leisure for any other good must equal the rate of transformation between leisure and that good. But, it is argued, indirect taxes *also* prevent the rates of substitution between pairs of goods, excluding leisure, being equal to their respective rates of transformation. Thus Henderson wrote:

> If a given revenue is required then the resources available to the consumer must be limited to the same extent by either method (i.e. direct or indirect taxation). But the method of indirect taxation has the further disadvantage of reducing the efficiency with which these resources are used, and therefore imposes an added burden.[2]

This argument is unsatisfactory because it assumes that the resources used are identical in both cases, as can be seen by the reference to '*the* resources available to the consumer'. In other words, it has to be assumed that the supply of labour is the same whether the taxation is direct or indirect. This amounts to saying that, for every individual, the cross-elasticity of demand for leisure with respect to all other prices is zero, i.e. leisure is not substitutable for any other good. To all intents and purposes, the assumption that the amount of labour does not vary has crept into an argument designed to show that direct taxation is better than indirect taxation, even when the supply of labour is admitted as a variable. This might not matter if it were really plausible to suppose that it would, under no conditions, vary much. But this is not a plausible supposition.

Consider a perfectly competitive economy with three goods, one

for simplicity of exposition. We could in principle treat the government as an 'economic man' with a consistent set of utility curves.

[1] Loc. cit. [2] Loc. cit., p. 545.

being leisure. Designate leisure by Z and the other two goods by X and Y. Let S and T stand respectively for the marginal rate of substitution and the marginal rate of transformation. We can now distinguish three cases as follows:

I. Direct taxation. Here we have

$$S = T \text{ for the pair } (X, Y),$$
$$S \neq T \text{ for the pair } (X, Z),$$
$$S \neq T \text{ for the pair } (Y, Z).$$

II. Indirect taxation on one good other than leisure. Letting the taxed good be X, we have

$$S = T \text{ for the pair } (Y, Z),$$
$$S \neq T \text{ for the pair } (X, Y),$$
$$S \neq T \text{ for the pair } (X, Z).$$

III. Unequal indirect taxation on both goods other than leisure. Here we have

$$S \neq T \text{ for all three pairs.}$$

A comparison of Cases I and II makes it sufficiently obvious that no argument against indirect taxation can be perfectly general. The two cases are quite symmetrical. Unless special assumptions are made, whatever can be said about one can be said about the other. But even if Case III is considered to be what is normally meant by indirect taxation, nothing appears to follow.

Let us illustrate this. In Fig. XXIII ABC is the production surface after subtraction of the government's fixed demands. It is assumed that the government succeeds in manipulating the budget surface so that the community's chosen point on that surface is also a point on the production surface ABC. If the chosen point were above the surface the government would not be getting the goods it required; if below it would be getting more than it required.

The points Q_0, Q_1, Q_2, Q_3, and Q_4 are points on the surface. AA', BB', and CC' are surface lines along which one of the three 'optimum conditions is satisfied. Thus at any point on the line CC', the partial rate of substitution (leisure constant) of Y for X equals the partial rate of transformation (leisure constant). These contract lines, if projected on to the planes BOC, AOC, and AOB respectively, would be analogous to ordinary contract curves. The point Q_0 is the only point at which all the optimum conditions are satisfied. Case I lands us on the line CC' between C and Q_0. Case II lands us either on AA', between A' and Q_0, or on BB', between B' and Q_0. Case III brings us to some point which lies on none of the contract lines. Part of Fig. XXII is embedded in Fig. XXIII. The plane surface $TQ_2Q_1T'O'$ appears in both diagrams.

The advocates of direct taxation or subsidization have to claim that every point on CC' is better than any other point on the production surface. It is intuitively obvious that there is no reason whatever for claiming that points on the line CC' are superior to those on the lines AA' and BB'. The lesser claim might, however, be made that points on a contract line are superior to points not on a contract line.

FIG. XXIII

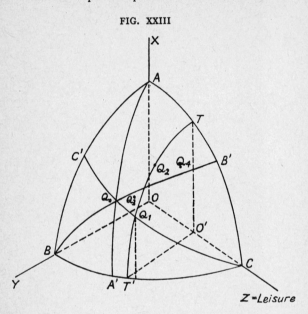

What, then, can be said about the relative superiority of points such as Q_0, Q_1, Q_2, Q_3, or Q_4? First, Q_0 is 'superior' to any other point because all the 'optimum' conditions are satisfied.[1] In other words, a 'community-indifference' surface is tangential to the production surface at Q_0, and cannot lie below the production surface at any other point. Secondly, the 'community-indifference' surface appropriate to Q_1 cannot lie below the production surface in the neighbourhood of the point Q_2. This is because it is tangential to the line $T'Q_1Q_2T$ at Q_1. Thirdly,

[1] By saying one point is 'superior' to another we mean that its 'community-indifference' surface passes outside (farther from the origin than) the other point in the neighbourhood of that point; which implies that the potential losers by a move from the latter to the former would be unable profitably to bribe the potential gainers to oppose the change. Therefore no point x can be 'superior' to any other chosen point y if the indifference surface of x is below the production surface in the neighbourhood of y.

it is quite consistent, both that these two conditions should be fulfilled and that the same indifference surface should or should not lie below the production surface in the neighbourhood of a point such as Q_3. There therefore appears to be no reason whatever to support any claim that Q_1 must be 'superior' to Q_3. A movement from Q_1 to Q_3 would reduce the amount of leisure. But it is also conceivable, given suitable production and indifference surfaces, that the indifference surface of Q_1 should lie below the production surface in the neighbourhood of a point like Q_4, where the amount of leisure is increased. The conclusion is that nothing whatever can be said about the 'superiority' of direct taxation unless it is certain that the amount of leisure will not change.

We have seen that Professor Henderson based his argument on the contention that the supply of labour would be constant. This means, in terms of Fig. XXIII, that it is presumed that a change from direct to indirect taxes would always cause a movement from a point like Q_1 to one like Q_2, leisure remaining constant. Taken to its logical extreme, such a contention is highly paradoxical. It implies that the amount of labour supplied is a function only of the quantities of goods consumed by the government. In the limit this implies that people would work as much even if income-tax was 100 per cent. of all incomes, consumption goods being supplied free! In general, it must be said that the 'purely theoretical' case against indirect taxation is non-existent.

We have seen that there is no general theoretical argument against indirect taxation. There is, on the other hand, quite a lot to be said in favour of it, apart from the paternal reason that people do not always know what is good for them. It is a cheaper method of taxing the poorer classes, and it cannot be so easily evaded as income-tax. Adjustments of indirect taxation can be made more rapidly than adjustments in direct taxation. It is therefore useful in regulating effective demand. In abnormal times, as when it is desired to cause a shift in the propensity to consume, it is useful to have indirect taxation which can be rapidly increased or decreased. If people take such shifts to be temporary, then the desired effect may be achieved. Again, in abnormal times, when shortages prevent output being adjusted until price is equal to marginal cost, indirect taxation (which then sins against no 'optimum' conditions) may prevent some undesirable redistributional effects. It may thus be used as an anti-profiteering weapon.

Taking everything into consideration, we can hardly complain if administrators have largely ignored 'the case against indirect taxation'. This is not to say that there may not sometimes, in particular cases, be a good case against indirect taxation. A typical argument is 'Why tax luxuries? It would be better to increase the progressiveness of income-tax, and leave those who remain comparatively rich to direct production as they will.' It is left to the reader to judge how strong this argument is, bearing in mind the above arguments and also the fact that some luxuries may give rise to external diseconomies. Possibly, for some people, the validity of the argument would turn on this question of whether the particular luxury gave rise to external economies, or diseconomies, of consumption. It should also be noted that indirect taxation of luxuries shifts the real income of people with equal money incomes in favour of those who have larger families.

If any general statement can be risked, it is simply that the best taxes are those on goods for which the demand is least elastic. The same holds true for subsidies. Income-tax, which is analogous to a subsidy of leisure, is not exceptional. Only in so far as the demand for leisure is highly inelastic is it a good tax. The purely theoretical 'case against indirect taxation' is an illusion. It is a particular case of a more general illusion that adjusting outputs until prices are equiproportional to marginal costs is sufficient for an improvement, or would be sufficient for an improvement if the distribution of wealth were not adversely affected.

INDEX OF AUTHORS

8622